D0787045

# Junctures

## in Women's Leadership

# ⟨ Business ⟩

## Junctures

Case Studies in Women's Leadership
Alison R. Bernstein, Series Editor

The books in this series explore decisions women leaders make in a variety of fields. Using the case study method, the authors focus on strategies employed by each woman as she faces important leadership challenges in business, various social movements, the arts, the health industry, and other sectors. The goal of the series is to broaden our conceptions of what constitutes successful leadership in these changing times.

# Junctures
in Women's Leadership

# ⟨ Business ⟩

Edited by Lisa Hetfield and Dana M. Britton

RUTGERS UNIVERSITY PRESS
NEW BRUNSWICK, NEW JERSEY, AND LONDON

Library of Congress Cataloging-in-Publication Data

Junctures in women's leadership : business / editors, Lisa Hetfield and Dana M. Britton.

pages cm.—(Junctures: Case studies in women's leadership)

Includes bibliographical references and index.

ISBN 978-0-8135-6594-1 (hardcover : alk. paper)—
ISBN 978-0-8135-6593-4 (pbk. : alk. paper)—ISBN 978-0-8135-6595-8
(e-book (web pdf))—ISBN 978-0-8135-7573-5 (e-book (epub))

1. Women executives—United States.  2. Leadership in women—United States.  3. Social responsibility of business—United States.  4. United States—Biography.  I. Hetfield, Lisa, editor.

HD6054.4.U6J86 2016
338.092'520973—dc23
2015024450

A British Cataloging-in-Publication record for this book is available from the British Library.

Visit our website: http://rutgerspress.rutgers.edu

Manufactured in the United States of America

# Contents

# Foreword to the Series
## Junctures: Case Studies in Women's Leadership

Throughout history, women have always been leaders in their societies and communities. Whether the leadership role was up-front such as hereditary queens and clan mothers, as elected officials, or as business executives and founders of organizations, women have participated at the highest levels of decision making. Yet, up through most of the twentieth century, we seldom associated the word *leader* with women. I might even argue that the noun *leader* was one of the most masculinized words in the English language. When we thought of leaders, our minds seldom conjured up a woman.

Fortunately, there has been a recent shift in our thinking, our images, and our imaginations. In the United States, credit may go to those women in the public eye like Gloria Steinem, Oprah Winfrey, Cecile Richards, and even Eleanor Roosevelt, who have blazed new trails in politics, media, and statecraft. Now leadership is beginning to look more gender neutral. That said, it is important to remember that, in many parts of the world, women leaders, including prominent feminists, have risen to power more rapidly than seems to be the case here. I think of Gro Bundtland in Norway, Helen Clarke in New Zealand, Michelle Bachelet in Chile, and others. These leaders certainly raise new and interesting questions about linking feminism with powerful political leadership. We in the United States also have Sheryl Sandberg to thank for using the word *feminist* in the same sentence as *leadership*.

Despite progress in the past few decades, women have not reached any kind of rough parity with men in terms of positional leadership—that is, the form of leadership that is appointed or elected and recognized as powerful and influential in coeducational public life. Women continue to be dramatically underrepresented in all major domains of leadership from politics to Fortune 500 companies, to labor unions, to academic administration, and even in fields where they are the majority, like in health care professions, teaching, or the arts. Scholars like Deborah Rhode and Nannerl O. Keohane note that, at the rate the United States is going, there will not be a convergence toward parity for an additional three centuries. Given the need for outstanding leadership at all levels and sectors of society, and given the huge waste of talent that exists when so many capable women are not encouraged to move into senior leadership positions, we cannot afford to wait for parity even three decades, let alone three centuries!

If we wish to accelerate the process of gender parity in producing leaders in the twenty-first century, what steps might we take, and what role can academia play in helping to increase the pool and percentage of women leaders? Historically, women's colleges, according to pioneering research by Elizabeth Tidball and others, graduated disproportionate numbers of women leaders up through the 1970s. More recently, business schools, which were largely male bastions, have educated a share of women leaders.

Today, in interdisciplinary fields such as women's and gender studies, examining the concept of leadership and teaching women students to be more effective leaders in a given profession or context is highly contested. For example, *Ms.* magazine noted in 2011, "Only a handful of the more than 650 women's studies programs at colleges and universities provide practical and theoretical knowledge necessary for the next generation to make a significant impact on their communities and world" as leaders. Many feminists and women scholars have negative associations with traditional ideas of leadership, arguing that the concept is elitist, individualistic, and hierarchical and justifies putting work ahead of family and parenting. Moreover, traditional leadership studies often have failed to take account of structural and contextual frameworks of unequal power and privilege, especially around gender and race. And yet approaching the study of leadership with a gender-sensitive lens is crucial if we are to make more progress toward a fairer and more just distribution of power and opportunity for women and men alike.

Which brings me to the genesis of this series, Junctures: Case Studies in Women's Leadership. The volumes in the series are designed to provide insights into the decision-making process undertaken by women leaders, both well-known and deserving to be better known. The case studies run the gamut from current affairs to past history. The Rutgers Institute for Women's Leadership (IWL) consortium, a group of nine separate units at the university, including Douglass Residential College, the Department of Women's and Gender Studies, and the Center for American Women in Politics, is sponsoring this series as a way to provide new pedagogical tools for understanding leadership that has been exercised by women. Each volume will consist of a dozen or so case studies of leaders in a specific field of endeavor. The focus is not on the woman leader per se but rather on the context that surrounded her decision, the factors she considered in making the decision, and the aftermath of the decision. Also, even though the series is focused on decision making by women leaders, it is not designed to demonstrate that all decisions were good ones or yielded the results expected.

The series does not promote the notion that there are biologically determined differences between women's and men's decision-making practices. There is no such thing as a "women's" approach to leadership. Nothing universally characterizes women's approaches to leadership as opposed to men's. Neither gender is genetically wired to be one kind of leader as opposed to another. That kind of biologically determined, reductionist thinking has no place in this series. Nor does the series suggest that women make decisions according to a single set of "women's values or issues," though there is some evidence to suggest that once women reach a critical mass of decision makers, they tend to elevate issues of family and human welfare more than men do. This evidence, collected by the Rutgers

University's Center for American Women in Politics, also suggests that women are more likely to seek compromise across rigid ideologies than are men in the same position.

Our series of case studies on women in leadership is not designed to prove that simply electing or appointing women to leadership positions will miraculously improve the standard-of-living outcomes for all people. Few of us believe that. On the other hand, it is important to examine some questions that are fundamental to understanding the values and practices of women leaders who, against the odds, have risen to shape the worlds in which we all live. The series employs the "case study" method because it provides a concrete, real-life example of a woman leader in action. We hope the case studies will prompt many questions, not the least of which is, What fresh perspectives and expanded insights do these women bring to leadership decisions? And, more theoretical and controversial, is there a feminist model of leadership?

In conclusion, the IWL is delighted to bring these studies to the attention of faculty, students, and leaders across a wide range of disciplines and professional fields. We believe it will contribute to accelerating the progress of women toward a more genuinely gender-equal power structure in which both men and women share the responsibility for forging a better and more just world for generations to come.

Alison R. Bernstein
Director, Institute for Women's Leadership (IWL) Consortium
Professor of History and Women's and Gender Studies
Rutgers University / New Brunswick
April 2015

Carolina Alonso Bejarano, Grace Howard, Laura Lovin, Kathleen E. McCollough, Rosemary Ndubuizu, Amanda Roberti, and Stina Soderling. Many more have helped to make this book possible. We are especially grateful to Mary Ellen Clark, Cynthia Daniels, and an anonymous reader for their invaluable reviews and to our research assistants, Marie Ferguson and Kim LeMoon, for their careful support in preparing the manuscript.

Our own partnership as coeditors has been a rewarding and enjoyable collaboration. We are inspired by the achievements of the women profiled here and dedicate this book to aspiring leaders— men and women—who will forge new paths, create new ideas, and expand our understanding of feminist leadership.

# Acknowledgments

The seeds for this book were sown over ten years ago when directors of the Rutgers University Institute for Women's Leadership consortium voiced the need for leadership case studies focused on women. We are grateful to Alison R. Bernstein, the director of the Institute for Women's Leadership (IWL), and Mary K. Trigg, the IWL director of leadership programs and research, for turning this idea into a proposal for a book series of case studies on women's leadership. Marlie Wasserman, the director of Rutgers University Press, gave her enthusiastic endorsement for the project. We are indebted to Mary S. Hartman, Edwin M. Hartman, Donna Griffin, and Bernice Venable, whose early confidence and generous financial support made this book and the forthcoming series possible.

The twelve women featured in our book have given us a rich collection of leadership examples. We thank them for their courage and determination. We are deeply grateful to the six women who took the time to speak candidly with us about their lives and leadership: Subha Barry, Barbara Krumsiek, JoAnn Heisen, Rosaline Marston, Diane McCarthy, and Avid Modjtabai. We thank Margaret Lanning and Paul Turner at Wells Fargo for their encouragement and assistance. We are also grateful to Joseph Blasi for his introduction to the world of employee ownership and guidance in understanding the details of employee stock-ownership plans.

We are fortunate that our case-study coauthors joined the project to research and draft compelling stories. Our hats are off to these talented graduate-student scholars and collaborators: Crystal Bedley,

in practice than the bare statistics on women in top corporate leadership suggest, and they provide readers with a diverse range of real-life decision making by women in power. We hope they provide lessons for a new generation of women (and men) leaders.

Dana M. Britton
Lisa Hetfield

## Notes

1 Graduate Management Admissions Council, *2012 Application Trends Survey Report* (Reston, VA: Graduate Management Admissions Council, 2012), http://www.gmac.com/~/media/Files/gmac/Research/admissions-and-application-trends/2012-application-trends-survey-report.pdf.

2 Stacy Blackman, "MBA Admissions: Strictly Business," *U.S. News & World Report*, August 19, 2011, http://www.usnews.com/education/blogs/MBA-admissions-strictly-business/2011/08/19/more-women-head-to-school-for-mbas.

3 Calvert Investments, *Examining the Cracks in the Ceiling: A Survey of Corporate Diversity Practices of the S&P 100*, March 2013, http://www.calvert.com/nrc/literature/documents/BR10063.pdf.

4 Spencer Stuart, *Spencer Stuart US Board Index*, 2012, http://content.spencerstuart.com/sswebsite/pdf/lib/Spencer-Stuart-US-Board-Index-2012_06Nov2012.pdf.

5 Alexander Patel, "HBS Dean Pledges to Double Female Protagonists in School's Case Studies," *Harvard Crimson*, January 31, 2014, http://www.thecrimson.com/article/2014/1/31/HBS-women-case-studies/.

think about diversity and business success. Alice Waters's devotion to good food and community involvement inspired her to take a leadership role in the "slow food" movement and to create "The Edible Schoolyard," a model school program to nourish and enrich students' lives. In a more indirect way, almost all of these women have used their positions to serve their communities by participating in local community organizations and philanthropic boards.

We intend this book to provide a broader perspective on and a broader representation of leadership than that typically found among standard business school cases. Women appear as protagonists in less than 10 percent of the case studies produced by the Harvard Business School, which distributes more than 80 percent of those case studies sold globally.[5] The case studies in this book teach leadership lessons, but contrary to any notion of a distinctively feminine style, they do not speak in a unitary voice. Some of these women suggest that women's leadership is different from men's, as in Avid Modjtabai's sense that women leaders can more readily access "EQ," or emotional intelligence. However, though their efforts have led to expanded opportunities for women, few among this group identify themselves explicitly as feminists. In fact, some explicitly disavow the term; though JoAnn Heisen spent much of her career working to advance women at Johnson & Johnson, she describes herself as neither "bra burner" nor social advocate. We leave it to readers to tackle the question of whether and how the work of these women might be read (or not) as feminist.

Even so, some themes around leadership appear in multiple women's stories. There is an emphasis on the importance of a vision of leadership structured by strong corporate cultures, for example, for JoAnn Heisen at Johnson & Johnson and Avid Modjtabai at Wells Fargo. There is a deep commitment to collaboration, inclusion, and consensus building that comes through in almost all of these stories, from Subha Barry's formation of a multicultural marketing team at Merrill Lynch to Diane McCarthy's team leadership at Verizon during the aftermath of Hurricane Sandy to Roseline Marston's leadership in the flatter, more accountable organizational model of an employee-owned company. Taken together, these twelve case studies illustrate a more inclusive vision of leadership the age of thirty-five. All of these women relied on support networks to help them achieve success, from stay-at-home husbands to (more commonly) paid caregivers.

To say that individuals' personal life experiences are powerful influences on who they are as leaders and the decisions they make is hardly novel. Yet for women seeking to succeed in business and lead change, this truism has particular significance. Women's lived experiences are distinct from those of their male counterparts. From their experiences come unique business ideas and the passion to address women's needs and interests. Madam C. J. Walker (1867–1919) was born in Mississippi, the daughter of former slaves, orphaned at seven, and divorced at twenty, with a daughter to raise on her own. Like many women of her era, at a young age she suffered from hair loss. This experience led to the creation of her famous hair-growth product and the development of a network of women marketers and consumers. Sara Blakely, born in Florida in 1971, was nurtured in a very different historical and social context, yet her entrepreneurial success was sparked by her own need for undergarments that flattered her shape and suited her lifestyle. Like Madam C. J. Walker, she has been passionate about her product and motivated by her deeply held belief that it benefits women. Martha Stewart developed a multimillion-dollar media empire by transforming the relatively small publishing niches of cooking, baking, horticulture, entertaining, crafts, and holidays into one category: "lifestyle." Dubbed "America's goddess of graciousness" by the *Wall Street Journal* in 1985, Stewart infused her publications with personal anecdotes and woman-to-woman stories, making her readers feel "at home" with her. This marketing strategy helped make hers a remarkable comeback story after she served a prison sentence for obstruction of justice.

Many of the women in these case studies see their efforts as connected to broader goals of changing the world for the better. Jane Ni Dhulchaointigh, the inventor of sugru, intends her product as an antidote for our wasteful "throwaway" culture. Frustrated by women's persistent underrepresentation in corporate leadership, Barbara Krumsiek used her analytic skills and business expertise to develop the Women's Principles to transform the ways companies to the investment agendas of companies, and ultimately nations, as Barbara Krumsiek has done at Calvert Investments. They are creating networks of women in leadership, such as the one JoAnn Heffernan Heisen established at Johnson & Johnson. They are leading technological innovation, as Avid Modjtabai has done for Wells Fargo. And they are inventing and marketing products that change our lives in realms as diverse as lingerie (Sara Blakely's Spanx) and advanced polymers (Jane Ni Dhulchaointigh's sugru).

One of the questions these stories raise is whether gender—and race and class—makes a difference in how we think about women's leadership. Does it matter that these are *women* leaders? Does it matter than many are immigrants or women of color? Taken together, these cases provide no single answer to this question. Some of the women on whom we focus are clear that their experiences with discrimination motivated their own leadership. Certainly this is true in an explicit way for Madam C. J. Walker, who navigated racism and sexism in the Jim Crow era to become America's first self-made woman millionaire. Diane McCarthy, who began her career as a wireline technician for AT&T, experienced sexual harassment as one of the few women integrating a heavily male-dominated occupation. And inequalities, though the women often do not name them as such, also thread themselves through the immigrant experiences of Roseline Marston and Subha Barry; the childhood of Ursula Burns, who was raised by a single mother in poverty; and the early career of JoAnn Heisen, who was told by her boss that she did not deserve the same compensation as men with families to support.

Unlike men, as these women ascended the corporate ladder, all of them contended with expectations that they would marry and become the primary nurturers and caretakers of homes and children. Barbara Krumsiek and JoAnn Heisen both faced supervisors and coworkers who believed they should be at home raising their children; Subha Barry's male colleagues took bets on whether she would return from maternity leave (until she beat them, literally, at their own game); Roseline Marston was a trailing spouse who chose her job on the basis of the location of her children's day care, raised them as a single mother, and became president of her company by

# Preface

By some measures, women are more successful as leaders in business than ever before. In 2014, twenty-four women were serving as CEOs of America's five hundred largest companies—up from one in 1998. The pipeline to leadership positions also appears strong. Women now make up about half of the applicant pool for master's programs in management, accounting, and marketing/communications.[1] At the Harvard Business School, which first admitted women in 1970, about 39 percent of the MBA class of 2013 was women.[2]

Despite this apparent improvement, women are still strikingly underrepresented in the ranks of top business leadership. As of 2013, 68 percent of S&P 100 companies had no women at all in their highest paid senior executive positions.[3] Nine percent of S&P 500 boards of directors still have no women at all.[4] And even though there are more women than ever before leading the top five hundred US companies, women still hold only 4.8 percent of CEO positions. While much has been written about the progress of women advancing to leadership and the substantive impact of this change, more needs to be said and done to address the barriers that keep women from reaching the top. That is not the aim of this book.

This is a book about women who are leading change in business. Their stories illuminate the ways women are using their power and positions—whether from the middle ranks or from the top, whether from within companies or by creating their own companies. These women are transforming organizations, ideas, industries, cultures, and leadership itself. They are taking corporate social responsibility

# Junctures

## in Women's Leadership

**〈 Business 〉**

# JoAnn Heffernan Heisen

## Enabling Women's Leadership at Johnson & Johnson

### Grace Howard and Dana M. Britton

## Background

Johnson & Johnson is the largest and most diverse medical device and diagnostics company in the world. It is the sixth-largest consumer health company and the fifth-largest biologics company; it encompasses more than 275 separate operating companies in more than sixty countries.[1] Founded in 1866 by brothers Robert Wood Johnson, James Wood Johnson, and Edward Mead Johnson, Johnson & Johnson has been listed as one of *Working Mother* magazine's "Best Companies for Working Mothers" for all twenty-eight years of the ranking and has won numerous awards for its environmental consciousness and diversity initiatives.

JoAnn Heisen's work on Johnson & Johnson's Women's Leadership Initiative not only elevated the status of women within the company but also linked advancing women to good business strategy. Heisen helped to develop a principle that would be adopted by other corporations around the world—the notion that women's advancement is good for business. Yet when Heisen came to work at Johnson & Johnson (J&J), she was one of the very few women in the upper ranks of the company; certainly gender diversity was not at the top of its corporate agenda. How did fostering women's success within J&J become important to Heisen? What strategies would she use to raise awareness of women's positions and growing importance within the company? What alliances would be crucial for her success? And how would she spread her model for enabling women's leadership throughout J&J's far-flung network of companies?

## Heisen's Early Life

JoAnn Heffernan Heisen was nine years old when her father, only forty-one, died of brain cancer, leaving his wife and four children with no source of income. Heisen's mother had quit her job after getting married, as many women did in the 1940s, and now faced raising four children, aged eleven years to eleven months old, entirely on her own. The sudden death of Heisen's father, who entered the hospital with a brain tumor the day after his wife gave birth to their youngest child, fundamentally changed the family. After twelve years out of the workforce, her mother was forced to find a job. Luckily, she was able to get work as a secretary for the government, and the family scraped by on her small income. Shaped by this experience, Heisen was determined to become a woman who could take care of herself. She keenly understood the vulnerable situation women of her mother's generation were in once they left the workforce—if their husbands left them, were injured, or died suddenly, the family could be left with nothing. Heisen knew that she never wanted to experience that kind of economic vulnerability.

## Pre–Johnson & Johnson Career

In 1972, JoAnn Heffernan Heisen graduated from Syracuse University at the top of her class with a BA in economics. She set out to find a job in finance in New York City at a time when conversations about women's place in business were still relatively novel. The second wave of the women's movement was just beginning. Women were still formally excluded from most graduate business and professional schools, from training programs in banking and brokerage firms, and from the men's clubs in which clients were courted and deals were made. Indeed, by some estimates, there were fewer than seventy professional women on Wall Street in the late 1960s, and little had changed by the time Heisen began to look for a job.[2]

Though aware of the women's movement, these early women pioneers in business navigated a complicated relationship with feminism. Most were not active feminists in any organized sense, though almost all experienced discrimination in their own careers. On August 26, 1970, Women's Rights Day, a small group of Wall Street women had protested in front of the New York Stock Exchange, handing out literature in support of the Equal Rights Amendment. Even for these women, however, equal rights meant equality in business rather than radical social change. First and foremost, they sought equality of opportunity and salary with their male counterparts. A *New York Times* writer's assessment in 1970 was that the women's liberation movement in the financial community was "amoebic and poorly organized."[3]

Pressure to hire women was building on Wall Street firms in the early 1970s, however, when the Equal Employment Opportunity Commission began to file cases of gender discrimination against a number of large companies, including some on Wall Street.[4] It was in this environment that JoAnn Heisen interviewed with Chase Manhattan Bank. She recalls that Chase "needed to hire a few women" at that time because it was "the right thing to do."[5] Determined to get the job, Heisen remembers asking at that first interview when she should start and on what floor her office would be located. She was hired. As was common for both men and women at the time, Heisen expected that she would stay with this company for the entirety of her career and hoped that with dedication and hard work she would climb the ladder of achievement within the company and eventually retire.

After five years at Chase Manhattan Bank, Heisen encountered a bump in the road, however. She believed that all was going well at work and that she had been doing a good job for the company. When time came for her annual evaluation meeting, she was aware that employees in her group were generally receiving a 4 percent raise. Yet at her meeting, her boss informed her that though she had received "glowing" performance reviews, she would get only 1 percent. She describes the experience: "I said, 'I don't understand.' [And my boss said,] 'Well, you know, John is married and he has two kids, and Jim is married and has one kid on the way. I only have so much of a pool. And I have to give it to the guys who have family obligations, and you're a single woman.' And I looked at him, and I said, 'And who pays my rent in New York City?' You know? 'I do!'"

This was a consciousness-raising experience for Heisen and perhaps a key moment that fueled her future efforts as a leader. She knew that her experience was likely not unique, and she had also observed that there were few women at Chase at the upper levels of the company. At the time, she ascribed this to the individual ignorance of men on the management team. As she put it, "There was really no ill will [among my male coworkers and managers]; it was just a case of not understanding reality." Heisen's boss was drawing on widely held gendered "common sense" of the time in dividing the resources he had available; even now, she believes he had good intentions. Yet Heisen came to understand that even men who never meant to hinder women's advancement and achievement contributed to the problem of inequality. Men's lack of understanding of the lives and skills of women workers meant that women were less likely to be hired and, once in the company, less likely to advance and to be paid equally in comparison to their male coworkers.

At around this time, Heisen began to make connections with other women in business. A key turning point in her career came when she joined the Financial Women's Association of New York (FWA). The FWA had been created in 1956 by a group of eight women security analysts who had been barred from joining men's groups in finance. By the time Heisen joined, it was made up of more the one hundred women on Wall Street.[6] As Melissa Fisher describes it, "The primary goal of the FWA, from its inception, was occupational mobility, ensuring that women move up the corporate ranks on Wall Street. FWA women viewed the network as an elite, female, financially focused entity defined by business principles rather than as a pro-feminist organization oriented toward fighting gendered discrimination."[7] FWA women viewed themselves as professionals seeking to help themselves and other women to succeed. Serving as peer mentors for each other, they shared information about banking and finance and passed along the unwritten rules and customs that are part of the culture on Wall Street. These women helped each other to thrive, but the FWA also became a resource for banks and brokerages themselves. Indeed, the FWA served as a key recruitment pool for Wall Street firms under pressure to diversify.[8] Here Heisen found not only wonderful friends but also the support of a group of peers at a time when there were relatively few women working in her field. Over the years, Heisen rose within the ranks of the FWA, serving as a treasurer and then a committee chairman and finally the president. In her experience working with this organization and advancing in leadership positions, Heisen learned the skills necessary to successfully navigate the politics of the business sector in an environment where she did not risk "losing [her] day job."

Heisen describes the women involved with the FWA in the 1970s and 1980s as the trailblazers—the first women working for New York City banks and brokerage houses. Like Heisen, all struggled to work and to achieve success in the male-dominated world of finance, and most did not see themselves explicitly as feminists.[9] Instead they were resolved to achieve and advance in their careers in a way that was fair, and for them this meant receiving opportunities and rewards equal to those given to men. Heisen combined these goals with what would become her business case for advancing women: "I was never a bra burner. I was never a complainer. I would never say, 'This is not fair, and I'm going to sue you.' I was always, 'I will work my darnedest, and I will deliver for you. And if I deliver for you, it means the business gets better. And if the business gets better, then I hope I'm rewarded for helping you get your business better.' I was always business driven." Though Heisen rejected the strategies she ascribed to the feminism of the time, she nonetheless developed an argument for fair treatment that was couched in the language of the market—women should be given the chance to make businesses better, and if they did, they should be rewarded fairly and equally to men who did the same. For her, the case for equity was driven by the bottom line.

In 1982, Heisen was president of the FWA, where executive recruiters regularly attended meetings. One such recruiter asked if she would like to work for the American Can Company, in Greenwich, Connecticut. American Can was originally a manufacturer of tin cans, though by the mid-1980s, it had become a financial conglomerate and renamed itself Primerica (the company later became a part of Citigroup). Heisen was offered a new position in "investor relations," in which she would represent the company on Wall Street, take questions from analysts, and discuss quarterly earnings. The company was looking for someone who not only had skills in public relations but could readily answer investor questions and understood finance. Heisen says they needed a finance person who "knew how to talk." She took the job.

Heisen loved working for American Can. She excelled at her new position and advanced within the company, eventually rising in rank to report directly to the chairman. Despite these successes, eventually Heisen grew dissatisfied. As business had expanded and Primerica had become a Wall Street corporation, she says, "elbows had sharpened." The company's culture was changing and becoming less amicable and more cutthroat. This was not the same company that Heisen had joined in 1982. Again, an executive recruiter came calling—and in 1989, Heisen took a position with Johnson & Johnson.

## Johnson & Johnson

The offer at Johnson & Johnson was for a position as assistant treasurer. Though this seemed on the surface like a demotion—Heisen would go from reporting to the chairman of her company to reporting to the treasurer—she found it attractive because J&J was a much larger global company. But other aspects of the position drew her as well:

> I ended up taking the job with Johnson & Johnson because the minute you walk into the lobby, the company credo is carved in granite and stands twelve feet tall. Our first responsibility is to the patients, the doctors and nurses, mothers and fathers, and those who use our products. That's our first responsibility. Our second responsibility is to our employees, the men and women around the world who work with us. Our third responsibility is to the communities in which we live and work. We will support good charities, we will support schools, we will support the community. And we will pay our fair share of taxes. And our last responsibility is to the shareholder. Because if we do the first three things right, you have a great business, [and you will have a high] stock price. Whereas on Wall Street, the first responsibility is to make money. So I just knew Johnson & Johnson was for me.

Heisen rose quickly within the ranks at J&J. Within two years, she had been promoted to the position of treasurer; eventually she was promoted to corporate controller and ultimately became the first woman to serve on the chairman's executive committee.

Heisen was a rarity in the upper ranks of J&J in many ways. For many years, she was the only woman at her level in the company. At the time, J&J also had a strong ethic of promoting from within—most of the men with whom she worked had been hired in their twenties and grew up in the company. Then, as now, J&J is highly decentralized, with over two hundred operating companies around the world, forty-five in the United States alone. The men in management at all of these companies knew one another because they had met while moving up through the ranks. Meanwhile, Heisen had been hired at age thirty-nine—one of the only people J&J ever hired midcareer during that period. She had no such network.

Heisen was a rarity in another way as well. At the time she took the job with J&J, Heisen was married and a mother of three children: a three-year-old and nine-month-old twins. Immediately after joining the company, Heisen found out that she was pregnant again. Although she was well respected at work, she says her male colleagues were confused about how she could perform such a demanding job while taking care of her family—how could she abandon her children? Of course, she was not performing her domestic duties single-handedly. Her husband (they subsequently divorced) was unemployed outside the home—she says they told people he was a "consultant" who worked from home—and she managed child care with the help of two nannies. Like most of the men with whom she worked at the time, Heisen was a parent and the sole breadwinner for her family. Unlike them, she violated the rules of gender by having a husband (secretly) at home and "abandoning" her children to the care of someone else.

Still, Heisen says she worked because she loved her job, and she knew she was good at it. She was the most senior woman at Johnson & Johnson. She served as treasurer for the entire company, including its hundreds of operating units all over the world. In this very visible and important position, she was becoming well known within the company. Though Johnson & Johnson was known as a family-friendly company workplace, there were very few women occupying the highest positions within the company. Heisen realized that this lack of experienced women in senior positions prevented her, and the other women at the company, from having an "old boys' network," a vital part of producing good business outcomes and advancing within the company.

### Founding the Women's Leadership Initiative

Heisen wanted an "old girls' network." Drawing on the FWA model she knew well, in 1990 she reached out to the fewer than thirty women at the vice president level and above at Johnson & Johnson operating companies—women she had never met but knew by name—and suggested that they get together to talk business. She invited these women to a meeting at J&J world headquarters in New Brunswick, New Jersey, to discuss opportunities for advancing the company and utilizing the strengths and talents of the company's women. This was the beginning of the Women's Leadership Initiative. Heisen intentionally framed her invitation—the women would meet about advancing the business first and advancing women second. She knew that with an invitation in hand to visit company world headquarters (a prestigious offer in itself) to discuss business, signed by the corporate treasurer, the women would face less scrutiny from their male colleagues. She then followed up with phone calls to the women, encouraging them to set up business meetings with relevant colleagues during the day while they were in New Brunswick. This helped to diffuse any animosity the women might have received for attending a "women's club" meeting.

The business of the Women's Leadership Initiative (WLI) took place during an evening session. At these meetings, the women would have a networking cocktail hour and a dinner. This was followed by a slideshow presentation by one of the women on some aspect of business in her J&J company, for example, market share, patent protection, research and development, and marketing. Mirroring the FWA networks that had helped Heisen advance in her company and her career, she formed such a network at J&J. She created a structure in which women formed connections throughout the company with people on whom they could call to answer questions. Women met each other and shared their experiences, but they also learned about aspects of J&J's other businesses that they could apply to their own.

By 1993, Heisen came to believe that she and the other women of the WLI had a responsibility, as the most senior women in the company, to help other, less senior, women at Johnson & Johnson. As beneficiaries of this new "old girls' network," Heisen wanted these women to go back to their own operating companies and start programs and initiatives to help other women succeed. It was an ambitious vision for a company of the size of J&J. To get the support of her chairman for the WLI, Heisen, "always a numbers person," drew on her new networks to prepare a presentation that would drive home the importance of women to the company:

> [I had numbers on] how many women in the workforce and how many women were graduating from college and how many women were in health care and how many mothers make all the decisions about health care for their family and how many women and mothers made all the decisions about consumer purchases. I had all the statistics, and I'd get them by calling up the one person at one of our companies who had them for her business plan and calling up the one person down at another company who had them for projections.

This presentation proved persuasive enough to raise the interest of the chairman; at Heisen's invitation, he and the eight other men on the executive committee attended the next WLI cocktail hour. Though the men were nervous about attending a meeting with twenty-five women, Heisen (as usual) appealed to their business sense. She provided them with background information on each of the women, highlighting their successes and their expertise. She assured the men they would not be stopping by the militant feminist hour. Instead they would be meeting with women colleagues from all over the company to discuss business. Heisen recounts what happened next: "And the next day at the executive committee luncheon, I said, 'Wasn't last night successful? Nobody complained. For that one hour everybody was discussing business.' And the chairman said, 'Yes, you're right! It was all about business.'"

By 1995, WLI meetings had grown in size as more and more women joined the company or were promoted to levels of vice president or above. Heisen invited each of these new women into the "old girls' network," hoping to make them feel like they were not so alone in this large, decentralized, primarily male-dominated corporation. Still, women held only 14 percent of the positions at the level of vice president and above at any Johnson & Johnson company.[10] In that year, with the support of the chairman, Ralph Larsen, Heisen held a WLI conference in New Brunswick. In line with her vision of advancing the next level of women at J&J, she invited all of those who held the position of director or above in any of the operating companies. To her surprise—and the chairman's shock—she discovered that there were more than three hundred women at this level. She envisioned the conference as a working meeting focused on making the business better and advancing women in J&J, not a "bitch and moan session." She asked the chairman and the other men on the executive committee to make an appearance to show their support, and the chairman agreed also to give a fifteen-minute welcoming speech.

On the morning of the conference, the chairman delivered his remarks warmly, though he made it clear to Heisen that he would be able to be at the conference only from 8:30 to 8:45, as he had a conference call at 9:00 a.m. in his office across the street. He concluded his remarks and walked to the back of the room. Heisen, as she had planned, began a presentation of the results of a survey she had conducted before the conference to collect demographic data on the women in the room. The anonymous survey asked the participating women questions about their work histories inside and outside the company, their marital status, whether they or their husbands were the primary breadwinners in their household, and the number and ages of children in the household. As she continued the presentation, she noticed that the chairman had remained at the back of the room watching. She says,

I can see him because I'm at the podium. He's at the back door. And he's looking at his watch, and he knows that it's a quarter of nine—so he could wait five minutes, ten minutes, and then run across the street to his office. So I start with the demographics of how many years women have been with J&J. I have pie charts. "Here's how many women have been here so many years. Here's how many women are the breadwinners in their family. Here's how many women are single with children. And here's how many women who have been with J&J for how many years and how many had made transfers." And he was looking at this. And then it was 9:05, then it was 9:15. . . . And I'm still making this presentation—and he's still there. So he obviously missed his conference call. But he came to me later and said that was so eye-opening for him. He said to me many times over the years, he realized at that moment that, quote, "the horse was out of the barn" and that women had so much potential. And he had—he'd seen me, and he knew maybe ten of us senior women by name—but he had no idea we had such bench strength throughout the corporation. He had no idea. And he said it was just a matter of time, that women were going to run J&J.

Thereafter, the WLI received the support of the chairman and the top-level executives at J&J.

After the conference in 1995, the women who had attended were charged with attracting, developing, and retaining talented women at J&J to improve the business. Upon returning to their individual operating companies, the women hosted afternoon sessions—luncheon meetings—to identify areas of focus for their own Women's Leadership Initiatives. These included issues like work and family balance, the advancement and inclusion of minority women, career development, and communication skills. Those women who developed their own Women's Leadership Initiatives at their companies often invited Heisen to come to their companies and give keynote speeches. She accepted, using her powerful position as a bully pulpit to legitimize their concerns:

> So I would agree to come. And then the president would say, "Since JoAnn Heisen is coming to our company, we'd better be on our best behavior. I'm going to encourage all my male senior executives also go to this meeting so they can meet JoAnn Heisen." I was in an extremely fortunate position. But I also—without naming names—knew senior women in other large public corporations who said, "Not my job. My job is to prove that women can be a senior executive. And I've got to perform well all the time so that I don't let down the other women. But I can't take this on in my corporation. The HR department should take that on." And I kept trying to explain that if I lobbied for women's opportunities at J&J, what were they going to do, fire the most senior woman? Fire the most visible woman? No. Not as long as I did my job.

Heisen's work on the WLI was double-edged. Though she used her powerful position to draw attention to women's concerns in J&J, she did so at a cost that many women at her level did not, or could not, choose to bear.

### Promotion to CIO and the Challenge of Sustaining and Building the WLI

In 1997, Heisen's career path took an unexpected turn when the chairman named her the new chief information officer (CIO) for J&J, in charge of all information technology (IT) for the corporation, worldwide. Like many corporations at the time, J&J was updating its IT business operations and needed someone to coordinate its efforts across its more than two hundred companies. Heisen says she rejected the offer of promotion many times. She was at that point in her life a single mother with four children. Her entire career had been built on her skill and expertise in finance. She had no background in IT. Still, the chairman insisted. He was not asking her to become the CIO (an acronym she feared really meant "career is over"); he was telling her. He felt that in performing her job as treasurer and in organizing the Women's Leadership Institute, Heisen had shown the skills necessary for the position. She was knowledgeable about the worldwide operation of the company and was well respected. She knew how to create a new strategy, budget, organize, lead people, and delegate. Now, with a $1.6 billion budget, she was tasked with bringing the worldwide IT operations of J&J up to date.

Beyond the not-insubstantial fact that Heisen had little background in technology, her new position presented two challenges for her work to advance women's status within J&J. Her substantial global business responsibilities meant that she was now less able to be actively involved in building and supporting initiatives at J&J companies in the United States. Additionally, she was now working directly in areas of the world in which there were few, if any, women at the upper levels of J&J's operating companies and in some cases strong cultural norms against women serving in positions of power (or working outside the home at all). Still, with the support of her chairman, she took the position and became the global head of information technology for J&J.

## Resolution

Heisen's new responsibilities were critical to Johnson & Johnson's operations. She was in charge of information technology for the entire company, responsible for centralizing major parts of J&J's IT operations and standardizing others. Her chairman had brushed aside her concerns that she had no background in technology, trusting instead in her abilities as a leader. She describes her leadership style:

> In my role as chief information officer, I collected the best and brightest. I'd get people around the table and say, "Guys, I don't have all the answers. The chairman has asked me to take on this role and responsibility, but I need you. I need you to give me your best work, to give me your best thoughts, and together, as an IT global

team, we're going to figure out the best thing for all of J&J. And around this table, everyone speaks, and the doors are closed. Things don't leave this room. But Jim, if you have an idea, I want to hear it. Beth, if you don't agree with Jim's idea about how it should be run, I want you to take your time around the table and tell me why it doesn't work." And I believe that the best idea, presented with facts and data, will convince people. Because Jim might be the first one to speak. And he has an idea. But by the time eight other people have spoken, he might say, "You know what? Your point is well taken." So I said, "I really believe that we have to be in this together. We all have to buy into it together, but we have to listen to each other." So I would say I was inclusive.

By "inclusive," Heisen meant that she gathered the best and brightest, listened, and then led. She worries that women often suffer from "paralysis by analysis": "Part of women's problems are that sometimes we're too inclusive. And we want to involve everybody, and then we keep putting off making a decision. Women have to learn to be decision makers." Heisen spent nine years in this role, much of it on the road, visiting J&J's far-flung network of operating companies. At the end of her term, the IT infrastructure of J&J had been transformed.

Though the new position had the potential to take Heisen out of her role as advocate for women in J&J, in fact, as she always had, she used her position to press for change. As CIO, Heisen was in a unique position to connect with women working for J&J all over the world and to make her case for the global operating companies to become actively involved in advancing the position of women. She recounts her strategy:

[In whatever country I visited] I'd be there for two or three days on business. I again had the bully pulpit, and I could tell them weeks in advance, "I am going to be in Paris meeting with the five presidents of our French companies, and I would like for you to come to dinner with me." When I met with them for dinner, I would say, "Now we're going to talk about women's leadership. What are you doing in France for the women who work in your companies?" And they almost fell over. They had heard about how I was sponsoring this Women Leadership Initiative, and they'd say, "I thought that was just in the US!"

Heisen checked in regularly with these men, and when she returned at intervals in her role as CIO, she would again hold dinners in which she would monitor their progress. As she had throughout her career, Heisen collected data on the numbers of women at various levels in the companies and used these data to support her case. She also became a voracious reader of research on gender and business success, drawing on studies of the ways diverse companies were able to leverage that diversity for success.

Wherever Heisen went, she used her position—and her data—to spread her message and the WLI. She found that the perception of women's advancement as strictly a US affair was particularly pronounced in Japan. There, the presidents of J&J's companies initially viewed the exclusion of women—particularly married women—from jobs in corporations as about culture, and they were shocked that Heisen would question this practice. Even so, she persisted:

I would go to Japan to discuss something, and [that evening] we would always have a private room in a restaurant. There would be seven men and me. I'd say, "I'd like to go around the table and ask you how many women you have working for you. How many people are in your sales force, and how many women?" And in general, it was, "I have four hundred men in my sales force, and I have no women." "I have two hundred men in my sales force. I have no women." "I have one hundred men in my sales force." And I'd say, "I'm going to ask you that question in six months when I come back." So I was back six months later; they would say, "I have one hundred, and I now have two women." "Oh, I have four hundred, and I now have one woman." But one president says, "I have five hundred, and I now have twenty women." And everybody at the table says, "What do you mean you have twenty women?" And that president said, "You know? It's—what JoAnn Heisen said. The women in Japan are so eager to have a job in a corporation. We only get the best. [Other large Japanese companies] never hire women.

So when we went out to universities to hire women, we had our pick of the very best. And then when they came on board, they wanted to show us they could sell!" A couple of years went by. [Then at our usual dinner meeting], he said, "Every year we have the president's sales and marketing trip. Of our five hundred sales reps, we recognize the top ten performers. This past year, of the top ten sales reps, seven were women." And as a consequence, the Japanese Bureau of Business gave that J&J company the very first award for the "Most Female-Friendly Company in All of Japan." Their company was featured in so many news magazines, they got every award. So that was great. But you know, the results they got from hiring those women showed that in the end it was all about business!

This story is worth recounting at length because it encapsulates the rationale and the goal of the WLI as Heisen framed it—advancing women is not an end in itself but is valuable to the extent that it leads to success for the company. For her, the WLI was and is ultimately "all about business." Throughout her years as CIO, she continued to spread the message and the model of the WLI—ensuring that her return visits yielded results. Her efforts paid off. The WLI model was well institutionalized in J&J's US operations, and her position as CIO allowed her to disseminate it internationally.

In 2005, the WLI celebrated its tenth anniversary with eight conferences, worldwide. More than eight hundred people attended the conference in New Brunswick, New Jersey, alone. Many were women whose bosses had been at those dinners with Heisen, but many were senior men who had bought into her message (or at least understood its importance in the company's culture) or junior men sent by their (male and female) bosses. By bringing women from across the corporation together, by demonstrating the utility of women's advancement as a business strategy—and using the leverage of her position to spread her message—Heisen had made a difference at Johnson & Johnson. From 14 percent in 1995, by 2002, the number of women at the executive level at the company had more than doubled, reaching 30 percent.[11]

After Heisen served nine years as the chief information officer, the new chairman of the board, William Welden, appointed her to the position of chief global diversity officer. She spent two years in that position before retiring. She used those years to further institutionalize the WLI, as well as to help implement a broad slate of other diversity initiatives.

Though Heisen had spent her entire tenure at J&J working—in addition to her "day job"—to advance the position of women in J&J, she is adamant that her efforts were "all about the business." She understands that not all women would have taken on this responsibility, however. When asked why this was so important to her, she answered,

> Growing up in a modest family with some disadvantages, each time—whether it was just going to college or getting that first job at Chase—I thought I was so lucky. I felt I was so lucky in my life and in my career. And you can't take all the credit for yourself. Somebody believed in me. It is the model of reach down and pull up. Reach down and pull up. As I'm climbing, let me help the next lady up. Let me help the next lady up, because she'll reach down and help the next lady up. And again, it's all about the business. It's all about the business. If we make the business stronger, we'll still be here.

Here Heisen invokes the language of "lifting as we climb," as it was articulated by Mary Church Terrell, first president of the National Association of Colored Women, founded in 1896. In some ways, this is ironic, as Heisen herself claims no particular identity as a member of any kind of liberation movement—feminist, civil rights, or otherwise—nor does she believe that she herself faced any particular discrimination.

There is no question, however, that her ideas and actions drew on and advanced the goals of equality espoused by these movements, at least in her own very large corporation. Though she would not use the word herself, Heisen's leadership on these issues might be read as a kind of "market feminism." She is one of a pioneer generation of women in finance and business who, as Fisher puts it, "introduc[ed] feminism in understandable and palpable ways into the marketplace so that (predominantly) male corporate CEO's and executives [could] view the marketplace as a space in which they [could] simultaneously pursue gender equality and profit."[12] By making it "about the business," Heisen was able to sell gender equality at J&J. Her constant use of the bully pulpit provided by her position and her ability to disseminate the WLI model created a "business case" for diversity and, in the process, helped to change the face of the company.

## Notes

1 Johnson & Johnson, "Johnson & Johnson History," n.d., http://www.jnj.com/about-jnj/company-history (accessed May 15, 2014).
2 Melissa S. Fisher, *Wall Street Women* (Durham, NC: Duke University Press, 2012).
3 Marilyn Bender, "Women's Lib Bearish in Wall St.: Movement Is Subdued and Impact Is Slight," *New York Times*, October 11, 1970.
4 Fisher, *Wall Street Women*.
5 All direct quotes are taken from an interview with JoAnn Heisen conducted by Lisa Hetfield and Dana Britton on January 9, 2014. The editors are grateful to JoAnn Heisen for her comments on an earlier draft of this chapter.
6 Melissa S. Fisher, "Wall Street Women: Engendering Global Finance in the Manhattan Landscape," *City & Society* 22 (2010): 262–285.
7 Fisher, *Wall Street Women*, 49.
8 Ibid.
9 Ibid.
10 Smith College Executive Education for Women, "The J&J Story," n.d., http://www.smith.edu/execed/?q=programs/smith-custom-programs/case-study (accessed May 15, 2014).
11 Ibid.
12 Fisher, *Wall Street Women*, 17.

## Bibliography

Bender, Marilyn. "Women's Lib Bearish in Wall St.: Movement Is Subdued and Impact Is Slight." *New York Times*, October 11, 1970.
Fisher, Melissa S. *Wall Street Women*. Durham, NC: Duke University Press, 2012.
———. "Wall Street Women: Engendering Global Finance in the Manhattan Landscape." *City & Society* 22 (2010): 262–285.
Johnson & Johnson. "Johnson & Johnson History." n.d. http://www.jnj.com/about-jnj/company-history (accessed May 15, 2014).
Smith College Executive Education for Women. "The J&J Story." n.d. http://www.smith.edu/execed/?q=programs/smith-custom-programs/case-study (accessed May 15, 2014).

# Sara Blakely

## Reinventing Women's Shapewear with Spanx

### Amanda Roberti and Lisa Hetfield

## Background

Sara Blakely may be associated with Spanx—one of the most well-known and often-used undergarments in our popular culture—but it was a different garment that led her to become the youngest self-made woman billionaire in the United States and the first to take the Giving Pledge to donate at least half of her wealth to charity. It was a pair of rarely worn ivory pants that inspired Blakely to invent what is now known as Spanx. She simply wanted to develop a garment that she could wear under those ivory pants that would not show her panty line or cellulite. She wanted to look good and feel confident yet avoid the restrictiveness and discomfort of old-fashioned girdles and other antiquated foundation wear.

Blakely did not enter the world of entrepreneurship through a clearly defined path of business know-how or fashion merchandising. In fact, as a twenty-seven-year-old Disney amusement park ride operator turned fax-machine saleswoman, Blakely's life before inventing Spanx was a lesson in determination and imagination. Her life after Spanx entered the mass market, however, is another story: one that would remind young women everywhere to take risks, remain true to oneself, and as Sara Blakely would say, "trust your gut."[1]

### Early Life

Sara Blakely was born in 1971 and raised in Clearwater, Florida, by her father and mother, who were employed as an attorney and an artist, respectively. Looking back on her childhood, Blakely often references her natural and creative entrepreneurial spirit—charging her neighborhood friends to enter her haunted house for Halloween and operating a lemonade stand, among other ventures. She was exposed to mass media early; her father worked on *Mays v. Twigg*, a trial involving two children who were swapped at birth. "That was a very high-profile case," Blakely recalled. "I'd be at my dad's office, and the phone would ring. And it would be Diane Sawyer calling, because everyone was vying for the interview."[2] Blakely's father was influential in her development as an entrepreneurial risk taker. At the family dinner table, he would ask Sara and her brother, Ford (also an entrepreneur), what they failed at that day. In an interview by Diane Sawyer for ABC's *World News*, Blakely recounted that she would say, "I tried out for this sport, and I was horrible!" to which her father would respond, "Way to go!" and give her a high five. "It just completely reset my definition of failure. So for my brother and me, failure is not trying."[3]

Popular and smart in high school, Blakely was both a cheerleader and a champion debater. Despite an otherwise typical upper-middle-class childhood, Sara suffered a series of tragic and unfortunate events during her teenage years. When she was sixteen, she witnessed her best friend get hit by a car and die; her parents separated; and two other friends died shortly after. Not surprisingly, these events stimulated a period of self-reflection. She began to think about life and mortality. "It kind of gave me a sense of urgency, I think," Blakely said. "I don't want to take any day for granted." Blakely was able to use these challenging experiences as a catalyst to delve into motivational "self-actualization."[4] She spent countless hours listening to the motivational speaker and author Wayne Dyer's books on tape, drawing much from his work. She was so impressed with them that she asked the principal at Clearwater High School to include them as part of the curriculum. She reported in an interview with Clare O'Connor for *Forbes* that her friends were less impressed with the tapes.[5] "People used to fight over who had to ride home with me at night after a party," said Blakely. "No one wanted to be in my car—they'd be, like, 'Oh no! She's going to make us listen to that motivational crap!'"[6]

After high school, Blakely went on to attend Florida State University, where she joined a sorority and took legal-communications courses. Blakely also retained her entrepreneurial streak after graduating from high school. In 1990, she began her first business venture, an unofficial club for kids at the Clearwater Beach Hilton. Charging eight dollars per child, Blakely watched the kids at the hotel while their parents enjoyed the facilities. She was unlicensed, inexperienced, and uninsured, but she escaped the hotel's notice for three summers before getting on the radar of the general manager when she attempted to give him a sales pitch for her club.

After graduating from Florida State in 1993, she set her sights on becoming an attorney like her father. She took the LSATs, but after receiving low scores twice and failing to get into law school, she had to reevaluate what she wanted to do. Blakely spent a few months working at Disney World, operating the rides, but quickly realized that this was not where she imagined herself in terms of building a life or profession. As Blakely told Zoe Wood for the *Observer*, it was not exactly a glamorous position: "I would see friends I hadn't seen for a while and I'd be wearing these big Mickey Mouse ears with my name on. . . . They'd say, 'Sara, is that you?' And I'd reply, 'Yes, now get on the ride.'"[7]

Shortly thereafter, Blakely was hired by Danka Business Systems, an office-equipment supplier that has since become part of Ricoh Company. She worked there for seven years, selling photocopiers and fax machines by cold-calling customers and making door-to-door sales calls. Although the experience was "humbling," as Blakely told Robert Trigaux in an interview for the *Tampa Bay Times*, it gave her a chance to refine the sales skills and persistence that would be essential to starting Spanx and fostering its extraordinary growth.[8]

"I was given four ZIP codes in Clearwater and a cubicle and told to sell $20,000 worth of fax machines a month," she said. "I can't hear that I am on that [*Forbes* billionaire's] list without laughing. . . . I can't help but think of the days when my job was to cold-call people in Clearwater to try and sell them fax machines and how many of them said 'No, no, no,'"[9] Later, Danka transferred her to Atlanta, Georgia, where she eventually founded Spanx and made her home. However, she did not know this yet—her journey was just beginning. Blakely applied her moxie and natural ability to lead and worked her way up the corporate ladder at Danka, eventually making her way to sales manager.

During this time, the fun-loving Blakely also dabbled in performing amateur comedy at local comedy clubs. "[As a teenager] I was really flat-chested," she said. "You have to develop a sense of humor if you're in a beach town with no boobs." Her standup act—observational humor that she compares to Seinfeld's and Cosby's—often began with her flinging a pair of pushup-bra pads into the audience. "It would defuse everything, and disarm them," she said.[10] Her approachable charm, positive attitude, and quick, often self-effacing, wit proved to be a winning combination and one that led to her eventual success in the shapewear industry.

As Blakely recounts her story, it all started in 1998 with a pair of Arden B ivory pants hanging in her closet that she wanted to wear to a party. Like many women, she wanted to look smooth and flawless in her pants—a difficult goal to accomplish, especially in pants of such a light color. And also like many women, she did not believe that the only way to a firm body was with a long-term commitment to Jane Fonda–esque workouts, which were popular in the 1980s and early 1990s. A pair of control-top pantyhose was really the only option for Blakely that night, but they were not ideal. For one thing, the southern heat made it virtually impossible to wear pantyhose as an undergarment. One just got too hot. Also, the seamed toe was unsightly sticking out of an open-toe shoe. Thinking quickly, and perhaps driven by a bout of frustration, Blakely cut off the feet of her control-top pantyhose and wore them under her ivory pants. However, during the course of the night, the modified pantyhose kept rolling up. Immediately she knew that this problem pointed to a gap in the market. There was no undergarment that was both comfortable and breathable. She also knew that there must be other women looking for this same nonexistent underwear. Girdles were antiquated, to say the least, and the then-current shapewear on the market was as limited as it was uncomfortable. Elastic waists created bulges and rolls and could make a woman look and feel miserable. The now-energized Blakely sought to make a light-weight, wearable shapewear garment that would not shift or roll up and that would help women feel spectacular wearing their favorite clothes. She envisioned that it would be a best-kept secret among girlfriends.[11]

Blakely spent countless long nights at the library researching everything about women's undergarments and shapewear, including fabric and old styles. Her research was self-directed, as was the draft of her patent for the first prototype of Spanx—the footless pantyhose. For Blakely, it was imperative to develop an undergarment that would stand up to the heat of the Deep South. Having worked at physically demanding jobs in the southern heat—as a ride operator at Disney World and hauling fax machines and printers at her sales job with Danka—Blakely knew the extreme discomfort of wearing pantyhose. With some research under her belt and a prototype in mind, Blakely took a week off from work and got down to business. She spent innumerable hours at the Georgia Tech library, this time researching hosiery manufacturers, patents, and girdles. She even went to fabric stores to find the best stretch material for her first product. And though she had no formal business training, Blakely's solo research led to writing her own patent and incorporating her shapewear business by the summer of 2000.[12]

While Blakely's subsequent success may in retrospect suggest a calculated and straightforward path, she understood the role of failure in achieving goals. She recalled that her father often encouraged her and her brother to try new things and not to be afraid of failing. It was this fatherly advice that instilled in Blakely the determination, persistence, and moxie to pitch her newly developed and exhaustively researched Spanx prototype via cold calls to hosiery manufacturers. This is also where her sales expertise and her standup-comedy skills came in handy. She made calls to numerous manufacturers and mills looking for one to produce her Spanx footless pantyhose. All rejected her proposal. Despite the rejections, Sara took it upon herself to visit a manufacturer in person, carrying the prototype in her signature red backpack. Although the owner initially dismissed her, two weeks later, she received a call back informing her that he would produce her prototype. This reversal was due in part to the owner's teen daughters, who persuaded their father that the crazy idea had potential and urged him to say yes to Blakely. The Highland Mills hosiery factory in Charlotte, North Carolina, was the first factory to produce a yet-to-be-named Spanx product. Currently, there are factories in fifteen other countries.[13]

It should be noted that neither at this point nor any other point to date did Blakely seek outside investors. The launch of Spanx was fully funded with her own scrupulously saved $5,000 nest egg. Blakely still owns 100 percent of the company, though she openly admits now that this was due more to her unfamiliarity at the time with business and investment matters than a conscious strategy. The entrepreneurial spirit that Blakely embodies evolved from the combination of her personality, parental advice, and her application of lessons learned in life. Her hard work, ambition, and common-sense approach to simple but important problems—like finding a decent shapewear enabling women to feel good in their clothes—were all working together to launch her into a new career and a new chapter of life. Indeed, with a manufacturer on board, Spanx went from being just a dream to being a reality.

### Building the Brand, Seeking a Mass Market

Once Blakely had a manufacturer that would make her product, it took her and the hosiery mill a year to create a prototype that met her standards for comfort. Blakely was now ready to delve into building the Spanx brand. She knew that there was much to gain from being imaginative and creative in her approach to generating and launching her distinctive product. She also knew that there was much to gain from a word-of-mouth reputation and advice given woman to woman.[14] One of the notable ways Blakely developed the Spanx brand was by applying her own sense of authenticity through original packaging and design. Spanx's bright-red packaging is adorned with a blond, ponytail-wearing cartoon figure named Sunny, a cartoon version of Blakely. Blakely shrewdly chose an illustration that would stand out among the rest of the subdued-colored schemes of the other packaged tights and shapewear.

The packaging reflected the youthful edge that Blakely sought to bring to the shapewear industry, as well as the idea that a woman need not be embarrassed about or hide her foundation garments.

On the contrary, she could, in fact, talk with her girlfriends about how good her Spanx make her feel. The descriptions, names, and cartoon inserts were all designed to draw women in on a basic, down-to-earth level that maintained the humor and ease behind Spanx.[15] Even the name Spanx was a concerted effort to grab attention with wit and lightheartedness. Though Blakely has noted that the x in Spanx was intended to make it easier to trademark, the x sound was all about directing attention and recognition.[16] Blakely admits, though, that while trying to market her product to stores, many had hung up on her upon hearing her utter the word "Spanx," assuming it was a joke. Embarrassingly, her very own mother once inadvertently directed a room full of ladies to an adult website with a different spelling of "Spanx."[17] Again, Sara Blakely's combination of gut instinct and a savvy sense of women's perspectives proved to be effective, as the name Spanx has grown to be nationally and internationally recognized.

Blakely continued to develop and market her product, which in its original iteration was like a pair of pantyhose without the feet. She relied on the personal, door-to-door strategy that she had developed selling fax machines, and she invested her personality into the Spanx brand. While promoting Spanx at department stores, Blakely was known for her legwork—literally. She was not shy about lifting a pant leg to show her Spanx or plastering her own derrière, clad in her ivory pants, in poster-size signs advertising Spanx's "no-lines" underwear as "before" and "after" shots.

Blakely targeted a wide array of stores including high-end department stores like Neiman Marcus and Saks Fifth Avenue, among others. Again, Blakely's life-learned skills of good humor, determination, creativity, and an unmistakable attitude toward failure were crucial. Blakely applied these important qualities when she was cold-calling department stores, receiving hang-ups upon hearing the name "Spanx," or having unsuccessful business meetings. Though Blakely sought to get the Spanx product in high-end stores, she also appealed to bargain stores such as Target with what eventually became the Spanx budget line, called Assets. In this way, women at a wider range of points in the economic spectrum could be reached. In short, Blakely believed that all women were in need of such a comfortable and useful foundation garment, and she was determined to make Spanx available to everyone.[18]

Blakely eventually started enjoying moderate success visiting department stores and getting her Spanx products on the shelf. Remarkably, Blakely was still working full-time at her office-supply sales job during the day, only to come home at night and send out packages of Spanx. She needed that one thing that would propel her into higher realms of success: to quit her day job and devote all her energy completely to Spanx.

Blakely left her job at Danka in October 2000 and took a risk to invest all of her time and effort into building her business. Without a full-time job occupying her days, Blakely was able to travel to department stores advertising her product day in and day out for hours on end. Blakely has often noted that she never spent a dime on advertising but relied on in-person meetings and word of mouth. With the prototype for the footless pantyhose in hand, Blakely secured a ten-minute meeting with a buyer at Neiman Marcus. She flew to Dallas for the interview, part of which was conducted in the ladies' room so that Blakely could personally demonstrate the effectiveness of her product. By the end of the pitch, she came away with an order for three thousand pairs of hose. In an article for the *Daily Mail* by Victoria Wellman, Neiman Marcus CEO Karen Katz notes Blakely's "character and charm" during the pitch: "Sara's effort was to solve an age-old problem for women in a modern way. . . . We were smitten from the beginning."[19]

Though Spanx's entry into department stores was an enormous break for Blakely and, indeed, a critical moment in her career, an important hurdle still remained: she would need to sell much more than three thousand pairs of Spanx. How could she take her fledgling business to the next level? What would it take to make the leap to reach that mass market that Blakely was sure existed? She was still primarily a quirky one-person enterprise with little capital and no major connections. Her staff at this point consisted of herself, a boyfriend, and temporary help from a few friends. How could she move from successful, store-to-store pitching to getting the message to millions? How could she expand into mass markets without losing the personal touches and girlfriend-to-girlfriend approach that made Spanx so authentic? What should she do next?

## Resolution

Sara Blakely's story is a case study in self-made business success. Her leadership strengths derive from her distinctive blend of creative energy, sense of humor, and self-confidence. She builds on personal life experiences and her willingness to share these experiences in person-to-person encounters as well as a deep commitment to being her irreverent self. She developed her company on the basis of three key strategies: positioning her product as a benefit to women's self-esteem and well-being; developing unique market messaging to turn a previously hidden women's product into a humorous shared "public secret" among girlfriends; and understanding and mobilizing the power of popular culture to market her products. Her core leadership strength—taking risks and persisting in the face of failure—along with her strategic approaches are evident from the humble beginnings of the Spanx company to the billion-dollar enterprise it became.

### Taking Off and Taking Risks

When confronted with the challenge to promote Spanx to a mass market, the best strategic move Blakely could think to make was to persuade a well-known, well-liked, big-name celebrity to get behind her product. This person would have to be a positive role model, a person with recognized, credible understanding of public life and body-image issues. She would also have to be extremely influential in reaching millions of women. Though the pool of famous women was rich with amazing possibilities, Blakely set her sights on, arguably, the most respected and influential of them all: Oprah Winfrey.

For Blakely, there was simply no better celebrity than Oprah. Not only was Oprah extremely influential, but her body and weight have long been the subject of media scrutiny. From early in her career, Oprah understood that the public spotlight is often directed at celebrity bodies—especially women's bodies—and had developed a distinct strategy of openness in talking about her own encounters and experiences with body image. Oprah had the trust of masses of women who watched her show, read her magazine, and shared her struggles with body image.[20] A mere two weeks after quitting Danka, Blakely implemented her new marketing plan. She sent a basket of Spanx to Oprah Winfrey's stylist, Andre Walker.

Just as Blakely had hoped, Walker gave the Spanx to Oprah, who in turn became a huge fan of the shapewear. Oprah raved about Spanx, added it to her "favorite things" list in 2000, and invited Blakely to appear on the show.[21] This endorsement launched Spanx and Sara Blakely to an entirely new level. Other famous women began endorsing Spanx products and mentioning Spanx by name on the red carpet. More department-store offers came rolling in. Blakely's practice of putting herself out front, confronting early rejection and seeming dead ends with determination, and trusting her instincts regarding women's needs proved to be the very strategy that enabled her success. Her vulnerability was indeed her strength. Her authenticity, creativity, and confidence in her intuition showed through in her leadership and entrepreneurial style. Because of this, Blakely found herself on a new level of success.

Not every public appearance went so smoothly, however, as Blakely found out in 2001 while being interviewed for the BBC. Wanting to make a strong impression on the UK audience but unaware of local colloquialisms, Blakely gleefully spoke about how Spanx is "all about the fanny. It smooths your fanny, it lifts it, and it firms your fanny." Not knowing that *fanny* is UK slang for the vagina, Blakely was quickly corrected by the host, who reminded her that the correct word would be *bum*. True to her trademark good humor and down-to-earth personality, she later laughed off the incident in an interview with *Newsweek*'s Kara Cutruzzula, stating, "It's important to be willing to make mistakes. The worst thing that can happen is you become memorable."[22]

Thanks to Oprah's endorsement, as well as the growing mentions of Spanx by other A-list celebrities, this minor snafu did not stop Blakely's growing success. In 2002, she made an appearance on the home shopping channel QVC to advertise the second product in her collection: Power Panties, a midthigh short. Incredibly,

Blakely sold about eight thousand pairs within six minutes.[23] It was clear, at this point, that her success in building the Spanx brand was reaching a critical mass—she needed to scale up her production. To expand, she knew she would need to bring new people on board with business skills and acumen. Spanx only had a few staff members, all of whom were business outsiders whom Blakely had hired largely based on her own intuition about their knowledge of style and abilities.

In 2002, Sara's boyfriend at the time and the chief operating officer of Spanx met the Coca-Cola licensing executive Laurie Ann Goldman while she was searching an Atlanta department store for some much-coveted fishnet Spanx. The two exchanged business cards. Soon thereafter, Blakely took yet another leap, hiring Goldman as a consultant for the budding company. Goldman's expertise in marketing for the soft-drink giant positioned her to provide the Spanx organization with some much-needed guidance and business know-how. On a personal level, Goldman's frustration with not finding the Spanx product she wanted spurred her interest in becoming a part of the Spanx enterprise.[24] Goldman rose quickly through the small company, eventually becoming the CEO the same year. Because Blakely had no prior business knowledge or training, Goldman provided the needed business skills and organizational development to Spanx, enabling the company to project and set ambitious yet attainable goals. Blakely and Goldman worked as a dynamic team, building the Spanx brand in new directions and to greater heights of success.

During Goldman's tenure at the company, she set forth a business plan for Spanx, often balancing and professionalizing Blakely's more spontaneous approach. Though Goldman had joined Spanx when it was just getting off the ground—a five-person operation out of Blakely's apartment—it quickly turned into a multimillion-dollar industry.[25] Goldman was instrumental in expanding the company globally, as well as taking the reins for three months when Blakely participated in a reality show. In 2014, Goldman decided to step down as CEO of Spanx after a very exciting and successful twelve-year run.[26] At the end of Goldman's tenure, Spanx made about $13.3 million per year in sales. Though the two women's leadership styles could not be more different, Goldman and Blakely leveraged their different approaches together to grow Spanx into the company that Blakely dreamed it would one day become, one that is an internationally recognizable powerhouse but that still maintains the brand as an approachable, dependable, and open-secret-between-girlfriends style.

## Keeping It Personal and for the Benefit of Women

As of mid-2012, Spanx continued to run with an unusually small corporate workforce in Atlanta—162 people, 131 of whom were women. The company's pink offices, adorned with staff photos, flowers, boudoir-esque mirrors, and themed conference rooms, suggest that this company thinks outside the traditional corporate box—or cubicle. Blakely's employees are encouraged in many ways to take part in the creative process: coming up with new ideas and products, getting inspired in one of the corporate office's "theme" rooms, or even looking to family members for inspiration.[27]

While the Spanx corporation may be thinking outside the box, as of 2012, it was thinking inside malls. Spanx stores opened in at least three different shopping malls on the East Coast, adding a new aspect to the Spanx empire. These stores—in Tyson's Corner, Virginia; King of Prussia, Pennsylvania; and Paramus, New Jersey—represented the next avenue for expanding the Spanx brand. The stores incorporate the variety of shapewear and activewear for women, as well as the men's line, in a way that could not have been achieved in the often rigid and limited space of a department store.[28] The stores retain the "emotional" or "girlfriend-to-girlfriend" appeal that is associated so strongly with Spanx.[29]

Blakely's consistent messaging and down-home approach to her business are reinforced in the brick-and-mortar stores, as well as in their helpful greeters and signage laden with self-affirmation statements. For Blakely, the success of Spanx has always been predicated on her keen sense of women's increasing openness and willingness to discuss their bodies. Underlying the functionality of Spanx is the idea that this is not your grandmother's girdle. Blakely may have researched shapewear going back to the days of laced-up corsets and matronly, uncomfortable, and embarrassing girdles, but she has always focused on making modern women feel good about their bodies and be unabashed about wearing Spanx. In this way, Blakely has reinvented girdles and foundation garments into slimming shapewear and set her products apart from the discomfort and shame associated with previously dominant fashion modes focused on unreal body images. This message, along with Blakely's woman-to-woman and women-for-women approach, resonates across diverse groups of women. Spanx now has about two hundred different products of all kinds, from the shapewear that began it all to activewear and swimsuits—men's and women's. Spanx is sold in over fifty-four countries.[30] The website and stores are clear indicators that Blakely continues to infuse her humor, playfulness, and woman-friendly attitude into her business and brand. Blakely's big-name endorsers and Spanx enthusiasts are displayed in the website's description of the popular Power Panties, using their very much recognizable first names (Madonna, Gwyneth, Oprah), reminiscent of the "girlfriend" familiarity that Blakely used from the start. Additionally, with product names like Bra-llelujah,[31] Undie-tectable, and Skinny Britches, the brand incorporates the intended goals of her various products in a humorous way. These names are not exclusively the creative genius of Sara Blakely but are a collaboration of her coworkers, employees, and even their spouses. Blakely has been known to encourage her employees to be creative, share ideas, and seek inspiration wherever they can find it. Blakely's husband, the former rapper and current entrepreneur Jesse Itzler, whom she married in 2008, has described his wife as 50 percent Lucille Ball and 50 percent Albert Einstein.[32] This apt description may be the best way to understand her unique business career and success.

Of course, with every good idea comes competitors or even imitators. Other companies—mostly lingerie and undergarment companies—have tried to share in the market success of Spanx by introducing their own shapewear products. In 2013, Blakely found her company involved in a legal dispute with another shapewear company, founded by a cast member of the reality TV show *Real Housewives of New York*. This legal matter revolved around patenting of the shapewear. Specifically, a letter from the competitor company includes allegations that Spanx had "knock[ed] off" a camisole.[33] This issue was even brought into the public, with the competitor company posting an open letter to Blakely on its website. However, despite any potential disputes or personal jabs, Spanx retains a very specific reputation that keeps the company on top of the shapewear industry; it is a reputation that Blakely meticulously and consciously built and maintains. Her vision of a business that is friendly, feel-good, and supportive translates to her products and to her customers. In fact, Blakely's approachability has inspired Spanx customers to share stories of all kinds—even if it means lifting up their own pant leg to show Blakely that they are proudly wearing their Spanx. Blakely also has taken that important customer feedback to create new and improved—or "Slimproved," as the Spanx website states—products.

The uplifting feeling that many women have come to associate with Spanx has also made the business part of the "lipstick effect" of recession-proof personal goods. In the world of business and marketing, the "lipstick effect" refers to items that continue to fly off the shelves, or at least do not suffer such great losses, despite a recession. Opening new storefronts during a recession might not sound like the best strategy, but Spanx enjoyed success because it offered people that little feel-good pick-me-up. And that positive attitude is entrenched in every facet of Spanx. Customers who are able to visit one of the Spanx stores can stand in front of a mirror with Sunny and hear empowering affirmations. Understanding Blakely's life story, one can see where her spirit of self-motivation, authenticity, creativity, confidence, and determination are clearly woven into every bit of the Spanx brand; and it works.[34]

### From Business Success to Philanthropic Leadership

Risk-taking proved an important factor in Blakely's success, from quitting her full-time job to focus on Spanx to showing up at department stores with her product to hiring business outsiders to allowing others to take the reins. Blakely also took a big risk when she chose to use a woman-to-woman approach to her business. Her long-term use of a low-end website despite a growing digital world and her unapologetic authenticity reinforces that being personable and being confident in yourself can often lead to great things.

Though Blakely's own rise to success and her current position of power were mostly self-directed, her whole brand and company model is built on the foundation of sisterhood and her belief in the solidarity of women in different ways. Thus, Blakely felt strongly that philanthropic support of young women entrepreneurs and rising leaders was an important mission for her personally and for her company. Blakely's status as the youngest woman billionaire entrepreneur also provides an important example for other women interested in entering management, especially given the continued underrepresentation of women at the highest levels of business leadership.[35]

A large component of Blakely's identity as a leader is her commitment to "paying it forward." As she is now a well-known woman leader in the business world, Blakely is part of a host of philanthropic ventures focusing mostly on women. In fact, Blakely has an interesting approach to philanthropy. In an interview with *Forbes*, Blakely quipped with characteristic candor, "I feel like money makes you more of who you already are. . . . If you're an asshole, you become a bigger asshole. If you're nice, you become nicer. Money is fun to make, fun to spend and fun to give away."[36]

The Sara Blakely Foundation was started by Blakely in 2006 in an effort to reinvest in women around the world. She started this foundation with a $750,000 check she earned by participating, and coming in second place, on the TV show *Rebel Billionaire* with Virgin Mobile's Richard Branson. Since then, Blakely has focused on donating to women and girls in African countries and in US cities, such as the Empowerment Plan of Detroit, to which she donated $100,000. She has also contributed $1 million to Oprah Winfrey's Leadership Academy, a gift that no doubt celebrates her appreciation of Oprah's role in taking the Spanx product to a mass market.[37]

Blakely also began Giving Women a Leg Up, which, according to the "Leg Up" spotlight on the Spanx website, offers sponsorship of women entrepreneurs in the spirit of her own beginnings. Giving Women a Leg Up has been investing in several women entrepreneurs per year since 2010. The women are featured prominently on the Spanx website and in the catalogue, which has an extensive readership. Most of these women come from humble beginnings and have created interesting, creative, and eco-friendly products. Additionally, in keeping with the idea of donating to women-focused and women-led businesses, Blakely donated $10,000 in 2012 to the National Association of Women Business Owners (NAWBO).

Most notably, in 2012, Blakely made headlines when she joined the Giving Pledge, a philanthropic venture started by Bill and Melinda Gates and Warren Buffet. In order to join this venture, the signers must promise to give at least 50 percent of their net worth to charitable causes. According to *Forbes*, Blakely will be donating half of her $1 billion net worth. After appearing on the cover of *Forbes*, Blakely recalls that she was approached by Bill Gates to join the Giving Pledge. She admittedly had been saving her profits, looking for an organization that would help guide her on how to pursue humanitarian and philanthropic ventures.[38] Blakely's Giving Pledge letter is an indication of both her gratitude and her humanity. She writes on the Giving Pledge website, "Since I was a little girl I have always known I would help women. In my wildest dreams I never thought I would have started with their butts. . . . With this pledge, my goal is the make the world a better place . . . one woman at a time."[39] Blakely's letter goes on to talk about the gratitude she feels for having been dealt a good hand, while acknowledging that not everyone is so lucky. Her hopes in signing up for the Giving Pledge focus on empowering women and "unleash[ing]" their potential.

Blakely is also positioned to use her power and growing name recognition with the success of Spanx to continue the conversation about body image. Throughout the tenure of Spanx in the mass market, Blakely has sought to bring the use of shapewear garments into the public consciousness. Whereas women's shapewear has long been hidden, often thought of as humiliating, Blakely has transformed shapewear for the twenty-first-century consumer, making it modern, comfortable, and something women do not have to be embarrassed about wearing. Underpinning the use of Spanx shapewear is the ideology that Blakely has instilled into every facet of the business: every woman deserves to feel confident and look fabulous. This "you go, girl" approach is very appealing to a diversity of women, especially as the pressure of the beauty industry and societal expectations often focus on bodily imperfections and unrealistic standards of beauty.

## Notes

1 Jane Mulkerrins, "All Spanx to Sara," *Daily Mail*, April 6, 2013, 28.
2 Alexandra Jacobs, "Smooth Moves: How Sara Blakely Rehabilitated the Girdle," *New Yorker*, March 28, 2011, http://www.newyorker.com/magazine/2011/03/28/smooth-moves.
3 "Spanx Entrepreneur Shares Advice," *ABC News*, March 10, 2012, http://abcnews.go.com/WNT/video/spanx-entrepreneur-shares-advice-15889928, video.
4 Clare O'Connor, "How Spanx Became a Billion-Dollar Business without Advertising," *Forbes*, March 12, 2012, http://www.forbes.com/sites/clareoconnor/2012/03/12/how-spanx-became-a-billion-dollar-business-without-advertising/.
5 Clare O'Connor, "Undercover Billionaire: Sara Blakely Joins the Rich List Thanks to Spanx," *Forbes*, March 7, 2012, http://www.forbes.com/sites/clareoconnor/2012/03/07/undercover-billionaire-sara-blakely-joins-the-rich-list-thanks-to-spanx/.
6 Lisa Phillips, "Sara Blakely," *Current Biography* 74, no. 1 (2013): 10.
7 Zoe Wood, "Sara Blakely: A Woman with a Great Grasp of Figures," *Observer*, March 10, 2012, http://www.theguardian.com/theobserver/2012/mar/11/observer-profile-sara-blakely-spanx.
8 Robert Trigaux, "Forbes Says Spanx's Sara Blakely, of Clearwater, Is World's Youngest Self-Made Female Billionaire," *Tampa Bay Times*, March 7, 2012, http://marketplace.tampabay.com/news/business/forbes-says-spanxs-sara-blakely-of-clearwater-is-worlds-youngest-self-made/1218862.
9 Ibid.
10 Jacobs, "Smooth Moves."
11 Feifei Sun, "The New Shape of Retail," *Time*, September 10, 2012, http://content.time.com/time/magazine/article/0,9171,2123314,00.html.
12 O'Connor, "Undercover Billionaire."
13 "Billion Dollar Ideas: How Spanx's Sara Blakely Made a Billion," CNN Money, July 7, 2013, http://money.cnn.com/video/news/2013/07/26/n-spanx-sara-blakely-billionaire-profile.cnnmoney/, video; O'Connor, "Undercover Billionaire."
14 "Billion Dollar Ideas."
15 O'Connor, "How Spanx Became a Billion-Dollar Business."
16 O'Connor, "Undercover Billionaire."
17 Jacobs, "Smooth Moves."
18 O'Connor, "Undercover Billionaire."
19 Victoria Wellman, "No Advertising, No Investment and No Debt: How Spanx's Sara Blakely Became the Youngest Self-Made Woman to Join Forbes' World

Billionaires List," *Daily Mail*, March 8, 2012, http://www.dailymail.co.uk/
femail/article-2111708/Spanxs-Sara-Blakely-Youngest-self-woman-join-Forbes
-World-Billionaires-list.html.

20  O'Connor, "How Spanx Became a Billion-Dollar Business."

21  Clare O'Connor, "Top Five Startup Tips from Spanx Billionaire Sara Blakely,"
    *Forbes*, April 2, 2012, http://www.forbes.com/sites/clareoconnor/2012/04/02/
    top-five-startup-tips-from-spanx-billionaire-sara-blakely/.

22  Kara Cutruzzula, "My Favorite Mistake: Spanx Founder Sara Blakely," *News-
    week*, May 7, 2012, 52.

23  Mulkerrins, "All Spanx to Sara."

24  Colleen Leahey, "SPANX CEO Out after Building the Mega-Brand," *Fortune*,
    February 11, 2014, http://fortune.com/2014/02/11/spanx-ceo-out-after
    -building-the-mega-brand/.

25  O'Connor, "Undercover Billionaire."

26  Leahey, "SPANX CEO."

27  Mulkerrins, "All Spanx to Sara."

28  Katherine Davis, "Can Spanx Stores Fit into America's Malls?," *Bloomberg Busi-
    nessweek*, November 30, 2012, http://www.businessweek.com/articles/2012-11
    -30/can-spanx-stores-fit-into-americas-malls.

29  Sun, "New Shape of Retail."

30  Mulkerrins, "All Spanx to Sara."

31  A staff member's husband came up with the "Bra-llelujah" name. Mulkerrins,
    "All Spanx to Sara."

32  O'Connor, "Undercover Billionaire."

33  Clare O'Connor, "Spanx Billionaire Sara Blakely Trades Lawsuits as Reality TV
    Star Threatens Patent 'War,'" *Forbes*, March 13, 2013, http://www.forbes.com/
    sites/clareoconnor/2013/03/13/spanx-billionaire-sara-blakely-trades-lawsuits
    -as-reality-tv-star-threatens-patent-war/.

34  Sun, "New Shape of Retail."

35  According to Catalyst, an organization focusing on women and business,
    women occupy only 4.8 percent of all Fortune 500 CEO positions currently.
    "Fortune 500 CEO Positions Held by Women," Catalyst, June 23, 2014, http://
    catalyst.org/knowledge/fortune-500-ceo-positions-held-women.

36  O'Connor, "Undercover Billionaire."

37  Olivia Fleming, "Billionaire Spanx Founder Sara Blakely Will Donate Half of
    Her Fortune to Charity as the First Woman to Join Warren Buffett and Bill
    Gates' Giving Pledge," *Daily Mail*, May 10, 2013, http://www.dailymail.co.uk/
    femail/article-2322201/Billionaire-Spanx-founder-Sara-Blakely-donate-half
    -fortune-charity-woman-join-Warren-Buffett-Bill-Gates-Giving-Pledge.html.

38  Clare O'Connor, "Spanx Mogul Sara Blakely Becomes First Female Billionaire
    to Join Gates-Buffett Giving Pledge," *Forbes*, May 7, 2013, http://www.forbes
    .com/sites/clareoconnor/2013/05/07/spanx-mogul-sara-blakely-becomes-first
    -female-billionaire-to-join-gates-buffett-giving-pledge/.

39  Sara Blakely, "My Giving Pledge," Giving Pledge website, n.d., http://giving
    pledge.org/pdf/pledge-letters/Blakely_Letter.pdf (accessed March 18, 2014).

# Bibliography

"Billion Dollar Ideas: How Spanx's Sara Blakely Made a Billion." CNN Money, July 7, 2013. http://money.cnn.com/video/news/2013/07/26/n-spanx-sara-blakely -billionaire-profile.cnnmoney/. Video.

Blakely, Sara. "My Giving Pledge." Giving Pledge website. n.d. http://givingpledge .org/pdf/pledge-letters/Blakely_Letter.pdf (accessed March 18, 2014).

Catalyst. "Fortune 500 CEO Positions Held By Women." June 23, 2014, http:// catalyst.org/knowledge/fortune-500-ceo-positions-held-women.

Cutruzzula, Kara. "My Favorite Mistake: Spanx Founder Sara Blakely." Newsweek, May 7, 2012, 52.

Davis, Katherine. "Can Spanx Stores Fit into America's Malls?" Bloomberg Business-week, November 30, 2012. http://www.businessweek.com/articles/2012-11-30/ can-spanx-stores-fit-into-americas-malls.

Fleming, Olivia. "Billionaire Spanx Founder Sara Blakely Will Donate Half of Her Fortune to Charity as the First Woman to Join Warren Buffett and Bill Gates' Giving Pledge." Daily Mail, May 10, 2013. http://www.dailymail.co.uk/femail/ article-2322201/Billionaire-Spanx-founder-Sara-Blakely-donate-half-fortune -charity-woman-join-Warren-Buffett-Bill-Gates-Giving-Pledge.html.

Jacobs, Alexandra. "Smooth Moves: How Sara Blakely Rehabilitated the Girdle." New Yorker, March 28, 2011. http://www.newyorker.com/magazine/2011/03/28/ smooth-moves.

Leahey, Colleen. "SPANX CEO Out after Building the Mega-Brand." Fortune, February 11, 2014. http://fortune.com/2014/02/11/spanx-ceo-out-after-building-the -mega-brand/.

Mulkerrins, Jane. "All Spanx to Sara." Daily Mail, April 6, 2013, 28.

O'Connor, Clare. "How Spanx Became a Billion-Dollar Business without Advertising." Forbes, March 12, 2012. http://www.forbes.com/sites/clareoconnor/2012/ 03/12/how-spanx-became-a-billion-dollar-business-without-advertising/.

———. "Spanx Billionaire Sara Blakely Trades Lawsuits as Reality TV Star Threatens Patent 'War.'" Forbes, March 13, 2013. http://www.forbes.com/sites/ clareoconnor/2013/03/13/spanx-billionaire-sara-blakely-trades-lawsuits-as -reality-tv-star-threatens-patent-war/.

———. "Spanx Mogul Sara Blakely Becomes First Female Billionaire to Join Gates-Buffett Giving Pledge." Forbes, May 7, 2013. http://www.forbes.com/sites/ clareoconnor/2013/05/07/spanx-mogul-sara-blakely-becomes-first-female -billionaire-to-join-gates-buffett-giving-pledge/.

———. "Top Five Startup Tips from Spanx Billionaire Sara Blakely." Forbes, April 2, 2012. http://www.forbes.com/sites/clareoconnor/2012/04/02/top-five-startup -tips-from-spanx-billionaire-sara-blakely/.

———. "Undercover Billionaire: Sara Blakely Joins the Rich List Thanks to Spanx." Forbes, March 7, 2012. http://www.forbes.com/sites/clareoconnor/2012/03/07/ undercover-billionaire-sara-blakely-joins-the-rich-list-thanks-to-spanx/.

Phillips, Lisa. "Sara Blakely." Current Biography 74, no. 1 (2013): 9–14.

"Spanx Entrepreneur Shares Advice." ABC News, March 10, 2012. http://abcnews .go.com/WNT/video/spanx-entrepreneur-shares-advice-15889928. Video.

Sun, Feifei. "The New Shape of Retail." *Time*, September 10, 2012. http://content
.time.com/time/magazine/article/0,9171,2123314,00.html.

Trigaux, Robert. "Forbes Says Spanx's Sara Blakely, of Clearwater, Is World's Youngest Self-Made Female Billionaire." *Tampa Bay Times*, March 7, 2012. http://
marketplace.tampabay.com/news/business/forbes-says-spanxs-sara-blakely-of
-clearwater-is-worlds-youngest-self-made/1218862.

Wellman, Victoria. "No Advertising, No Investment and No Debt: How Spanx's
Sara Blakely Became the Youngest Self-Made Woman to Join Forbes' World
Billionaires List." *Daily Mail*, March 8, 2012. http://www.dailymail.co.uk/femail/
article-2111708/Spanxs-Sara-Blakely-Youngest-self-woman-join-Forbes-World
-Billionaires-list.html.

Wood, Zoe. "Sara Blakely: A Woman with a Great Grasp of Figures." *Observer*,
March 10, 2012. http://www.theguardian.com/theobserver/2012/mar/11/
observer-profile-sara-blakely-spanx.

# Madam C. J. Walker
## Leadership Grounded in Social and Racial Uplift

**Rosemary Ndubuizu and Lisa Hetfield**

## Background

In 1912, Madam C. J. Walker was not yet an African American household name. Although her popularity in black political circles rose steadily due to her success with her beauty-product company, she still yearned for acceptance and respect within black business circles. She desired inclusion not only because she wished to demonstrate that black women were economically and politically vital to black liberation struggles of her day but also because she wished to demonstrate how black women can model a different type of business leadership. She wanted to build on her business success to become a force for social change.

One black leader—Booker T. Washington—continued to frustrate her attempts to gain full entry into black business circles. As the founder and leader of the National Negro Business League, Washington held an important foothold on the hearts and minds of black business leaders, influencing their political practice as well as their business decisions. Typical of the day, black business leaders like Washington paid scant attention to the rising influence of black women business leaders like Walker. She knew that if she won his recognition, more doors of economic opportunity and public leadership would be opened to her.

How would Walker, with her humble beginnings as the daughter of emancipated slaves whose first career was as a laundress, be able to penetrate Washington's elite business circle while still maintaining her own signature business style? How could she inspire politically conscious leadership within her own company, particularly in her black female sales agents? Ultimately, how could Walker use her success to forge a model of black women's leadership that championed black enterprise and social uplift?

### Sarah Breedlove, a Black Exoduster in Search of Greener Pastures

Madam C. J. Walker was born Sarah Breedlove on December 23, 1867, in Delta, Louisiana, at a time when the state and the country were undergoing rapid change. Unbeknownst to baby Sarah, this undercurrent of political and economic change following the end of the Civil War would have immense impact on her future. Sarah's parents, Owen and Minerva Breedlove, were both readjusting to their lives as emancipated slaves.

Louisiana, one of the original seven Confederate states, was acclimating to its brief life under military rule following the Confederacy. No longer considered legal and physical chattel, newly emancipated black men like Owen Breedlove were granted constitutional protections in 1864 and officially offered the right to vote in Louisiana in 1867. Black women like Minerva and even her newborn daughter, Sarah, would not be granted the right to vote until 1920.

Life was no "crystal staircase" for newly emancipated blacks. The Breedloves raised their six children on the meager returns they received from harvesting cotton on the plantation where they had once been slaves. Denied any property or access to the wealth that they had helped their former owner accrue through their enslaved labor, Owen and Minerva raised their family in a small shack with the hope that their children would be able to create lives that were not tied to their former lives of enslavement. Minerva Breedlove died in 1874, and Owen passed away the following year, both due to unknown causes.

Sarah Breedlove remembered her childhood as bleak: "I had little or no opportunity when I started out in life, having been left an orphan and being without mother or father since I was seven years of age."[1] After the death of her parents and with only a few months of formal schooling, she had to move in with her older sister and brother-in-law. With limited resources, Breedlove's brother-in-law ruled with an iron fist, forcing her to supplement the household income by working. The poor returns from plantation work forced Breedlove and her sister's family to seek opportunities in the comparatively more urbanized Vicksburg, Mississippi. There she soon found work as a laundress. According to her biographer A'Lelia Bundles, the work of laundress was almost exclusively given to African American women, since white women with any disposable income had renounced the work as too laborious.[2]

Breedlove's rough home life was not the only challenge that she had to confront. The reality of white supremacy and the country's entrenched commitment to segregation and discrimination was ever present after the end of Reconstruction in 1877. Southern blacks endured a never-ending onslaught of white-led and state-sanctioned terrorism. Mississippi was home to some of the most brazen white supremacists. In Breedlove's new hometown of Vicksburg, she was exposed to the horrors of violence inflicted on scores of African Americans. The historian Paula Giddings recounts the omnipresent threat of white violence and black death in Mississippi during the 1870s: "No southern state carried out its violent intentions more openly than Mississippi, whose white supremacists felt little need to mask themselves or their extralegal intentions."[3] Politicians and lay white Americans alike used various tactics, legal and extrajudicial, to ensure black subservience in all aspects of American life. Black business owners were not exempt from the rage of white supremacists. The historian Paula Giddings argues that the black business owners earned a special type of ire and hatred from white supremacists since their work symbolized independence from white America's economic chokehold on black life.[4] Black grocery stores were burned, and black farmers were routinely threatened or lynched.

Breedlove, surely frustrated by her limited financial resources and the abusive treatment she received at the hands of her brother-in-law, moved out of her sister's home and married in 1882. Later, Breedlove claimed that she "married at the age of fourteen in order to get a home of [her] own."[5] Three years into her married life with Moses Williams, the couple welcomed a daughter, Leila, into their common-law union. Moses died six years into their marriage. The cause of his death remains unknown, but there is speculation that he died at the hands of a white lynch mob. The lack of details surrounding Moses's death does not blunt the harsh reality that Sarah succinctly captured: "I was left a widow at the age of twenty with a little girl to raise."[6] She knew that if she wanted a better life, she would have to leave Mississippi. Like the twenty thousand other black Exodusters (the name given to African Americans who migrated north from states along the Mississippi River in the late nineteenth and early twentieth centuries), Breedlove, with her baby in tow, left for St. Louis, Missouri, a bustling town with an established black business elite.

Once in St. Louis, Breedlove joined a local church, St. Paul African Methodist Episcopal Church. There she benefited from the supportive role the church played in her life: "By Sunday, her only day off, Sarah welcomed the release that church always brought her, for she had long embraced the power of prayer. As a newcomer in a fast city and as a recent widow, she needed the solace it brought."[7] But beyond this important supportive role, the church afforded Breedlove multiple opportunities to engage with St. Louis's black elite. Although still a laundress, she frequently mingled with the black elite during church events.

Perhaps motivated by the prospect of earning a living similar to that of the church's more affluent members or perhaps simply yearning for different employment opportunities, Breedlove started dreaming of more lucrative career alternatives. Her pursuit of upward mobility started with two simple questions: "What are you going to do when you grow old and your back gets stiff? Who is going to take care of your little girl?"[8] Resolute but unclear about next steps, Breedlove reflected, "This set me to thinking, but with all my thinking I couldn't see how I, a poor washerwoman, was going to better my condition."[9]

## From Laundress to Sales Agent to Entrepreneur

Breedlove did not have much time to think of alternative careers when she first moved to St. Louis. She had to grapple with sustaining a healthy household for her daughter. This was no small feat, considering that in 1894 she married John Davis, a man who struggled with alcoholism and frequent unemployment. His violent rages were an open secret in her St. Louis neighborhood. But her religious commitment continued to provide her with consolation. She worked with church members to raise funds for local residents who were in need. In her local fundraising efforts, she gained the respect of her church members—and perhaps indirectly gained the confidence she needed to branch out on her own and look for alternative work.

It was during this time that Breedlove experienced rapid hair loss. In those days, black women often concocted homemade hair products to maintain their hair. While the story of how she developed her hair-growth product remains the subject of much controversy, Breedlove proudly claimed that her product's formula came to her in a divine dream. "In that dream a big black man appeared to me and told me what to mix for my hair. Some of the remedy was from Africa, but I sent for it, mixed it, put it on my scalp and in a few weeks my hair was coming in faster than it had fallen out."[10] She insisted that initially she was not looking to place her product on the market; she simply wanted a product that would prevent her continued hair loss.

Breedlove, however, would have had many reasons to take her product to market. Religious and cultural influences pressured women to regard long hair as a mark of beauty. White constructions of beauty that emphasized long hair were particularly challenging for African American women. Moreover, hair care was something Breedlove certainly had to notice while observing the middle-class congregants in her St. Louis church. "Hair care—or lack of it—was a carefully calibrated indicator of class, no more so than among middle-class blacks, who warily watched the steady flow of Deep South newcomers, most of them unsophisticated, uneducated and haphazardly groomed as Sarah had been when she first arrived."[11] An editorial from the *St. Louis Palladium*, May, 26, 1906, decried black women migrants' appearance: "With the approach of summer comes the annual appearance of heads out of windows. On Lawton, Market, Morgan, Johnson streets . . . can be seen: HEADS. NAPPY HEADS! WOOLLY HEADS! COMBED HEADS! UNCOMBED HEADS! Heads of all descriptions, especially when a band is near by or the congregation of a church is being dismissed."[12]

This critical perspective on black women's hair was certainly challenged, particularly by black women activists like Fannie Barrier Williams, the educator and political and civil rights leader. In spite of vocal critics, the reality persisted—that black women were constantly taught to aspire to Western-inspired dictates of beauty. Breedlove was no exception. She clearly would have understood the use value of hair-growth products in black female circles and its relatively limitless profit potential.

By the early 1900s, Breedlove had given up her life as a laundress, left her second husband, and started full-time as a hair-care saleswoman. Perhaps to distance herself from the growing critique of black women who sought to change their appearance to mirror white women's middle-class standards, Breedlove called herself a "hair culturist." For her, "hair culturist" meant hair grower, not hair straighter. She got her start selling Annie Turnbo Malone's hair products, sold under the Poro Company name. Turnbo encouraged her sale agents—including Breedlove—to stress improved hygiene. Turnbo's improved-hygiene selling pitch claimed a clear connection between appearance and increased social status: "Better appearance means greater business opportunities, higher social standing, cleaner living and beautiful homes."[13] This concept of black uplift linked to social appearance was not new to Breedlove. She heard similar refrains from her fellow church parishioners.

Breedlove's two years as a Turnbo agent opened her eyes to the need and demand for hair products, as well as to her own sales abilities. She began to experiment with making her own hair products and, with the help of her third husband, began to sell her own products in 1906. She eventually changed her name to Madam C. J. Walker to accentuate how her hair products signified class and sophistication. In her brief tenure with Turnbo's company, she learned valuable sales skills and had begun to establish a market in Denver. Walker took her product to the Midwest, amassing a large following. She dazzled her audiences with her charisma and successful demonstrations of her product's benefits. Referrals and black-newspaper advertising bolstered her recruits. She set prices for her products so that "the very poorest may be benefitted."[14] Eventually, Walker left the Midwest and headed to "the heavily black South and the expanding cities of the North."[15] A key ingredient to Walker's success lay in her understanding that women wanted to be attractive, as well as in her fervent conviction that they needed to be financially independent.

## Building Support by Seeking Black Leaders' Endorsements

Walker never hesitated to travel to recruit more customers. She rode the rails east, west, north, and south—wherever she could get a showing of her products. Between 1906 and 1912, Walker perfected her sales pitch, ditched her philandering husband, and hired a trusted lawyer, Freeman Ransom, to run the day-to-day operations of her growing business. Since many of her customers were like her—southern migrants—Walker often appealed to their shared upbringing on the farm. Walker explained, "Do you realize that it is as necessary to cultivate the scalp to grow hair as it is to cultivate the soil to grow a garden?" "Soil that will grow grass will grow a plant," she advised. "If the grass is removed and the soil cultivated, the plant will be a very healthy one. The same applies to the scalp."[16]

In order to gain legitimacy and access to different black communities, Walker relied heavily on black institutions and their leaders' endorsements. For instance, Walker's church connections enabled her to tap into the national network of black churches. Her involvement with her church's women's auxiliary group likely gave her contacts with national black women's clubs. She frequently entered new cities through these connections and asked churches and club women to sign petitions supporting her work. One such petition read, "We, the undersigned, highly recommend Mme. C. J. Walker's work and worth." The letter of support continued, "As a hair grower she has no equal. . . . We found her to be a strictly honest, thoroughgoing business woman. Until her advent into this city . . . we did not believe in such a thing as a hair grower."[17] Walker's extensive outreach started to pay dividends. In 1908, two years after branching out on her own, she was earning close to $7,000 annually. The next year, she banked close to $9,000, the equivalent of over $200,000 when compared to incomes in 2015.

Local newspapers and black leaders started to take notice of Walker's rising prosperity. More women came to see her as they heard of her success with hair products. Her business continued to grow. A Louisville-based preacher, Charles H. Parrish, met Walker and was so inspired by her presentation that he encouraged her to reach out to Booker T. Washington for support. By 1909, Washington was a household name in African American communities and arguably one of America's most famous men. Born into slavery, Washington rose in prominence, in part, due to his self-help ideology. In his famous Atlanta Compromise speech in 1895, he told a largely white audience, "The wisest among my race understand that the agitation of questions of social equality is the extremest folly, and that the progress in the enjoyment of all the privileges that will come to us must be the result of severe and constant struggle rather than of artificial forcing." He insisted, "It is important and right that all privileges of the law be ours, but it is vastly more important that we be prepared for the exercise of those privileges."[18] In order to ready blacks for full citizenship, Washington called on blacks to create schools, businesses, and local economies. Repeatedly and publicly, he dissuaded explicit confrontation with whites, although privately he gave to causes that did just that, and instead advocated industrial education, the accumulation of wealth, and the conciliation of the South.[19]

Washington was the founder of Tuskegee Institute, a historically black college funded by wealthy white magnates including Andrew Carnegie, John Rockefeller, and Henry Rogers. In 1900, Washington founded the National Negro Business League (NNBL). NNBL held conventions annually, inviting black business leaders, big and small, to network and promote their products. Unlike women's club associations like the National Association of Colored Women (NACW) that linked black uplift with political agitation, NNBL stressed apolitical discussions about black commerce. Walker frequently attended conventions held by various associations, including NNBL. Under Washington's leadership, NNBL afforded Walker a unique opportunity to gain access to established black leaders and new markets. More than simply expanding her business connections with black leaders, Walker wanted the opportunity to convince NNBL members about the importance of black women's leadership. As a sharecropper turned black female entrepreneur, Walker knew she had an inspirational story to share. Walker understood that her amazing ascent in black enterprise would serve as an example of resiliency and defiance for black women because she intimately understood the "multiple jeopardy" that black women experienced due to "dual and systematic discriminations of racism and sexism," which thwarted their economic opportunities.[20]

For these reasons, involvement and respect within NNBL as a black female business leader eventually became Walker's overwhelming goal. Never one to shy away from an opportunity, Walker earnestly wrote Washington, inviting him to invest in her company. She penned, "[My plan] is to give employment to many boys and girls" and "make this [factory] one of the largest factories of its kind in the United States."[21] Timely with his response, Washington politely declined, claiming that his attention to Tuskegee was full-time, and wished her the best of luck in her endeavors. Undeterred, she later engaged him on several different occasions to convince him of her worth as a black woman business leader.

Shortly thereafter, Walker settled in Indianapolis and built her factory with her company's profits, since most banks frequently denied loans to up-and-coming black businesses. While establishing herself as one of the Indianapolis' black elite, Walker pledged a $1,000 donation to the construction of a new black YMCA. Her donation was historic and earned her the praise of numerous black leaders. Two years later, Walker reached out to Washington again. Although she had donated the money because she believed that the black YMCA would enrich black families' lives, she did hope her financial investment in black communities' development would please Washington, since charitable giving was a cornerstone of his black uplift work. In her second letter to Washington, Walker asked if she could promote her work at one of his sponsored black farmers' conferences. Washington once again rebuffed her. What made matters worse was that cosmetic manufacturers, particularly manufacturers of hair care products, were denied entry into NNBL. Washington had warned the *New York Age* editor Fred Moore about the heightened number of hair-care ads in black newspapers, which he feared would elicit "the ridicule of even our best white friends."[22] Perhaps at first, Walker did not know that Washington harbored such disdain for black women's hair products. This stance, however, was only part of the problem; Washington's vision of black leadership did not include black women. A woman's role in the movement was not meant to be as steadfast and visible as men's. But Walker was determined to win Washington's endorsement and gain entry into the Washington-approved convention's speaker circle.

## Resolution

Madam C. J. Walker had many strikes against her—an orphan at seven with very little education who started work as a laundress in times of acute racial discrimination. Yet through networking, aligning her products with self-improvement and uplift for women, and eventually focusing her philanthropic giving to inspire individual and black economic autonomy, she built a successful business and became a social change leader.

Walker drew from her personal experiences as a poor woman who migrated from the farm to the city and who experienced hair loss. Her early marketing strategy was to share her personal story to connect with and motivate other women like her. She was a consummate networker, whose powerful public-speaking skills and persistence are models for all who aspire to lead change. She traveled across the country and even to neighboring countries, teaching black women how to practice hair care. Walker's sharp business instincts led her to tap into the reservoir of black organizations and to broaden her reach. Black-led religious institutions, businesses, community organizations, conferences, political associations, and women's clubs were central to her outreach efforts. She gained legitimacy in black neighborhoods across the nation because she was deliberate and thoughtful about how to engage black social networks. Walker's penchant for motivational and culturally responsive presentations contributed to her large following. A key strategy in her business success was her investment in black female entrepreneurship, a strategy that was evident in her company's creation of agent-led chapters. Black female entrepreneurs could create chapters across the nation. These were group gatherings to share Walker's hair-care literature and products while also creating supportive self-care spaces. Walker's hair-care regime gave black women, during an era when the country enacted severe physical and economic repression, a physical space to talk, share, and care for themselves and other black women. This safe space also provided black women the chance to reflect on the political issues of the day and to organize to fight.

Walker needed more than a savvy business strategy to win Booker T. Washington's respect. Walker's requests for inclusion in NNBL and other Washington-sponsored business events were declined, so she chose a different tactic. She decided to visit Washington's home, uninvited. Against the counsel of her lawyer, Ransom, Walker went to Washington's house fortified with a letter of support from the highly praised secretary for Indianapolis's black YMCA. Her go-getter attitude was rewarded. Washington granted her ten minutes to speak to black farmers. She shared her story of her humble beginnings and encouraged the farmers to keep up the hard work. Even though Walker was afforded an opportunity to try her products on Washington's wife and niece and established a local chapter for her company in Tuskegee, Washington still had not heartily endorsed her work. She returned to Indianapolis hopeful that Washington would eventually support her work and status as a black commerce leader.

The thirteenth NNBL convention was set for August 1912. Walker was certain that Washington would readily invite her to present her product and share her rags-to-riches story with the convention's attendees. Still, Washington did not promise her any speaking time. Before she left to attend NNBL's conference, Ransom tried to dissuade her from speaking at the conference, but Walker went to the conference anyway. Two thousand attendees filled the convention halls. Washington controlled the agenda and handpicked endorsements. Walker patiently waited for Washington to identify her.

The acknowledgment never came. Even when her colleague George Knox, an NNBL member, tried to spontaneously recognize Walker's efforts, Washington silenced Knox and moved on. Clearly Walker would have to create an opportunity for recognition. On the last day of the conference, Walker interrupted Washington's speech. Staring directly at Washington, she stood up and said, "Surely you are not going to shut the door in my face. I feel that I am in a business that is a credit to the womanhood of our race. I went into a business that is despised, that is criticized and talked about by everybody— the business of growing hair. They did not believe such a thing could be done, but I have been proven beyond the question of a doubt that I do grow hair."[23]

Fired up, she continued, "I have been trying to get before you business people and tell you what I am doing. I am a woman that came from the cotton fields of the South. I was promoted from there to the wash-tub. Then I was promoted to the cook kitchen, and from there I promoted myself into the business of manufacturing hair goods and preparations. I am not ashamed of my past. . . . Everybody told me I was making a mistake by going into this business, but I know how to grow hair as well as I know how to grow cotton."[24] Walker's impromptu speech garnered a large applause from the audience.

But Washington remained unmoved. Still undaunted, Walker used her ties to the YMCA to extend an invitation to Washington to give a talk at the YMCA's dedication in July 1913. Washington accepted her invitation, and she spared little expense in hosting him in grand style. Finally, Walker won the endorsement she desperately desired. At the fourteenth NNBL convention in 1913, Washington identified Walker as a "striking example of the possibilities of Negro womanhood in the business world."[25]

Walker sought to leverage her connections with Washington to institutionalize her profession in black universities like Tuskegee. She repeatedly asked Washington to establish courses in Tuskegee that would teach hair styling and hair culture work. Now a supporter of Walker, Washington stopped short of institutionalizing this profession. But many other colleges readily took up Walker on her offer, providing courses in hair care.[26] Nevertheless, Walker's newfound favor with Washington afforded her the opportunity to share her vision for black women's entrepreneurship. Unlike Washington, Walker believed that her position as a business leader must be used to advance the political goals of women's equality. She knew she needed more than herself to advance this mission—she needed more black women to see themselves as black entrepreneurs and to join the movement for social and political equality. In front of NNBL attendees, she announced, "I am not merely satisfied in making money for myself, for I am endeavoring to provide employment for hundreds of the women of my race. I had little or no opportunity when I started out in life. . . . I had to make my own living and my own opportunity. But I made it. That is why I want to say to every Negro woman present, don't sit down and wait for the opportunities to come, but you have to get up and make them!"[27]

Walker also took this message of black female entrepreneurship to the pulpits. At various black churches throughout the country, she advised black women "to rise above the laundry and kitchen . . . and to aspire to a place in the world of commerce and trade."[28] By 1912, at least a thousand black women had decided to do just that as Walker's sale agents. Walker's biographers suggest that black women flocked to Walker because "many saw the work as a door to a better life."[29] These biographers cite one of Walker's black female sales agents to illustrate why the hair dressing/styling profession was so attractive. Maggie Wilson, one of Walker's top agents in Pittsburgh, opened up a trade for hundreds of other black women. It was work that enabled them to make "an honest and profitable living," work in which "they can make as much in one week as a month's salary would bring from any other position a colored woman can secure."[30] In order to become a sales agent, women had to take Walker's certification course. Once the agent's training was completed, she could then open her own beauty parlor selling Walker's products. These agents often replicated Walker's successful sales strategy: certified sales agents would contact the local Baptist or AME church, open a suitable beauty parlor, recruit endorsements from local civic organizations, present the benefits of Walker products at local events, train other potential agents, take orders, and move on to the next selling site. This marketing strategy, which largely operated through word of mouth and social networks, was by the mid-twentieth century to become a signature business marketing model, on which brands such as Avon cosmetics were based.[31]

Within ten years, Walker had built a veritable empire of black women entrepreneurs and potential community leaders. Instead of simply avoiding the increasing violence and discrimination that blacks confronted on a daily basis, as Washington advised in his Atlanta Compromise and espoused in his leadership role at NNBL, Walker insisted that black female employees fight for political equality head-on. She modeled this behavior through her political engagements. Her years of living in the violence-drenched South no doubt inspired her to support and advocate for black-equality causes. One particular cause dear to Walker's heart was the antilynching campaign. Open-minded and supportive of various political approaches to civil rights, Walker financed groups across the political spectrum. She gave to the National Association for the Advancement of Colored People (NAACP) and donated to the arguably more militant National Equal Rights League, led by political rabble-rousers like Ida B. Wells and William Monroe Trotter.

Seizing the role of race leader, Walker welcomed opportunities to speak against the rising tide of white-led, state-sanctioned terrorism against blacks throughout the country. She relocated to New York in 1916 and quickly got involved in the local organizing efforts against lynching. The national movement against lynching was gaining steam by the early 1900s due to the great organizing efforts of organizations like the NAACP and antilynching organizers like Ida B. Wells, the Reverend Hutchens Bishop, and many others. No movement would gain prominence without the participation of everyday people emboldened by their passion to fight for a better world and inspired by leaders who called for change. In New York, over eight hundred children joined more than twenty thousand black adults in their protest against lynching on July 28, 1917. Boy Scouts passed out protest fliers that stated, "We march because we want to make impossible a repetition of Waco, Memphis and St. Louis, by rousing the conscience of the country and bringing the murderers of our brothers, sisters and innocent children to justice."[32] Walker and other Harlem leaders traveled to Washington, DC, a few days after the New York protest to implore President Woodrow Wilson to speak against lawless violence against blacks. Wilson did not meet with them and instead referred them to one of his aides, Joseph Patrick Tumulty. In the meeting, Tumulty refused to commit Wilson to making a public statement against the lynching terrorism happening in black communities across the country.

Walker's commitment to financial investment in the growing civil rights movement was reflected in her agents' fundraising for justice efforts as well. In 1916, Walker decided to institutionalize her company's commitment to social justice by starting the National Beauty Culturists and Benevolent Association of Madam C. J. Walker Agents. Walker had two goals: to increase her agents' sales and to encourage them to contribute to social-betterment causes. Walker's years of involvement in church clubs and national club groups like the National Association of Colored Women inspired her to infuse a similar political-movement sentiment into her company. In short, Walker wanted for her agents the same public recognition and admiration she had earned for herself as a donor to Tuskegee and the YMCA.

In 1917, Walker established an association composed of decentralized chapters that would support charity work and fund organizing efforts against discrimination and segregation. Her organizing efforts were met with the success of the association's first convention. Walker agents shared their stories of success, charity work, and sales strategies. The convention's proceedings were similar to those of NACW and NNBL. Walker spoke on the final night. Reading her keynote speech, called "Women's Duty to Woman," Walker implored black women to remain unwavering in their "protest against wrong and injustice."[33] Walker's rousing speech inspired her agents to submit a telegram to President Wilson that read in part,

We, the representatives of the National Convention of the Mme. C. J. Walker Agents, in convention assembled, and in larger sense representing twelve million Negroes, have keenly felt the injustice done our race and country through the recent lynching at Memphis,

Tennessee, and the horrible race riot at East St. Louis. . . . We further respectfully urge that you as President of these United States use your great influence that congress enact the necessary laws to prevent a recurrence of such disgraceful affairs.[34]

Walker's political commitments and financial support won her the acclaim of many black elites and organizers. Once she opened her thirty-four-room villa in Irvington, New York, she entertained all types of black leaders. Her intense political engagement eventually earned her the ire of Secret Service officials. US government officials sent spies to monitor Walker's activities and attend her parties. Ransom constantly tried to discourage Walker's participation in political activities, particularly her organizing efforts associated with more militant leaders like William Monroe Trotter. Walker had to be careful about the company she kept, Ransom insisted, lest she risk hurting her company's brand.[35] Even with threats to her company's growth, Walker remained committed to working with all types of black leaders in pursuit of social and economic betterment for blacks, and she encouraged her agents to do the same. She repeatedly reminded her agents to "feel that their first duty is to humanity."[36] She compelled her agents to "do their bit to help and advance the best interests of the Race."[37]

## Notes

1   A'Lelia Bundles, *On Her Own Ground: The Life and Times of Madam C. J. Walker* (New York: Scribner, 2001), 38.

2   Ibid., 37.

3   Paula Giddings, *Ida, a Sword among Lions: Ida B. Wells and the Campaign against Lynching* (New York: HarperCollins, 2008), 90.

4   Ibid.

5   Bundles, *On Her Own Ground*, 40.

6   Ibid., 43.

7   Ibid., 46.

8   Ibid., 48.

9   Ibid.

10  Ibid., 60.

11  Ibid., 63.

12  Ibid., 64.

13  Ibid., 65.

14  Ibid., 89.

15 Ibid., 91.
16 Ibid., 98.
17 Ibid., 96.
18 Booker T. Washington, "The 1895 Atlanta Compromise Speech," in *The Booker T. Washington Papers, vol. 3*, ed. Louis R. Harlan (Urbana: University of Illinois Press, 1974), 583.
19 W. E. B. Du Bois, *The Souls of Black Folk* (New York: Oxford University Press, 2009), 39.
20 Deborah K. King, "Multiple Jeopardy, Multiple Consciousness: The Context of a Black Feminist Ideology," *Signs* 14 (1988): 43.
21 Bundles, *On Her Own Ground*, 100.
22 Ibid., 123.
23 Ibid., 135.
24 Ibid., 135–136.
25 Ibid., 148.
26 Nancy F. Koehn, Anne Dwojeski, William Grundy, Erica Helms, and Katherine Miller, "Madam C. J. Walker: Entrepreneur, Leader, and Philanthropist," Harvard Business School Case 807-145 (March 2007, revised April 2011), 21.
27 Bundles, *On Her Own Ground*, 136.
28 Ibid., 153.
29 Koehn et al., "Madam C. J. Walker," 18, citing U.S. Census Bureau, "Negroes in the United States," 1900 U.S. Census, http://www2.census.gov/prod2/decennial/documents/03322287no8ch2.pdf.
30 Ibid.
31 Ibid.
32 Bundles, *On Her Own Ground*, 207.
33 Ibid., 212.
34 Ibid.
35 Mark David Higbee, "W. E. B. Du Bois, F. B. Ransom, the Madam Walker Company, and Black Business Leadership in the 1930s," *Indiana Magazine of History* 89 (1993): 101–124.
36 Bundles, *On Her Own Ground*, 231.
37 Ibid.

## Bibliography

Bundles, A'Lelia. *On Her Own Ground: The Life and Times of Madam C. J. Walker*. New York: Scribner, 2001.

Du Bois, W. E. B. *The Souls of Black Folk*. New York: Oxford University Press, 2009.

Giddings, Paula. *Ida, a Sword among Lions: Ida B Wells and the Campaign against Lynching*. New York: HarperCollins, 2008.

Higbee, Mark David. "W. E. B. Du Bois, F. B. Ransom, the Madam Walker Company, and Black Business Leadership in the 1930s." *Indiana Magazine of History* 89 (1993): 101–124.

King, Deborah K. "Multiple Jeopardy, Multiple Consciousness: The Context of a Black Feminist Ideology." *Signs* 14 (1988): 42–72.

Koehn, Nancy F., Anne Dwojeski, William Grundy, Erica Helms, and Katherine Miller. "Madam C. J. Walker: Entrepreneur, Leader, and Philanthropist." Harvard Business School Case 807-145 (March 2007, revised April 2011).

Washington, Booker T. "The 1895 Atlanta Compromise Speech." In *The Booker T. Washington Papers*, vol. 3, edited by Louis R. Harlan, 583–587. Urbana: University of Illinois Press, 1974.

# Diane McCarthy

## Responding to Crisis through Connected Leadership at Verizon

### Kathleen E. McCollough and Lisa Hetfield

## Background

The threat of a "Frankenstorm," the result of an impending "monster weather combination," was the lead story for New Jersey forecasters on Friday, October 27, 2012.[1] Area residents were all too familiar with the potential dangers of such storms. One year prior, in late August, Hurricane Irene had left record flood levels throughout the state as a result of torrential rains, saturated ground, and overflowing rivers.[2] By Monday, October 29, residents knew without a doubt that an unprecedented storm was headed their way, or as Newark's *Star-Ledger* headline predicted, "State Forecast: A Catastrophe."[3]

The predictions proved accurate. On the evening of October 29, Hurricane Sandy's eighty-mile-per-hour winds made landfall near Atlantic City, New Jersey. As a late-season, posttropical cyclone, Sandy's high winds and unique angle of approach as well as a full moon combined to produce a record storm surge for New Jersey and the New York City area. The National Hurricane Center reported over $55 billion in damages, making the storm the second costliest in US history after Katrina.[4] Sandy impacted more than 346,000 structures in the New Jersey and New York area alone and decimated the region's power, water, and telecommunications infrastructure.[5] On Thursday, the *Star-Ledger*'s front-page banner headline describing the devastation was "PURE HELL." For the millions of residents without power and hot water who were facing a potential gas shortage and overnight temperatures reaching into the thirties, this headline was no exaggeration.

## McCarthy's Team Responds to Crisis

Behind the scenes of Hurricane Sandy, Diane McCarthy, Verizon's senior vice president of network and technology—service delivery and assurance, and her team were already hard at work to prevent damage to the telecommunications wireline infrastructure. Verizon Communication's operations span across two business divisions: Verizon wireless and wireline. The wireline division provides customers with communications products and services including local exchange and long-distance voice service, broadband video and data, IP network services, network access, and more.[6] In the aftermath of Sandy, one of the many tasks of McCarthy's team was to rapidly restore landline service to Verizon's wireline customers, twenty-three million in the Northeast alone.[7]

The Verizon team initiated its crisis continuity plans; as McCarthy says, "Everybody rolls their sleeves up. This is what we do."[8] The necessity to restore and rebuild multiple buildings involved not only massive plans but also cross-functional effort and communication between Verizon wireline and wireless, the city, and the power companies. One of the buildings needing immediate attention was Verizon's New York City headquarters at West Street in lower Manhattan. The headquarters was inundated with a storm surge that left behind a four-foot-high watermark in the lobby of the historic building and flooded the underground cable vault.[9] Another of the eighteen central switch hubs for Manhattan, the Broad Street hub, incurred even more extensive flooding. Outside Manhattan, post-Sandy repairs were hindered by downed power lines, trees and debris, closed roads, flooding, and even several feet of snow in some areas.[10] As a resident of the New Jersey shore, McCarthy found her hometown among the hardest hit.

## Verizon and Previous Experiences with Crisis

According to the company's published corporate history, Verizon Communications Inc., based in New York City, was formed on June 30, 2000, with the merger of Bell Atlantic and GTE Corp. The merger, one of the largest in US business history, was many years in the making, involving companies with roots going back to the beginnings of the telephone business in the late nineteenth century. Government regulation largely shaped the evolution of the industry throughout most of the twentieth century. Then, with the signing of the Telecommunications Act on February 8, 1996, federal law directed a shift to more market-based policies. With the merger of the two companies, Verizon was established to provide long-distance and data services nationwide. Thus, the devastation brought about by Sandy had wide implications for Verizon and its customers.

Hurricane Sandy, however, was not the first time McCarthy and her team had faced a crisis of this magnitude. The telecommunications infrastructure for the area had also been decimated after 9/11 and the previous August's Hurricane Irene. McCarthy recounts how the experience of 9/11 in particular prepared the team physically, emotionally, and strategically for how to handle crisis management. The Sandy-flooded West Street headquarters had been so close to the World Trade Center that the building had been hit with falling debris during 9/11.[11]

The leadership team working with McCarthy for Sandy included those team members who had been responsible for rebuilding the infrastructure in lower Manhattan after 9/11. These leaders had firsthand technical knowledge of what needed to be done to reroute, restore, and rebuild the lower Manhattan network. As an executive director during 9/11, McCarthy had been responsible for supporting wholesale carrier customers (e.g., AT&T, Sprint, Level 3) who had lost service to the financial exchanges on Wall Street. Wholesale involves the sale of goods to retailers themselves, who are often industrial, commercial, or institutional users.[12] As the liaison between Verizon and its wholesale customers, McCarthy was placed in the complex position of having to assist wholesale carriers in getting their customers back in service while also rebuilding for Verizon's retail customers. Her goal was to ensure parity in repairs for both wholesale and retail. Her successful navigation of this complex terrain was a challenge, but together the team worked "step by step, day by day, to get the Stock Exchange turned up in a week" after 9/11.[13] These challenges taught McCarthy how to balance conflicting demands, prioritize, and meet the most pressing needs of her customers and her team.

While previous catastrophic events had given the team experience with crisis, the Herculean effort often required to recover from these massive catastrophes was also contributing to widespread burnout within the company. These crisis events took a toll not only on Verizon's telecommunications infrastructure but also on its employees. McCarthy describes how the team had even coined the phrase "battle fatigue" to describe their feelings after dealing with Irene, a work stoppage, and then Sandy.[14] The need for this kind of crisis response was not supposed to be once a year. The recent work stoppage, although not at the level of a natural disaster, had also been disruptive for day-to-day operations. Management was loaned from across the country so that workers from Oklahoma might end up working in Queens, New York, creating additional stress for all involved. The lack of time for the team to recover from the last natural disaster had left many employees facing serious burnout and wondering, "How much more can we take?"

### Regulatory and Technical Change

Such crisis events, furthermore, are far from the only challenges faced by the Verizon team. The team also works on a daily basis to provide and improve service amid the massive regulatory and technical changes that have dramatically transformed the telecommunications industry over the past three decades. While McCarthy describes feeling honored to be in a position to influence positively customers in response to 9/11 and Hurricane Sandy, she emphasizes, "Every single day our customers depend upon us to keep them connected, and the true triumph is the network issues that never happen because of the diligence of a team of eighteen thousand that I'm beyond proud to lead."[15] In striving for the best possible service at all times, McCarthy used her leadership to play a pivotal role in transforming the Verizon Network Field operations team. Through continual revisions to process and tweaks to existing protocol, McCarthy was able to help steer the team in ways that worked to increase efficiencies while reducing expenses and improving service results.

In addition to recovery from natural disasters, the business of Verizon wireline has been redefined over the past few decades. A few of the major changes since the 1970s include "the development and diffusion of microwave transmission, digital switching, and optical fiber transport."[16] Since the mid-1990s, the diffusion of digital technology had contributed further to a "convergence of what were historically the separate services offered by cable and satellite companies, wireless carriers, and wireline telephone companies."[17] In turn, services have expanded "from analogue voice and limited data to digital voice, high-speed data, Internet access, video, narrowband/broadband wireless."[18] Verizon FiOS, or Fiber Optic Services, for instance, offers high-definition television and high-speed Internet services in addition to local and long-distance phone service.

Updates to the infrastructure played a role in the recovery from Sandy, as the company was tasked not only to repair damaged lines but also to replace the copper-line infrastructure with fiber or FiOS technology. "While the company has buried fiber optic lines beneath much of its territory, it still serves about a third of its footprint via century-old copper wire technology. Copper is not only slower than fiber; it's also more vulnerable to failing when wet."[19] Verizon's efforts to restore its infrastructure after Sandy in many cases also involved improving it by replacing the copper network with fiber technology.

Within this ever-changing industry, Verizon wireline has had to redefine itself, its product, and its services in order to anticipate customers' demands and meet their needs. McCarthy describes how she and other Verizon leaders have come to understand their role "as enablers of seamlessly connecting people and things to improve the quality of life": "Our networks are at the center of the connected world and we're working to build the platforms that will bring information and computing to anyone at any time on any device."[20] Within a company devoted to "seamlessly connecting people," McCarthy's own leadership style and career are founded on building and sustaining a network of professional and personal connections throughout her years of experience in the business.

## Laying the Infrastructure for Connective Leadership

When McCarthy describes the successes in her career, she points out that there was not a "single shining moment" but a compilation of contributions as she was able to work her "way up and across the business."[21] McCarthy's current leadership is grounded in thirty years of both making and keeping a network of supportive connections within Verizon and across the industry.

While McCarthy has become a well-known team builder and leader within the industry, the first six years of her career were marked by many challenges, most of which were due to a work environment that was noninclusive and lacked the corporate support to handle diversity. After graduating from Rutgers University with a degree in communications, McCarthy started in 1982 as a central office technician in Newark, New Jersey, at what was then AT&T Long Lines. In a nontraditional occupation for women at the time, McCarthy spent the first six years of her career as one of only a few female technicians in the field and often as the only woman in the building. While her parents raised safety concerns for their twenty-two-year-old daughter's assignment to the Newark central office, which was surrounded by a twelve-foot-high barbed-wire fence, McCarthy jokes that it was "much more dangerous inside the building."[22]

As one of very few female technicians, a position that created some difficult working conditions, McCarthy learned not only to persevere in the face of resistance and hostility but also how to command respect, garner support, and find her place within an ever-changing organization. At that time, the only way for a technician to receive qualification to work overtime was through his or her direct supervisor. McCarthy and her direct supervisor had several confrontations including an episode in which he made inappropriate comments on her appearance and was reported by a friend to the district manager. After her supervisor told the rest of the team that he was reprimanded due to the incident, she experienced a backlash from her coworkers. This incident made learning the necessary job skills more difficult because the position depended on hands-on learning from supervisors and coworkers with more experience. McCarthy notes in recounting this challenging time in her career today that subsequently an official process was developed so that current employees can get help when confronted with such difficult situations.

After six years as a technician in the union, McCarthy was offered a promotional opportunity in sales for New Jersey Bell, a move that provided her the chance to work more directly with customers. This move offered her not only experience in a new area but also the opportunity to learn new skills. While she found herself missing the technical aspects of the business, the sales position challenged her in ways that her technician position had not. Sales taught her how to conquer her fear of public speaking and allowed her to emerge as a high performer. After watching a video of herself presenting in front of group of people, McCarthy remembers telling her family, "I can't do this." Her family told her, "Well, then quit." Her response to this challenge was, "I can't quit. I just can't quit."

Overcoming her own difficulty with public speaking has also enabled McCarthy to mentor others to become more effective communicators. She notes, "You need to be put in situations where you have to speak in order to overcome your fear. You need to make mistakes and learn from them and get back up and do it over and over. You need to practice, practice."[23] McCarthy recounted how her boss would make her come to his office and make a presentation about what she had learned at sales training. McCarthy describes this as "a lesson in a lesson" and an invaluable space where she could gain confidence. In asking this same boss how she would be able to make her sales quota without a big staff support team, he responded, "A hundred thousand people work for you. This whole company works for you on behalf of your customer. You need to think differently about how you do your job. You are the customer's advocate."[24]

The next phase of McCarthy's career included the cultivation of relationships with leaders and mentors who had noted McCarthy's potential and displayed a desire to help her succeed. After taking maternity leave from her sales position, McCarthy made the decision to return to network operations rather than sales, as operations involved less travel and others had told her that her skills were of value to that area of the business. After several assignments, including dispatch manager for large union groups, McCarthy worked as the director to the senior vice president, in other words, as chief of staff. This movement up and across the organization helped McCarthy to gain experience in different areas of the business and to garner the support of mentors.

Ultimately, McCarthy rose to lead the teams that oversaw Verizon's wireline networks as well as to develop and implement Verizon's fiber-to-the-premises (FTTP) network behind its industry-leading FiOS data and TV services. McCarthy also led the global group responsible for Verizon's global voice, data, and IP wholesale and enterprise customers in more than twenty-six hundred cities in 150 countries on six continents. In addition, McCarthy became the chair of the board for the Common Ground Alliance (CGA), a consortium of industry stakeholders working together to protect underground facilities from damage. In her role as chair of the CGA, McCarthy worked to develop a sense of shared responsibility as well as increase the numbers of participants in the group. She notes that "the bottom line is the more people that are involved, the higher the success in preventing damage to buried facilities."[25]

When McCarthy is praised for her leadership, she points to the great benefit of having spent a long time with the same group of people, many of whom mentored her or whom she played a role in mentoring. McCarthy notes that one of her greatest contributions as a leader has been her influence in selecting and cultivating a team of the highest caliber through an "intentional focus on picking the best people." Reflecting on her previous roles in leading organizational change, she observes, "You change the people, or you change the people."[26]

## As Sandy Hit

As New Jersey Governor Chris Christie was ordering a state of emergency for New Jersey on Saturday, October 27, Diane McCarthy was arriving at Newark-Liberty airport from a business trip to Asia. Unlike with 9/11, the Verizon team knew that Sandy was coming. As each hour progressed, it become clear that the dire predictions for the storm were accurate, and the entire Verizon team was preparing accordingly. On Monday night, October 29, McCarthy and other Verizon leaders remained on teleconference calls until midnight, when they were forced to hang up as the storm surge hit lower Manhattan. At that point, everyone realized that the storm damage was going to be "devastating in terms of what they have to do."[27] McCarthy knew that her team would need her support. She had learned from previous experience that this level of damage necessitates working together with the Federal Emergency Management Agency (FEMA), the power company, wholesale customers, Verizon Wireless, and others.

The next morning, McCarthy woke up in her home at the Jersey Shore, only four blocks from the ocean. Her neighbor's one-hundred-year-old tree had fallen across her lawn, blocking her driveway. There was no power, and the state police were checking IDs at the entrance to her town to ensure that only residents and first responders were coming in and out. Much of the Jersey shore was devastated. In the wake of the storm, McCarthy's team was once again among the first responders. What should she do to lead her team most effectively? What steps should be taken to help restore services? Could the crisis-weary Verizon team once again perform up to the beyond-the-usual expectations? What ways could the team improve its ability to withstand future disasters?

## Resolution

We are often told that some people are born leaders; however, such a notion of leadership foregrounds those who command a scene or take charge. Diane McCarthy notes that her leadership style is "certainly not command and control."[28] In a state of constant change and occasional crisis, the telecommunications industry depends on a sense of shared responsibility cultivated by a leader who listens, establishes trust, communicates directly, and works collaboratively to create a collective vision and plan.

One of the greatest challenges before, during, and after major disasters is the ability to coordinate a large number of individuals and organizations with a lack of preexisting social networks to support the response.[29] In particular, research has found that in major disasters, "sharing information, willingness to collaborate, and shared values" are vital bases of effective information sharing and communication.[30] During Hurricane Sandy, for instance, Verizon's leadership partnered with "local authorities, power companies, government agencies and suppliers to ensure monitoring of critical facilities and kept effective lines of communications open."[31] Verizon offered additional response services by establishing various command centers throughout the region to facilitate response and communication.

After it was safe to dispatch technicians to the field, McCarthy's team worked to prepare a priority list to ensure that impacted parts of the network got back online quickly.[32] A major priority for Verizon wireline was the restoration of its inside plant network, particularly in New York City. This required the complete reconstruction of the buildings' power plants as well as the replacement and restoration of complex switching, transport, and telemetry systems. The West Street facility was restored within twenty-four hours of flooding, and the Broad Street facility, which was hit even harder, was fully restored soon afterward.[33]

An effective response depends on preexisting personal connections, mutual trust, and a shared plan. McCarthy and her team's previous experiences in response both to 9/11 and to Hurricane Irene had provided the organization with the necessary knowledge to develop and hone an effective crisis plan and response to Hurricane Sandy. The leadership team had firsthand experience with how to handle and respond to crisis events—many of them previously held the positions that they were now supervising and had established themselves as trustworthy leaders. McCarthy, for instance, recalls that her phone rang nonstop after 9/11 as she acted as a reliable communication hub between her customers and the Verizon engineers. As McCarthy had established trusted relationships with both her customers and the Verizon team, they could turn to her during the crisis to help them get the job done as soon as possible.

Previous experience had taught McCarthy and her team to anticipate and prepare for crisis events prior to catastrophe, rather than during or after. Verizon relies on plans and process around business continuity in response to various types of work stoppages for everything from service discontinuation to natural disasters. As soon as predictions for the storm began, McCarthy's team reacted by

> sending technicians, supplies, and equipment from around the country to potential impacted areas, making sure standby and portable generators were strategically located, tested, and fuel tanks were topped off, as well as sandbagging and securing all central offices and technical facilities that had the potential to flood. Verizon also staged a mobile communication center as well as COWs (Cells On Wheels) near the impacted areas for immediate post-storm support of residents, businesses and, of course, first responders.[34]

When Sandy hit, the team relied on both its emergency plans and a sense that they could "do it again."

The morning after Sandy, McCarthy began the removal of the tree across her driveway as well as worked to remove roadblocks at Verizon in order to allow her team to be able to do what it needed to do. She used her industry connections to obtain a letter from FEMA that allowed work crews to enter New York City. Once she was able, McCarthy also went out in the field and joined her team on the ground as it restored service. Her work in meetings, on the phone, and what she describes as "going to see my people" points to her ability to make the connections and to establish the trust across departments and organizations necessary for working collaboratively to get the mission accomplished.[35] McCarthy's response points to her role as a strong, respected, trusted, and seasoned team leader.

## Leadership Approach: Connections, Strategic Planning, and Collaboration

In an industry grounded in networked connections, McCarthy's connective and collaborative leadership approach during the crisis was founded on (1) a passion for personal connections built on trust, (2) strategic planning based on deep knowledge of the business, and (3) collaboration within, across, and outside the industry.

## Personal Connections

When McCarthy is praised for her individual success as a leader, she often circles back to praise her team. McCarthy's success as a leader before and during Hurricane Sandy appears most vividly not in an account of her efforts but through an email sent by one of her technicians to Verizon's chair and CEO, Lowell McAdams. In this email, the technician describes working throughout the night of Hurricane Sandy to protect and sandbag the central office on Fire Island from the storm surge. He expresses his own pride in volunteering to prevent further damage and praise for the efforts of his leadership team, as he directly names his supervisor and manager.

McCarthy's sense of shared pride in recounting this technician's story points to the way that she is able to both model and cultivate a collaborative and connective leadership. Showing appreciation and recognition works to build and sustain a team with shared values and mutual trust. She describes expressing appreciation as one of the practices that, in addition to rest, helped the team combat "battle fatigue."[36] Her active participation alongside her team also helped to demonstrate that they were "in this together."

Furthermore, cultivating personal connections based on mutual trust is critical to good mentorship. Mentoring is a leadership tool that allows McCarthy to leverage connections in order to improve her team's skills and knowledge, thereby building a stronger organization. She describes how she will give a new team member an assignment that is "narrow and specific": "What I do is call upon another leader who is very good at that task and say, 'Can you coach this person for me?'" This helps to build what McCarthy calls a "buddy system," or system of mutual support. For McCarthy, being a good leader is "all about making those connections."[37]

## Strategic Planning

McCarthy's comprehensive knowledge of Verizon's operations was learned on the ground through her experience working on teams in engineering, sales, and network operations. Within each of these areas, she has held a variety of staff and line positions with increasing responsibility, including central office technician, large business sales, and billing operations.[38] McCarthy's experiences across and up the business have provided her with firsthand knowledge of the perspectives held by a variety of stakeholders. This firsthand knowledge allows her to combine big-picture thinking with on-the-ground practical know-how.

One of the most critical components to the successful crisis response of McCarthy's team remains its business continuity and emergency management plans. These plans are continually honed to deal with a series of potential issues including severe weather, natural disasters, and commercial power outages. The planning process also allows the company to apply lessons/best practices from previous disasters to be better prepared for the future. For instance, in response to Sandy, the Verizon organization focused on improving its current infrastructure to prevent future damage— particularly its central switch locations in lower Manhattan, which had been hit hard by 9/11, Irene, and Sandy.

Verizon wireline responded to the repeated damage sustained to these locations in several ways. First of all, the company replaced more than three hundred thousand pounds of copper with fiber-optic cable. Fiber not only offers the capacity for higher-speed broadband but also is more easily replaced and resistant to seawater.[39] Furthermore, to address the problem of water picking up velocity, the team has partnered with the Dutch engineering firm Arcadis to create more sophisticated barriers than sandbags that may be set up in a day and that also provide a more formidable barrier.[40] While the company had already moved the West Street office's diesel generator to the tenth floor, the fuel tank and pumping system remained underground. This area has now been turned into an environment similar to a submarine, so that even if the floors above the pumping system are flooded, the building would still be able to run.[41] Good leadership uses the last crisis to prepare for the next.

Strategic planning enables McCarthy's team to safely and effectively get the job done both during a crisis and day to day. McCarthy's skill in process improvement ensures that the team is most effectively and efficiently servicing its customers. These plans form the infrastructure of the emergency response that allows the company to effectively mobilize, communicate, and safely complete necessary tasks.

## Collaboration

McCarthy's very early experience as the first woman on a team of unionized technicians, followed by years in customer service—with wholesale customers, in particular—forged a tough yet balanced perspective on finding profitable solutions to problems that benefit all parties, while maintaining the quality of the services offered. In turn, McCarthy's leadership style centralizes the way that a business exchange is also a relationship; furthermore, these relationships function best when they are collaborative and consider the needs of all parties. Her style of leadership also is built on a sense of mutual trust cultivated with her team, as she not only keeps her word but also lends support when needed. McCarthy's diverse experiences moving up and across the industry allowed her to develop an experiential understanding of the different needs and perspectives held by various stakeholders.

McCarthy notes that these recent crisis events have taught Verizon the necessity of "looking outside of [the] company and working with other companies and associations to find out what best practices they were using to really mitigate these events."[42] She points to one of the first steps in building collaboration: the recognition that you and your team do not know everything. As McCarthy puts it, "Team building is not only about your own team. Team building is whoever else is out there to help you when you have to rely on other people. Step one is recognizing the problem, and the problem is that you don't know everything." Then you move into action to "get people to want to help you."[43] This involves translating the problem and visualizing the solution for those who are unable to see it from their perspective.

Two recent examples of building a win-win strategy are shown in Verizon's copper-to-fiber migration and the switch to green energy. As Verizon migrates from copper to fiber, McCarthy notes, "Moving customers from copper to fiber has a significant upside for our customers and for Verizon, and we'll continue to aggressively pursue migration opportunities."[44] McCarthy and her team have focused on switching copper customers who have experienced ongoing service issues. These customers are given the "opportunity to migrate to the more reliable fiber platform at no cost whatsoever. The same products on a more resilient infrastructure at no additional cost— there is no downside." Another example of a win-win solution is the move at Verizon to onsite green energy. As McCarthy notes, "This investment helps reduce the load on our nation's power grid while enhancing our proven service continuity—even during network issues."[45] These solutions not only are a win for the Verizon team or its customers but also benefit what McCarthy calls the "collective good."[46]

## Conclusion

Through emphasis on personal connections, strategic planning, and collaboration—and drawing on a reservoir of trust, respect, and team loyalty forged over the years—Diane McCarthy was able to meet the needs of a recovery effort from Hurricane Sandy that demanded a persistent and resilient team with a shared purpose. McCarthy's leadership story is a case study in how a leader's development and prioritization of teamwork are essential during a crisis to sustain recovery efforts. McCarthy's leadership during the crisis of Hurricane Sandy was more about reducing the roadblocks for her team and allowing it to shine than about her being the hero out front leading the charge. She demonstrated that she is not afraid to join her team in the trenches when the need arises.

This case also emphasizes that effective crisis management depends on the investment—well before the crisis event—in improving process, establishing trust, and making critical connections across the industry. Building an effective team, however, takes time, intention, and investment in mentorship. McCarthy and her team were able to rise to the challenge during Hurricane Sandy because they had already spent years recruiting and developing the highest caliber team, plans/process, and infrastructure to see them through the crisis.

## Notes

1 Stephen Stirling, "The Rise of Frankenstorm: Potential Impact of Monster Weather Combination 'Borders on Rare to Unprecedented,' Climatologist Says," *Star-Ledger*, October 26, 2012.

2 Len Melisurgo, "Hurricane Irene: New Jersey's Forgotten Storm," *Star-Ledger*, August 27, 2013.

3 National Oceanic and Atmospheric Administration, "State Forecast: A Catastrophe," *Star-Ledger*, October 29, 2012.

4 Eric S. Blake, Todd B. Kimberlain, Robert J. Berg, John P. Cangialosi, and John L. Beven II, "Tropical Cyclone Report: Hurricane Sandy," National Hurricane Center, February 12, 2014, http://www.nhc.noaa.gov/data/tcr/AL182012 _Sandy.pdf.

5 Ibid., 17.

6 MarketLine Industry Profile, *Wireless Telecommunication Services in the United States*, December 10, 2013.

7 Gerry Smith, "Hurricane Sandy Delivers 'Another Catastrophe' to Verizon's Home, Complicating Network Repairs," *Huffington Post*, November 3, 2012, http://www.huffingtonpost.com/2012/11/03/verizon-sandy_n_2069033.html.

8 Diane McCarthy, in discussion with Lisa Hetfield and Dana Britton, January 13, 2014.

9 Smith, "Hurricane Sandy Delivers 'Another Catastrophe.'"

10 Ibid.

11 Ibid.

12 Eric Schoonover, "Whole Bandwidth: The Price Is Still Right," *Business Communications Review* 36 (July 2007): 32.

13 Diane McCarthy, in discussion with Lisa Hetfield and Dana Britton, January 13, 2014.

14 Ibid.

15 Ibid.

16 Jerry A. Hausman and William E. Taylor, "Telecommunication in the U.S.: From Regulation to Competition (Almost)," *Review of Industrial Organization* 42 (2012): 206.

17 Ibid., 206.

18 Ibid.

19 Ibid.

20 Sharon Vollman, "OSP Interviews Diane McCarthy," *OSP*, 2013, http://www .ospmag.com/issue/article/OSP-Interviews-Diane-McCarthy.

21 Ibid.

22 Diane McCarthy, in discussion with Lisa Hetfield and Dana Britton, January 13, 2014.

23 Ibid.

24 Ibid.

25 Vollman, "OSP Interviews Diane McCarthy."

26 Diane McCarthy, in discussion with Lisa Hetfield and Dana Britton, January 13, 2014.

27  Ibid.
28  Vollman, "OSP Interviews Diane McCarthy."
29  Paul T. Jaeger, Ben Shneiderman, Kenneth R. Fleischmann, Jennifer Preece, Yan Qu, and Philip Fei Wu, "Community Response Grids: E-government Social Networks, and Effective Emergency Management," *Telecommunications Policy* 31 (2007): 592–604.
30  Naim Kapucu, "Interagency Communication Networks during Emergencies: Boundary Spanners in Multiagency Coordination," *American Review of Public Administration* 36 (2006): 210.
31  Vollman, "OSP Interviews Diane McCarthy."
32  Ibid.
33  Aaron Elstein, Andrew J. Hawkins, Barbara Benson, Matthew Flamm, and Thornton McEnery, "What If Sandy Happened Today?," *Crain's New York Business*, October 18, 2013, http://www.crainsnewyork.com/article/20131018/NEWS/131019888/what-if-sandy-happened-today#.
34  Vollman, "OSP Interviews Diane McCarthy."
35  Diane McCarthy, in discussion with Lisa Hetfield and Dana Britton, January 13, 2014.
36  Ibid.
37  Ibid.
38  Vollman, "OSP Interviews Diane McCarthy."
39  Elstein, "What If Sandy Happened Today?"
40  Ibid.
41  Ibid.
42  Diane McCarthy, in discussion with Lisa Hetfield and Dana Britton, January 13, 2014.
43  Ibid.
44  Vollman, "OSP Interviews Diane McCarthy."
45  Ibid.
46  Diane McCarthy, in discussion with Lisa Hetfield and Dana Britton, January 13, 2014.

## Bibliography

Blake, Eric S., Todd B. Kimberlain, Robert J. Berg, John P. Cangialosi, and John L. Beven II. "Tropical Cyclone Report: Hurricane Sandy." National Hurricane Center, February 12, 2014. http://www.nhc.noaa.gov/data/tcr/AL182012_Sandy.pdf.

Elstein, Aaron, Andrew J. Hawkins, Barbara Benson, Matthew Flamm, and Thornton McEnery. "What If Sandy Happened Today?" *Crain's New York Business*, October 18, 2013. http://www.crainsnewyork.com/article/20131018/NEWS/131019888/what-if-sandy-happened-today#.

Hausman, Jerry A., and William E. Taylor. "Telecommunication in the U.S.: From Regulation to Competition (Almost)." *Review of Industrial Organization* 42 (2012): 203–230.

Jaeger, Paul T., Ben Shneiderman, Kenneth R. Fleischmann, Jennifer Preece, Yan Qu, and Philip Fei Wu. "Community Response Grids: E-government Social

Networks, and Effective Emergency Management." *Telecommunications Policy* 31 (2007): 592–604.

Kapucu, Naim. "Interagency Communication Networks during Emergencies: Boundary Spanners in Multiagency Coordination." *American Review of Public Administration* 36 (2006): 207–225.

MarketLine Industry Profile. *Wireless Telecommunication Services in the United States*. December 10, 2013.

Melisurgo, Len. "Hurricane Irene: New Jersey's Forgotten Storm." *Star-Ledger*, August 27, 2013.

National Oceanic and Atmospheric Administration. "State Forecast: A Catastrophe." *Star-Ledger*, October 29, 2012.

Schoonover, Eric. "Whole Bandwidth: The Price Is Still Right." *Business Communications Review* 36 (July 2007): 32–35.

Smith, Gerry. "Hurricane Sandy Delivers 'Another Catastrophe' to Verizon's Home, Complicating Network Repairs." *Huffington Post*, November 3, 2012. http://www.huffingtonpost.com/2012/11/03/verizon-sandy_n_2069033.html.

Stirling, Stephen. "The Rise of Frankenstorm: Potential Impact of Monster Weather Combination 'Borders on Rare to Unprecedented,' Climatologist Says." *Star-Ledger*, October, 26, 2012.

Vollman, Sharon. "OSP Interviews Diane McCarthy." *OSP*, 2013. http://www.ospmag.com/issue/article/OSP-Interviews-Diane-McCarthy.

# Jane Ni Dhulchaointigh
## Changing the World through Participatory Design

**Laura Lovin and Dana M. Britton**

## Background

Jane Ni Dhulchaointigh is the inventor of a material called *sugru* and CEO of the company FormFormForm, which makes and markets the product. Sugru is a silicone substance that was designed to stick to most materials—including aluminum, steel, ceramics, glass, wood, and some plastics. It has the moldable quality of children's modeling clay, and it can be shaped in virtually any form before it cures into strong yet flexible silicone rubber. The range of its use is unlimited, as the ever-growing online community of sugru users testifies. This community is filled with people who share their projects and ideas about how to fix or "hack" things with sugru. Stories on the company's website testify to the product's almost unlimited uses—users send in hacks that range from mending charging cables to fixing snow boots and wheelchair joysticks to creating glow-in-the-dark tent pegs. In 2010, *Time* magazine named sugru one of the top fifty inventions of the year—ranking it ahead of the iPad.[1]

Ni Dhulchaointigh chose a form of the Irish word for "play," *súgradh*, to name her invention. As she put it, "the word 'sugru' is the Irish word for 'play' and that's what it's all about—getting people to have a playful attitude toward life and to know that they can do something about their problems without having to wait around on others."[2] Sugru facilitates the simultaneous promotion of people's resourcefulness and creativity as well as the revival of a culture of repair as a mode of sustainable and socially responsible design. Anyone who has a couple of packages of sugru can not only repair but also modify, adapt, and improve the products they already own to fit their own uses better and last longer. When Ni Dhulchaointigh and her team were about to launch her product, she claimed, "We think that sugru can be something as big or bigger than duct tape, superglue or anything else that you use to repair." After December 2009, when Ni Dhulchaointigh sold the first one thousand packs of sugru in just about six hours, investors began to take notice. To date, her company has made more than two and a half million packages of sugru, sales have skyrocketed to more than $2 million, and the customer base expanded to impressive one hundred thousand across one hundred countries.[3]

The success of sugru was far from a certainty, however. It was an entirely new material—a sort of cross between duct tape and modeling clay—with no predetermined purpose. It was not a product in itself but was rather intended to fix or modify other products. Ni Dhulchaointigh was young, was without resources, and lacked formal experience in business. How would her strong belief in the utility of sustainable design guide the development of her product? How would she be able to amass the resources to launch it? And ultimately, how would she be able to reach her marketplace of users willing and able to invent uses for sugru?

## The Ideas behind Sugru

The arrival of sugru was well timed to coincide with the rising "do-it-yourself" (DIY) or "makers" movement. A newly found respect for repair and adaptation and a growing resistance to consumerism and its accompanying throwaway culture have been emerging in recent years. This enthusiasm for DIY is likely connected to the economic recession of the past decade and urgent environmental concerns. Inspired by these issues, many people are now taking the route of making good their old things instead of throwing them out and rushing to the store to buy a replacement. Ni Dhulchaointigh could be considered one of the pioneers of this newly emerged ethos, and sugru has helped to facilitate its growth. She describes sugru as the mark of our times and simultaneously a material that is still "slightly before its time."[4]

Ni Dhulchaointigh acknowledges that economic and environmental pressures are key to the contemporary makers movement, but at the same time, she argues that open-source and user-generated online environments have encouraged users to manipulate and customize physical objects. Since these conditions and changes are relatively new, the turn to creative fixing, repairing, and adapting is still under way. Ni Dhulchaointigh explains, "The last two or three generations have been sold this idea that everything is cheap. But in fact we just haven't been able to see the cost. I can't tell the future, but things are going to happen in the world that are much bigger than all of us—like climate change, oil, and, of course, recessions where people just don't have the money to buy stuff at the same rate. That means we will all need to be more resourceful."[5] Ni Dhulchaointigh is proudest about sugru when users reach out to her to share their fixes, as in the case of this woman: "Oh my god I would never think to try to do home repair and I tried sugru on the vacuum cleaner and I can't believe it works! I'm having so many ideas!"[6] Such messages are proof that sugru helps people to feel excited and empowered.

Ni Dhulchaointigh classifies the users and usages of sugru in three categories. In the first category, she places repairs to utilitarian objects, such as the case just described. The second category includes inventions or prototypes, and such is the case of "a dad who created a camera for his kids so they could learn photography. He put sugru on the walls of a snappy camera so it would bounce if his kids dropped it."[7] The third category consists of "new utilitarian things that absolutely anyone might have a need for."[8] Sugru has also become part of the design solutions for products manufactured and distributed by other companies. Recently, Zing Partners LLC, a manufacturer of massage devices, turned to sugru to customize its products by bonding two devices together without incurring new industrial-design and tooling costs.[9]

### Sugru: A Story of Design

Jane Ni Dhulchaointigh grew up on a farm in Ireland, among adults and children who were problem solvers. She recalls her childhood among machines and crops, working on the things that were broken.[10] In 2003, she was working toward her MA in product design at the Royal College of Art (RCA) in London. According to the company's website, Ni Dhulchaointigh came up with the idea for sugru when it occurred to her that she did not "want to buy new stuff all the time": "I want to hack the stuff I already have so it works better for me." While Ni Dhulchaointigh likes to describe herself as "playing and experimenting with materials," she was well aware that her involvement with each phase of the design process (thought, research, modeling, interactive adjustment, and redesign) was situated at that dynamic point of intersection. Ni Dhulchaointigh believes that "we all can be problem-solvers" and that the world needed a product that would make for "an easier and fun way for people to repair and modify things."[11]

These ideas were followed by experimentation with smelly silicone caulk and wood dust. The first version, which Ni Dhulchaointigh retrospectively describes as "pretty horrible," helped her to get a more comfortable grip on her knife and to get a kitchen stopper to do its job. Ni Dhulchaointigh describes her mood at this stage: "I knew that there was something a little bit magical. I just didn't know what it was."[12] As she could not take her mind off this product, she started imagining a world in which there was a better version of it. The product itself would be "a space-age rubber—super easy to shape, sticky, and durable; it needed to feel gorgeous." At her final graduation show, Ni Dhulchaointigh presented the prototype material for sugru. The version she presented in the final exhibition was made with finer powders and pigments. She also put together a book of cartoons showing one hundred ways this material could be used if it existed in the material form imagined by its designer.[13] The visitors too could see all kinds of uses, transformations, and improvements to mass-produced things that they already owned. When Ni Dhulchaointigh was flooded with questions—"How much is it?" and "Where can I get it?"—she says she knew that she had to make her concept real.

Transforming the prototype of her material into the gorgeous feel-super-sticky space-age rubber necessitated a lot of science. Chemistry was not Ni Dhulchaointigh's strong suit, but her sense for collaborative work was. "You can't know everything; you have to pull knowledge from other people," says Ni Dhulchaointigh.[14] Thus, she started building a team of seven that included two retired scientists with expertise in the US silicone industry. As far as business skills go, Ni Dhulchaointigh had run "entrepreneurial projects" from the age of nine or ten. Besides teaching swimming to children and assisting her grandmother with her shopping, she also capitalized on her artistic talents by selling paintings to her extended family. But to develop sugru into an award-winning product that has been used on all seven continents and the North Pole,[15] Ni Dhulchaointigh needed the partnership not only of scientists and other designers but also of Roger Ashby, a serial entrepreneur with a background in technology, engineering, and science.[16]

## FormFormForm—The Business

Ni Dhulchaointigh and Ashby started the company FormFormForm in 2004 to make and market sugru. A £35,000 Creative Pioneer grant received in 2005 from the National Endowment for Science, Technology and the Arts (Nesta), the United Kingdom's innovation think tank, got operations going. The first substantial steps were to lease a place and get the sugru formula ready for manufacturing. Ni Dhulchaointigh started experimenting with the first versions of her product in a studio in Bethnal Green in 2005. Early experiments with a contract laboratory were unproductive and expensive, and Ni Dhulchaointigh decided to learn chemistry herself and to set up a small laboratory with the rest of the money. In 2006, after two years of work, the team had come up with successful chemical formulations and applied for patents. The material was a new silicone trademarked as Formerol. Ni Dhulchaointigh explains, "First of all, the technology has been difficult to invent. But second of all, you know, we're not a big company with big budgets behind us."[17] As time went by, Ni Dhulchaointigh's materials were getting stronger and more stable. Trial users consistently told her, "Make it stick to more stuff!" By 2008, her team managed to perfect the product's adhesive properties.

## The Search for Investors

For the first four years, funding the project was challenging. Ni Dhulchaointigh worried that her small company would not be able to build a household name. She and her team started testing potential industrial uses for these materials and explored partnerships with leading glue or gardening companies on the world's market. At the same time, however, efforts to partner with multinational companies failed to yield success:

> My vision was really big and I felt strongly that sugru belonged with all the other products—like duct tape, superglue, and velcro—that people have in their toolboxes or kitchen drawers for those just-in-case moments. That's where we needed to be, but that's not something a small, two-person company can do, so we decided to explore a partnership. I started making friends with all the big glue companies and we put all our eggs in that basket because they were expressing so much interest and we were having loads of meetings. Then, in 2008, which was four years in, we had an almost-working material when we realized it was never going to happen. We kept having meetings, but nobody was putting money on the table. We hit a low point when I realized the business model wasn't going to work—it was too risky and too big of an investment for a company to take on a totally unproven concept.[18]

By early summer of 2008, Ni Dhulchaointigh began to reconsider her plan to affiliate with big companies and to look into possibilities to start her own brand. One of those summer days, while taking a bike ride, she thought of the word *sugru*. At the time, the fledgling company was in rather dire circumstances: "Our funding was running low, and we were still a way off with our development. We started pitching for investment again, but it was different this time. The recession meant we pitched to almost 100 investors. With the recession getting deeper, we were scraping by on our own over-draft. With no great signs from investors, we hit a low point."[19]

It was then that Ni Dhulchaointigh made a key decision; she decided to launch the company independently. Abandoning the idea of licensing the technology for the big money of big multinational corporations is the risk that Ni Dhulchaointigh took. She explained that this came with the understanding that things could be achieved by "thinking small" and attending to the company's own visions and talents: "Stop thinking big, think small. Make a brand that's gonna get us excited. Go back to the original idea. I think along the way we have come to think that this needs to be in the glue section; this needs to be mainstream if it's gonna work. But then, I think the realization was: actually, no, let's start small, let's make it for us, people like us. We managed to do that by creating a brand and a website, packaging and telling our story, basically."[20]

It took Ni Dhulchaointigh another year to find a private investor who trusted that her team could launch sugru by themselves. The team set a firm schedule of six months. During this interval, they transformed the research lab into a minifactory and bought a small industrial mixer of the kind normally used by chewing-gum manufacturers. Sugru proved difficult to package—as one employee put it, "Basically, we are packing glue"—so the team brought on board a friend who was an engineer to design and build a packaging machine. Ni Dhulchaointigh and her employees, friends, and family spent days and nights making and packing sugru. They also began to develop the packaging and marketing materials: "We designed a brand to get ourselves excited. We made videos, designed packaging and built a website. What we're quite good at is design, it's what we do, so we had a fantastic package design and a really great website design. When we went live it looked like we were much bigger than we were."[21]

Ni Dhulchaointigh and her team knew that the challenges to starting up a small independent business were formidable. They relied from the start on the power of the web to promote themselves. When the team went live, they sent packs to several key technology writers and reviewers, including one at London's *Daily Telegraph*. That writer, Harry Wallop, gave sugru a score of ten out of ten. The review immediately went viral and provoked further interest. In the United States, technology-oriented sites like *Wired* and *Boing Boing* also reviewed the material and linked to sugru's site. *Wired*'s reviewer, Charlie Sorrell, wrote, "Sugru is a brand new modeling clay that has me absurdly excited. Why? Because it is something I have wanted since forever, only I didn't even know it."[22] It took only six hours to sell the first one thousand packs. Ni Dhulchaointigh decided to put two thousand more packs up for preorder. These, too, sold in ten hours. The question of whether the product would sell had a clear answer. The new, more pressing one was how they could make more sugru.

The company's initial success soon drew the attention of investors. After having sold the one thousand packages of sugru, Ni Dhulchaointigh notes, "all of a sudden, we had our pick of some pretty awesome investors."[23] The money that came in during those initial days was promptly invested in creating infrastructure. Once sugru production started, the team found a warehouse, updated the website, and relaunched the product. Between 2005 and 2011, FormFormForm raised £1.25 million, including funds from twenty-two "angel" investors and an enterprise investment scheme managed by the British investment firm Lacomp. Sugru was trademarked with the free assistance of a patent attorney. The company also benefited from the financial and strategic advice of blue-chip experts, among whom was a senior manufacturing executive from Dell and a former head of health and safety from GlaxoSmith-Kline, and creative and enthusiastic young employees who represented the vibrancy and diversity of London's East End diasporas.[24]

After this somewhat uncertain beginning, the product has become a resounding success. According to Ni Dhulchaointigh's business partner Roger Ashby, the market valuation of the company came close to £10 million in 2011, a figure that brought to the early investors in FormFormForm a tenfold return. From the moment sugru entered the market, revenue numbers have been on a steadily rising trajectory. FormFormForm's projected sales in 2011 were £750,000.[25] And just a year later, at the end of 2012, the company reached £1 million in sales.[26] Sugru is still manufactured in the United Kingdom, in a former shoe factory in East London. Outsourcing is not an option due to the small number of units made and sugru's gluey consistency.[27] But since the US market amounts to half of the total sales, FormFormForm has leased a warehouse in Michigan. A significant part of the sales come from loyal, returning customers of the product, but sugru continues to expand its base of users. In 2013, the company cautiously expanded into retail. The first step was taken in the United Kingdom by entering B&Q, the largest DIY store.[28] In the United States, sugru sells nationwide in the Container Store, and it is also featured on the shelves of the MoMA Store in New York.

**Product as Movement**

Through sugru, Ni Dhulchaointigh believes she has the potential to change the world—not through political and social activism but by introducing a product that alters relations between humans and their material environment of objects and commodities. Sugru enables a radical rethinking of society's throwaway mind-set. It facilitates the drive of human beings toward creativity, innovation, and bettering their environment. The product is the tool she uses to challenge the consumerist ethos of the throwaway society. She describes sugru and the change she envisioned: "It is not a product for me—I was doing it because I really care about people fixing stuff, and I really wanted to make that change in the world. I really wanted to make a cultural change so that people will actually look after their stuff more, and if something breaks, they can fix it. Because people really do have the capability to fix things. People are amazingly inventful, creative, and resourceful—I think they have just forgotten that they are."[29]

Ni Dhulchaointigh's product facilitates a process of participatory design. Participatory design, like participatory leadership, is rooted in feminist principles that place collaborative, nonhierarchical modes of sharing knowledge at the core of learning about and changing the world. Her practice is resonant with the participatory themes and processes developed during the 1980s by the Matrix collective and the Women's Design Service (WDS) in London. These organizations functioned as resource centers that provided "technical help to address women's housing needs" as well as "to train future women architects in feminist architectural practice." Ni Dhulchaointigh's emphasis on control and empowerment further echoes accounts about "how tenants in public housing in New York City's Harlem organized to control and save the building they lived in" or "how residents' involvement in designing needed spaces in a public housing project in Chicago [had] been empowering."[30]

## The Challenge of Marketing a Movement

Once the ideas, the product, and the investors were in place, the next challenge that Ni Dhulchaointigh faced was building a brand. One of the biggest problems in growing the company came from the nature of the material itself. Sugru is not an end in itself; it is a product that enables future acts of design by its users. It literally enables "collaborative design," an act in which users are able to build on the efforts of those who made an object and in the process make it better. But this meant that consumers themselves had to participate in imagining uses for the product—an uncommon way of thinking in a prepackaged, throwaway culture. Persuading potential customers to imagine how sugru might be used was a challenge from the start.

This philosophy of fixing, rather than buying, created a second obstacle—how to market a product for sale while at the same time decrying consumerism. The irony of this approach is obvious. Sugru is not inexpensive; three five-gram packages retail for about twelve dollars. So the question was how to encourage users to leverage their own creativity to imagine what they could do with a product that had no predetermined uses, as well as to leverage what was basically an anticapitalist ethos to sell a consumer product. As a small company, FormFormForm had no budget for conventional advertising. So once the product was ready to ship, the immediate challenge was to get it into the hands of potential users.

## Resolution

Throughout the process of creating and marketing sugru, Ni Dhulchaointigh was firm in asserting the product's relation to the goals of environmentalism and the rejection of the throwaway society. Was the market ready for sugru? Ni Dhulchaointigh knew that sugru was a great product, but key to market success was how people perceived it. The company's commitment to empowering a creative and eco-friendly culture of mend, make, and improve is at the core of its deployment of online and social media marketing strategies. Sugru users had to think as designers, and in order to do that, they needed to be inspired. At Ni Dhulchaointigh's graduation show, she had paired her prototype material with a cartoon book of possible utilizations, but now ideas about sugru had to spread more broadly.

The Internet was the perfect medium for Ni Dhulchaointigh's goals. In 2008, she came up with a new slogan for her company: "The Future Needs Fixing." She wrote and posted her twelve-point "Fixer's Manifesto," which encapsulated her theory of design and critique of throwaway consumer culture. The manifesto begins, "If it's broken, fix it!" Readers were encouraged to "resist trends and needless upgrades" and not to "let companies treat you like a passive consumer" and told that "a fixed thing is a beautiful thing" and "disposability is a choice, not a physical characteristic."[31]

On sugru's website, those who are interested in the product are able to find inspiration. The e-tail channel of the sugru website (http://www.sugru.com) prompts its visitors to "hack things better!" The gallery is divided into ten sections: (1) How to get started; (2) Home improvements and DYI; (3) Outdoors and sport; (4) Make things magnetic; (5) Gadgets and tech; (6) Parents; (7) Photography; (8) Craft and making; (9) Cars and motorbikes; (10) Engineering and electronics. Users have submitted sugru hacks and fixes about how to customize ski poles, to fix a car's cooling system, to make bump-proof camera and phone cases, to patch up boots, to make mounts for iPods, to fix power cables of all kinds, to customize handles, to make rooms safer for babies, and the list goes on.

Part and parcel of sugru's initial concept and its marketing is reaching out to customers directly. Social media platforms supplemented the logistics that sugru had initially mobilized through the company's well-designed website and email campaigns. Facebook and Twitter brought new possibilities for building a community of users who loved to share their fixes and hacks.

Social media played a multiple role for Ni Dhulchaointigh: it gave her a platform for building the community of users that she envisioned as sharing their creations; it created visibility around her participatory design and social change processes; and ultimately, it constituted the best marketing tools and approach that the world has to offer. Sugru's online brand and Ni Dhulchaointigh's marketing strategy have been an absolute success. Sugru's novelty and meaningfulness have consisted in its ability to place "itself at the center of people's life."[32]

An integral part of the company's promotion strategy, the website displays photographs of what users make and posts videos that further spread the message about sugru. The feedback and photos received from the community of customers by email, tweets, and Facebook updates convinced Ni Dhulchaointigh that sugru goes beyond what its name indicates, which is mere play. It is an invention that is indeed playful and fun, but it is also useful. Tapping into human creativity, sugru soon became part of technical solutions to everyday problems. Ni Dhulchaointigh's favorite part of the month became the moment she went through the contributions of the community to prepare her monthly email update and to name the fix of the month. These fixes are particularly ingenious ways people have found to use sugru. For example, in July 2012, the fix of the month went to Joanne. She wanted to compete in a seven-hundred-kilometer-long canoe race up the Yukon River. She has no fingers on her left hand, and using a common paddle is impossible. A small modification to the paddle gave her a firmer grip and enabled her not only to compete but also to finish the race in three days and three nights of paddling.[33] Ni Dhulchaointigh explains, "The best thing about inventing something is to see people using it and finding it useful in their lives. Like seeing one of the Paralympic archers this year using it on his bow—we love that. Every day we get emails from people telling us how they use the product and that is what keeps us all going. I get surprises all the time when people are using sugru for things that I didn't even think about."[34]

The company's online strategy, Ni Dhulchaointigh admits, was a "make it or break it" endeavor. "How those people feel about us was determining whether we would go on."[35] Ultimately, the strategy has paid off. Amazing stories came in to the website revealing extraordinary creativity vis-à-vis people's relations with things. From the day of the sale of the first one thousand packs, people's responses on Twitter showed that there was a high level of excitement among consumers. Today, sugru has 10,541 followers on Twitter who share their fixes; sugru's Facebook page has more than eighteen thousand likes.

The company's online strategy offered a solution that has melded both its need to show users what they can do with the product and its critique of throwaway consumerism. The sugru community's sharing of hacks, fixes, repairs, and improvements gave the company invaluable feedback about what its product does, what it is most often and effectively used for, and why people buy it and love it. Social media enabled sugru to become a company that is perfectly attuned to its customers. Sugru's website and other social media platforms are spaces where users can share the results of their creativity and their fixes of items that might otherwise have been discarded. According to one observer, "The constraints of the promotional budget have been overcome by employing viral marketing on the net and by empowering the sugru user base. Sugru is as much about a new way of life as a new product!"[36] Ni Dhulchaointigh sees in e-tail a great and timely opportunity. For its capacity to connect with clients and to trade with people from across the world, she recommends it to all aspiring entrepreneurs. She points out, "Creativity is free. The people who know their thing, love what they do, whether musicians, designers or whatever, have a massive opportunity ahead."[37]

Despite the fact that the idea of sugru predates social media platforms, Ni Dhulchaointigh points out that sugru's life on the market was contingent on the existence and popularity of these new technologies, particularly Facebook (2004), YouTube (2005), and Twitter (2006). She explains, "When I had the idea for sugru, a very early insight into the product was that if you just provide the product, people won't do anything clever with it. . . . But if they're inspired by seeing things that other people have done then that means they will often have great ideas and solve problems." Back in 2003, building the sugru community would have been impossible. The online space took away all the geographic barriers that could have prevented ideas and communications from happening. Ni Dhulchaointigh continues, "I can get a message [in London] from somebody sitting at the kitchen table in Alaska working on their headphones and we have a bit of a banter about favorite songs."[38] Social media gave customers the rare opportunity to speak directly to the inventor and the managing director of the company. They also gave Ni Dhulchaointigh the means to convince people that they needed the new material she invented because it made them see the things that needed fixing around them. She accomplished that by creating online spaces of sharing and inspiration that placed the users and what they were doing at the forefront of the scene.

Ni Dhulchaointigh's journey from the workshop to the market, along with the feedback that she received from the users of sugru, clearly showed that design and technology are "intertwined and interdependent."[39] In Ni Dhulchaointigh's work, new technologies complement design, challenging the idea that there is a split between these spheres of human creative activity. Sugru also dissolves the conceptual boundaries and hierarchical relations between art as creativity that materializes ex nihilo and the incrementalism and everydayness of the creativity of repair, adaptation, and improvement. This allows us to see creativity outside paradigms that foreground the genius of the creator and the perfection of the creation, while leading to a celebration of everyday creations, repairs, and their material traces. Ni Dhulchaointigh's leadership unfolded both through her vision of creative employment and through her collaborative approach to entrepreneurialism.

# Notes

1 Deirdre Van Dyk, "Sugru," in "The 50 Best Inventions of 2010," *Time*, November 11, 2010, http://content.time.com/time/specials/packages/article/0,28804,2029497_2030629_2029789,00.html.

2 Tina Essmaker, "Jane Ni Dhulchaointigh," *Great Discontent*, July 10, 2013, http://thegreatdiscontent.com/jane-ni-dhulchaointigh.

3 Nick Glass and Tom Levitt, "Sugru: A Gripping Tale of Struggle and Success," CNN Tech, October 26, 2012, http://www.cnn.com/2012/10/25/tech/sugru/.

4 Sonya James, "Q&A: Jane Ni Dhulchaointigh, Inventor of Sugru, on Marketing Mending," *Smart Planet*, September 12, 2013, http://www.smartplanet.com/blog/pure-genius/qa-jane-ni-dhulchaointigh-inventor-of-sugru-on-marketing-mending/.

5 Ibid.

6 Ibid.

7 Ibid.

8 Ibid.

9 "Zing Partners LLC Begin Advanced Prototyping Using Sugru Forming Material," PRWeb, November 22, 2013, http://www.prweb.com/releases/2013/11/prweb11342119.htm.

10 Emma Sinclair, "How 'Best Invention' Sugru Went from B&Q to the North Pole," *Telegraph*, June 24, 2013, http://www.telegraph.co.uk/women/womens-business/10139032/How-best-invention-Sugru-went-from-BandQ-to-the-North-Pole.html.

11 "You Need Passion to Be an Inventor," thejournal.ie, September 8, 2012, http://www.thejournal.ie/readme/column-you-need-passion-to-be-an-inventor-588009-Sep2012/.

12 Glass and Levitt, "Sugru."

13 Sinclair, "How 'Best Invention' Sugru Went from B&Q to the North Pole."

14 Sugru, "Our Story," n.d., https://sugru.com/story (accessed March 12, 2014).

15 Explorers have taken sugru with them to Antarctica and the North Pole.

16 Sinclair, "How 'Best Invention' Sugru Went from B&Q to the North Pole."

17 Glass and Levitt, "Sugru."

18 Essmaker, "Jane Ni Dhulchaointigh."

19 Sugru, "Our Story."

20 HN London, "Jane Ni Dhulchaointigh—The Story of Sugru," Vimeo, http://vimeo.com/37306611 (accessed March 12, 2014), video.

21 Glass and Levitt, "Sugru."

22 Charlie Sorrel, "Sugru, an Amazing Silicon Modeling Clay for Makers and Hackers," *Wired*, December 9, 2009, http://www.wired.com/2009/12/sugru-an-amazing-silicon-modeling-clay-for-makers-and-hackers/.

23 Sugru, "Our Story."

24 Jonathan Moules, "Costing the Dream: FormFormForm," *Financial Times*, December 9, 2011, http://www.ft.com/cms/s/0/432b4618-1f31-11e1-ab49-00144feabdc0.html.

25 Ibid.

26  Sinclair, "How 'Best Invention' Sugru Went from B&Q to the North Pole."
27  Moules, "Costing the Dream."
28  B&Q is the equivalent of Home Depot in the United States.
29  Sugru, "Our Story."
30  Joan Rothschild, "Designed Environments and Women's Studies: A Wake-Up Call," *NWSA Journal* 10 (1998): 103–104.
31  Sugru, "Fixer's Manifesto," n.d., https://sugru.com/manifesto (accessed March 12, 2014).
32  Seo and social media management, "Unleash Your True Brand Potential," Wellheeled-executive.com, November 23, 2012, http://wellheeled-executive.com/unleash-your-true-brand-potential/.
33  For the full story and pictures see "[Fix of the Month, Aug 2012] A Mod to Take Part in an Epic Canoe Race That Is 715km Long," Sugru blog, August 15, 2012, http://sugru.com/us/blog/fix-of-the-month-aug-2012-a-mod-to-take-part-in-an-epic-canoe-race-that-is-715km-long.
34  Glass and Levitt, "Sugru."
35  99U, "Jane Ni Dhulchaointigh: The Magic Is in the Process," lecture from a Behance Conference, Vimeo, http://vimeo.com/72040407 (accessed February 2, 2014), video.
36  Parmy Olson, "How Facebook and Twitter Made 'Sugru' Sticky," *Forbes*, October 7, 2010, http://www.forbes.com/sites/parmyolson/2010/10/07/how-social-networks-made-sugru-sticky/.
37  "Success Is Sticking to Creativity," *Irish Times*, November 12, 2010, http://www.highbeam.com/doc/1P2-26354500.html.
38  Ibid.
39  Rothschild, "Designed Environments and Women's Studies," 101.

## Bibliography

Essmaker, Tina. "Jane Ni Dhulchaointigh." *Great Discontent*, July 10, 2013. https://thegreatdiscontent.com/interview/jane-ni-dhulchaointigh.

"[Fix of the Month, Aug 2012] A Mod to Take Part in an Epic Canoe Race That Is 715km Long." Sugru blog, August 15, 2012. http://sugru.com/us/blog/fix-of-the-month-aug-2012-a-mod-to-take-part-in-an-epic-canoe-race-that-is-715km-long.

Glass, Nick, and Tom Levitt. "Sugru: A Gripping Tale of Struggle and Success." CNN Tech, October 26, 2012. http://www.cnn.com/2012/10/25/tech/sugru/.

HN London. "Jane Ni Dhulchaointigh—The Story of Sugru." Vimeo. http://vimeo.com/37306611 (accessed March 12, 2014). Video.

James, Sonya. "Q&A: Jane Ni Dhulchaointigh, Inventor of Sugru, on Marketing Mending." *Smart Planet*, September 12, 2013. http://www.smartplanet.com/blog/pure-genius/qa-jane-ni-dhulchaointigh-inventor-of-sugru-on-marketing-mending/.

Moules, Jonathan. "Costing the Dream: FormFormForm." *Financial Times*, December 9, 2011. http://www.ft.com/cms/s/0/432b4618-1f31-11e1-ab49-00144feabdco.html.

99U. "Jane Ni Dhulchaointigh: The Magic Is in the Process." Lecture from a Behance Conference. Vimeo. http://vimeo.com/72040407 (accessed February 2, 2014). Video.

Olson, Parmy. "How Facebook and Twitter Made 'Sugru' Sticky." *Forbes*, October 7, 2010. http://www.forbes.com/sites/parmyolson/2010/10/07/how-social-networks-made-sugru-sticky/.

Rothschild, Joan. "Designed Environments and Women's Studies: A Wake-Up Call." *NWSA Journal* 10 (1998): 100–116.

Seo and social media management. "Unleash Your True Brand Potential." Wellheeled-executive.com, November 23, 2012. http://wellheeled-executive.com/unleash-your-true-brand-potential/.

Sinclair, Emma. "How 'Best Invention' Sugru Went from B&Q to the North Pole." *Telegraph*, June 24, 2013. http://www.telegraph.co.uk/women/womens-business/10139032/How-best-invention-Sugru-went-from-BandQ-to-the-North-Pole.html.

Sorrel, Charlie. "Sugru, an Amazing Silicon Modeling Clay for Makers and Hackers." *Wired*, December 9, 2009. http://www.wired.com/2009/12/sugru-an-amazing-silicon-modeling-clay-for-makers-and-hackers/.

"Success Is Sticking to Creativity." *Irish Times*, November 12, 2010. http://www.highbeam.com/doc/1P2-26354500.html.

Sugru. "Fixer's Manifesto." n.d. https://sugru.com/manifesto (accessed March 12, 2014).

———. "Our Story." n.d. https://sugru.com/story (accessed March 12, 2014).

Van Dyk, Deirdre. "Sugru." In "The 50 Best Inventions of 2010," *Time*, November 11, 2010. http://content.time.com/time/specials/packages/article/0,28804,2029497_2030629_2029789,00.html.

"You Need Passion to Be an Inventor." thejournal.ie, September 8, 2012. http://www.thejournal.ie/readme/column-you-need-passion-to-be-an-inventor-588009-Sep2012/.

"Zing Partners LLC Begin Advanced Prototyping Using Sugru Forming Material." PRWeb, November 22, 2013. http://www.prweb.com/releases/2013/11/prweb11342119.htm.

# Ursula Burns

## Restructuring an American Icon at Xerox

**Rosemary Ndubuizu and Dana M. Britton**

Appointed as the first African American woman to head a Fortune 500 company in June 2009, Ursula Burns should have been on cloud nine. But instead, in the middle of America's worst recession since World War II, she had to face the herculean task of revitalizing Xerox's relevance in a digital world that relied less and less on paper and copy machines, the company's signature products. Not only did Burns have to contend with Xerox's declining significance; she had to face the company's volatile investors, weakening stock price, relentless competitors, and nervous employees.

How could Burns revitalize a demand for Xerox's services when American and international companies feared making investments due to the global recession? How could she motivate Xerox employees to trust her leadership when many feared they would lose their jobs because of the recession? How could Burns calm Xerox's leading investors while encouraging them to trust her leadership during these trying economic times? Ultimately, what leadership skills would Burns need to direct Xerox to a financially brighter future?

### Humble Beginnings: From Lower East Side Projects to Columbia University

Ursula Burns was born in 1958 in New York to Panamanian immigrant parents. She was the second child of three. Her father left the family when she was young, though she says she never felt "slighted" by her father's absence, joking, "[My mother] could be a pain in the rear end and all over me and stuff like that. But I never felt we needed someone else in the household."[1] Her mother, Olga Burns, raised her children in a public housing project on the Lower East Side. Despite their limited resources, she raised her children to believe in their dreams. Olga and her children set about "creating a little world of [their] own," in which she told her children, "Where you are is not who you are."[2] Olga Burns operated a home day-care business and scraped and saved to finance her children's Catholic school education. If she did not have the money to pay for services like health or dental care, she bartered cleaning or child-care services instead. For Ursula Burns, her mother did "whatever the hell she needed" to keep the family going.[3] Ursula Burns credits her mother for her straight-talking leadership style; Olga Burns always said what was on her mind.

Ursula Burns says her mother never asked for much in return— she simply expected her children to strive for excellence. Ursula rarely disappointed on this end, and in school, she shined. "I was really good at reading, writing, math," she unabashedly admits. "I was particularly good at math."[4] Nearing the end of high school, Burns met with her guidance counselor to identify her postcollege career. She particularly asked for advice on careers that would complement her strong science and math background. The counselor gave her three stereotypical choices: she could become a nurse, a teacher, or a nun.

Disturbed and dissatisfied, Burns went to her local library to research alternative career options. She settled on engineering. After finishing high school, she received a scholarship to attend Brooklyn Polytechnic Institute (now part of New York University). When she graduated in 1980 with a bachelor's in mechanical engineering, she was selected for a summer internship with Xerox. The next year, Xerox helped pay for her graduate education at Columbia University, where she earned a master's degree in mechanical engineering. She never dreamt that her brief internship would turn into a thirty-plus-year career at Xerox. But she did know that wherever she settled, she would be successful, because she was simply fulfilling her mother's wishes: "My mother was always very clear that we would get an education and be successful."[5]

## Xerox's Commitment to Diversity Lays the
## Foundation for Burns's Ascent to Leadership

The company that became Xerox was born in the frustration of a student. Chester Carlson, born in 1906, was a physicist turned patent attorney turned inventor. When studying for his law degree in the 1930s, he copied reams of material in longhand because he could not afford to buy law books. Frustrated but intrigued by the puzzle of solving a complicated technical problem, he put his physics training to use developing a machine that would produce perfect copies of documents on plain paper. After many false starts, in 1942, he received a patent for a process he called "electrophotography." In attempting to develop and market his process, he was turned down for funding by more than twenty companies, including IBM and General Electric, neither of which believed there was a profitable market for copiers. Carlson then took his product to Joseph C. Wilson, the heir to Haloid Photographic Company, and to John Dessauer, its chief of research. Wilson and Dessauer saw the value of Carlson's invention, and Haloid poured millions into research and development. In 1955, anticipating large-scale production, Wilson expanded the company's capacity by acquiring a large parcel of land in a suburb of Rochester, New York. This was to become the company's permanent headquarters.

To brand Carlson's copying process, Haloid coined the term *Xerography*, which derives from the Greek root meaning "dry writing." In 1959, on live TV, the company introduced the Xerox 914, the first plain-paper photocopier. The company quickly found a market, and the Xerox 914 has sometimes been described as the most successful single product of all time.[6] Though early machines were expensive, Xerox pioneered a marketing strategy through which companies could rent machines and pay a fee for the number of copies they used. This led to the widespread adoption of the company's technology and the defeat of its emerging competition. The company was to have a virtual monopoly on the market for business copiers for the next several decades. Revenues skyrocketed, and Xerox quickly became a household name, as well as the generic term for the process of copying itself. After the success of the Xerox 914, Haloid changed its name to the Xerox Corporation in 1961.[7]

In 1963, there was a series of violent race riots in Rochester, where the company was headquartered. The shock of this violence, as well as the changes wrought by the civil rights movement, "helped awaken senior Xerox managers to the seriousness of racial inequities and conflicts in the United States." Joe Wilson, the company's original CEO, and Peter McColough, who was then president of Xerox, "shared a common belief in fairness and a moral commitment to affirmative action."[8] In 1968, they wrote a letter to all Xerox managers taking the company's own share of responsibility for exacerbating racial tensions: "We, like all other Americans, share the responsibility for a color-divided nation; and in all honesty, we need not look beyond our own doorstep to find out why. In Rochester, one of the first American cities scarred by racial strife, Xerox continues to employ only a very small percentage of Negroes. In other major cities, including some that have suffered even greater violence, we employ no Negroes at all." The letter went on to outline a strategy that made every Xerox manager accountable for rectifying the situation by actively recruiting African Americans. It read, in part,

> The full and unqualified cooperation of all Xerox managers is expected in reaching our minority hiring goals. Corporate Personnel has been given the responsibility for implementing our plans, and for establishing an accountability system through which top management—beginning immediately—can regularly assess progress in all divisions, departments and subsidiaries of the corporation. Today there are 22 million Negroes in the United States. The exclusion of many of them from our society is a malignancy that the nation cannot endure. . . . We are fully aware, of course, of the progress that Xerox has already made in assisting the civil rights movement. But it simply has not gone far enough. We must do more because Xerox will not add to the misery of the present condition of most Negroes. It will not condone the waste of a great national resource. It will not compromise the conviction on which the success of this enterprise and of the nation depends.[9]

Under Wilson and McColough, the company engaged in other efforts to support the civil rights movement, including supporting African American–owned companies and funding media designed to raise awareness of racial inequities.[10]

The company's emphasis on diversity as a core cultural value, as well as a result for which managers were accountable, persisted long after Wilson's leadership tenure ended in 1971. African American workers themselves began to organize to demand racial equality in recruiting and to pressure the company to implement mechanisms to support African American employees once they were on the job. For instance, in 1969, a group of African American workers in San Francisco organized and negotiated with Xerox's regional management to implement an interview process that would allow a black Xerox employee to be present whenever white managers interviewed a black candidate.[11] In the early 1970s, a group of black employees in Rochester met with Xerox's senior management to create an organizational plan that would ensure the introduction and support mechanisms for marginalized groups. The company responded by creating a Minority Advisory Committee (MAC), which was later renamed the Employee Resource Advisory Committee. Originally, this committee was staffed with the top black executives in Xerox. Recalling that time, Barry Rand, one of the black male committee members, admits that the members of MAC were "race forward" and grew up during the civil rights movement, infusing "civil rights activism . . . into the corporate boardroom."[12] Latino workers also organized to influence Xerox's management and hiring practices. By the 1980s, Xerox had several affinity groups for women, blacks, and Latinos, and senior executives had the responsibility for sponsoring them. These support networks enabled underrepresented employees to share support, advice, and information. These networks were eventually institutionalized as caucuses, many of which still operate today.

Later, as the company's chief executive officer (CEO), Ursula Burns credited the company's commitment to diversity for its ability to weather the challenges it was to face. "One of the things that Xerox found out early," Ursula reflects, "is generally, if it's good for society, it's generally good for business." She reasoned, "You can't be a bad citizen and get great employees. You can't be a non-diverse environment and get the one or two women or one or two African Americans or Hispanics that you need who are great. You have to actually embrace the entire thing to have it work well. And so I think that our position in the world, which is still in the Fortune 500, still in a very good position and the leading diversified service company in the world, is based on the fact that we are a good citizen. A good corporate citizen around the world."[13] Today, Xerox is one of the most diverse of all Fortune 500 corporations; more than one-third of its 3,819 executives are women, and 22 percent are minorities.[14] Xerox's commitment to inclusive corporate culture, which was stated in no uncertain terms by its founding CEO and then actualized by mechanisms of accountability and the efforts of employees of color, set the stage for the appointment of Burns as CEO—the first African American woman to lead a Fortune 500 company.

## Ursula Burns Challenges Xerox's Leadership Culture

After graduating from Columbia University in 1981, Ursula Burns returned to Xerox and served in various positions in product development and planning. In 1989, she decided to participate in a meeting that arguably ignited her meteoric rise in Xerox's leadership ranks. In a Quality of Work Life council meeting, a space dedicated to discussing how Xerox could improve the work experience for its employees, an employee expressed concern that Xerox's diversity initiatives lowered the company's standards by leading to the hiring of unqualified employees. Wayland Hicks, whom Burns did not know at the time, was running the meeting. According to Burns, Hicks patiently listened to this employee's complaint. He then explained his position that the diversity initiatives were good for the company and did not lower its standards.

Burns says she was stunned and appalled that Hicks took the question seriously. Never one to shy away from a debate, she raised her hand and challenged him: "Why give the question the dignity of a response?" He tried to respond to her concerns, but Burns was still unsatisfied. After the meeting, she found out that Hicks was vice president of marketing and customer operations.

She knew then that she had essentially initiated a public argument with one of the most powerful people in the company. A few weeks later, Hicks called Ursula Burns into his office. She was certain she would be either fired or reprimanded.[15] But Hicks admitted that she was right to be concerned with the question but wrong for dismissing the opportunity for productive engagement around the issue. Then he offered her an opportunity: become his executive assistant. At first mention of the offer, Burns scoffed to herself, "Why would I ever want to do that?"[16] She had a master's degree in mechanical engineering, and she silently feared that she would become a glorified secretary with no leadership or advancement opportunities. But despite her reservations, she accepted the offer.

To the people at the upper levels of the company, however, her position as an executive assistant had a very different meaning. It was a clear sign that she was being groomed for future leadership positions. Anne Mulcahy, who was later to become Xerox's first woman CEO, said that Burns's hire as executive assistant was "a significant signal to everyone. That was the first sign she was really on the executive track," she recalled. The consultant Reginald Brown Jr. agreed: "These were jobs in the company that division presidents put their best people in. Most of them were white males, so to have an African American female in such a position of power, you knew early on she had great potential."[17] For Burns, the job was the education of a lifetime. Alongside Hicks, she flew to various Xerox sites throughout the world, participated in decision-making meetings, and executed exciting work. Hicks later commented, "Burns was enormously curious. She wanted to know why we were doing some things at the time, and she was prepared in a way that I thought was very refreshing."[18] Although Hicks came from a completely different racial, economic, and political background from Burns, their working partnership evolved into a worthwhile mentoring relationship. Hicks shared leadership lessons with Burns often. One of the most important lessons was about how to manage people effectively. He encouraged Burns not to browbeat employees but to listen to and value the concerns they shared.

Burns continued to absorb Hicks's leadership advice but remained unafraid to speak her mind within the company. In 1991, she was sitting in on a meeting with top management, including Xerox's president, Paul Allaire. In this meeting, Allaire repeated a familiar litany of financial problems at the company and recommended that Xerox institute a hiring freeze. Burns raised her hand. She inquired, "If you keep saying, 'No hiring,' and we hire 1,000 people every month, who can say 'No hiring' and make it actually happen?"[19] Allaire silenced her with a deafening stare, Burns recollected, and he continued with the meeting. Sometime shortly thereafter, Burns was summoned to Allaire's office, certain her sharp tongue would get her in trouble this time. Instead, Allaire offered her a position as his executive assistant. Again, Burns wondered if this was an advantageous move. She had just married a fellow Xerox employee, Lloyd Bean, and she wanted to pursue other opportunities in the company. When she told Allaire about her reservations and asked why she should take the position, Allaire hesitated and then responded, "Because I'm the CEO, and I asked you to do it." Burns accepted the offer, later admitting, "It was one of my first lessons in not getting too big for your britches, not assuming that you know all the answers. When the CEO of a company asks you to do something, you should be honored."[20]

Allaire served as Burns's leadership mentor too, advising her to nurture employees' confidence. He counseled her, "Giv[e] people credit for ideas that they didn't have, but you sold to them, to give them ownership."[21] She also learned about the realities of corporate leadership at the highest levels: "The assignment taught me that there was a lot more to business than just engineering or just pricing and forecasting. There was all this political stuff that CEOs and business leaders are involved in. I also discovered that the level of stress involved in leading was significantly higher than I thought it was, and the level of control was significantly lower."[22] Her position in the upper echelons of the company also gave her opportunities to build relationships with other women and people of color on the fast track to leadership. One example was her relationship with Anne Mulcahy. Mulcahy and Burns developed a strong partnership—and friendship. The two discussed the difficulties of being a woman in a major company. Burns credits Mulcahy for teaching her that leaders have insecurities too: "[Anne] was a great person to talk to. She showed me that she had insecurities as well—and dealing with those insecurities are part of being a leader."[23] This advice served Burns well when she transitioned into other leadership positions at Xerox. By 1999, she was appointed to the position of vice president for global manufacturing.

Her promotions should have been cause for celebration. But Burns was rising to the top of a company that was imploding. In 2000, Xerox was drowning in mounting debt ($17.1 billion), in its seventh quarter of losses, and its stock price was plummeting; over two years, it fell from $63.69 to $4.43.[24] Xerox's leaders were leaving the company for positions elsewhere. And to add to this list of woes, the Securities and Exchange Commission (SEC) was conducting an investigation into accounting irregularities at the company.

How did Xerox end up in this situation? Analysts have concluded that a series of shortsighted and ultimately ineffective leadership decisions led the company to the point of near bankruptcy. The company had been complacent in the face of competition and dramatically changing markets for its products. As one journalist suggested, Xerox's initial success as a leading copy-machine producer contributed to its eventual troubles: "Xerox is one of those storied tech companies—think IBM, Motorola, Hewlett-Packard—that rested on its laurels and resisted change."[25] When the digital age dawned in the 1980s, Xerox leadership passed up opportunities to invest in the personal computer technology that its own research center had invented. During the same period, Xerox's competitors in Japan edged out Xerox's dominance in the copier market. When Allaire retired in 1999, the company hired an outsider, Rick Thoman, the former chief financial officer of IBM, to lead Xerox into the digital era. But the company continued to lose revenue on a massive scale, and Thoman's tenure was short-lived. He was fired after thirteen months, and Allaire was reinstated as the interim CEO. Allaire then tapped Mulcahy as his successor. Mulcahy was stunned: "I never expected to be CEO of Xerox. I was never groomed to be CEO of Xerox. It was a total surprise to everyone, including myself."[26]

Once appointed as CEO in 2000, Mulcahy formed her leadership team. She appointed Ursula Burns as senior vice president for corporate strategic services. When Burns was asked to serve in this position, she had already decided to leave the company, accepting another job offer with more money. "It was not because of more money," Burns insisted when she reflected on why she was ready to resign. "It was just, 'What's going on here? What is this place?'"[27] Burns continued, "We had lost complete faith in the leadership of the company. We didn't have any cash and few prospects for making any."[28] She knew that Xerox's future was uncertain, but a few close colleagues, including Mulcahy, convinced her to stay.[29] Ultimately, Burns's mother's axioms of perseverance and loyalty motivated her to accept Mulcahy's offer: "I have been to almost every country in the world. . . . I have more than I ever imagined, and it all came from a partnership between me and this company. So what do you say when times are tough? 'Thank you very much, I'll see you later.' That's not what my mother taught me."[30]

Together, Mulcahy and Burns spearheaded Xerox's turnaround. While Mulcahy traveled around the country trying to woo investors, persuading Xerox's executive leaders to stay, and fighting for the company's investment-grade status, Burns worked on the "guts of the company."[31] Burns implemented a massive overhaul of how Xerox operated: she had to oversee how the company brought parts and built its products and to reduce production costs by $1 billion, while still increasing productivity.[32] Always the straight talker, Burns would call out any employee who was not meeting the company's expectations. Mulcahy recalled, "She'd say, 'Jim, you blew it; tell us what happened.'"[33]

During Burns's tenure as senior vice president, she outsourced Xerox's manufacturing operations to a Singapore-based company, Flextronics, to cut costs. To complete the deal, she had to massively downsize Xerox's workforce. In contract negotiations with Xerox's two thousand unionized workers in Rochester, she was as frank as possible. "I told them the truth, in as much detail as I could, about what was happening," Burns recalled. Mulcahy applauded Burns's approach: "She literally convinced the union that it was going to be either some jobs or no jobs. For anyone. It was survival. There was no other way."[34] Burns did what several previous Xerox CEOs had failed to accomplish: she negotiated a deal with the union, downsized the workforce by close to 40 percent, outsourced Xerox's

manufacturing, and closed the remaining manufacturing operations. And for the first six weeks of these negotiations, she did so
while recuperating from an emergency hysterectomy, first from her
hospital bed and then from her living room.

As Burns busied herself with executing the company's ambitious
restructuring plan, Mulcahy worked on closing the chapter on the
sticky legal issue of the SEC's investigation. By 2002, the company
had finally concluded the investigation and paid a record $10 mil-
lion in fines, and Mulcahy cleaned house in the financial department, eventually hiring a new chief financial officer. Once the fog of
the SEC investigation cleared, the company slowly gained financial
backing again. Burns's work in restructuring also started to pay dividends. The company's costs fell, productivity increased, and profits rose. By 2007, Xerox seemed to be on a firmly upward trajectory.
Burns was promoted to president, and two years later, Mulcahy
announced her retirement and appointed Burns to take her place
as CEO. Burns's appointment marked two historic firsts: the first
African American woman to head a Fortune 500 company and the
first woman-to-woman CEO succession.

But once again Burns's jubilant moment was dampened by the
company's next big crisis. Burns was appointed in the middle of
the Great Recession, during a global financial crisis. Customers were
not buying. She was also overseeing the company's biggest investment yet: the $6.4 billion acquisition of Affiliated Computer Ser-
vices (ACS), a firm specializing in business process outsourcing. To
investors, it appeared that the company was making a risky move in
a tumultuous economic climate, and Xerox's stock price fell. All of
this was compounded by the reality of stiff competition and stunted
growth—Accenture, Automatic Data Processing (ADP), IBM,
and others were clamoring to take larger shares of the business-
processing market themselves. Investors and competitors were not
the only ones vying for Burns's attention—employees were dissatisfied with the company's mandated pay cuts and layoffs.

Ursula Burns took the helm of a once-great American company
that now seemed to be rocking from crisis to crisis. She had little time to enjoy the fact of her ascendance to CEO; instead, she
"had a war to fight."[35] She had to build trust about the massive

restructuring that she and Mulcahy had initiated, regain credibility with investors and employees, and hold her competitors at bay. Most of all, she had to get Xerox growing again.

## Resolution

As a result of the work that Mulcahy and Burns had done to turn the company around, and then the decisions Burns made about even more dramatic changes, the company began to grow slowly. Much of that growth resulted from the ACS deal, though at the time it seemed like an extremely risky decision. Burns built consensus carefully. First, she sought to convince investors and colleagues at Xerox that this was a smart investment by reframing Xerox's business mission. The copy-machine market was dying, and business process outsourcing was potentially a $500 billion market. Burns sat down with her investors and explained why this move was the right choice. "We announced that we were spending a bit of money, a lot of it in the form of stock, so investors were not too thrilled about the dilution, obviously. But they were also just confused. Who is ACS? What is business-process outsourcing? And why are you engaged in it?"[36]

Burns's strategy was to link the acquisition to the company's original mission. From the beginning, she explained, "Our company [has used] technology to transform business processing." Burns met with various investors, explaining to them that Xerox had always been in the business of simplifying business: "That's what Chester Carlson did when he created the copying machine. He was just pissed off that he had to write [things] seven times. He didn't say, 'Well, I'm going to create an industry.' That business process was not what he did for a living. He was a friggin' patent attorney! . . . So he created this technology, and the rest is history."[37] Xerox would continue Carlson's tradition of simplifying business, though it would now do so by managing customer infrastructure and back-office responsibilities for companies.

Ultimately, Burns hoped that the combination of the two companies would produce a synergy that would allow Xerox to grow.

She believed that combining Xerox's research expertise with ACS's market would lead to innovations that would set the company apart from the competition. She was right. In the first few years after the acquisition, Xerox researchers had produced technology that enabled the company to become the country's leading producer of the automated-toll technology E-ZPass. Xerox also now manages the infrastructure for municipalities' parking enforcement and call centers for various companies. Because of Burns's commitment to tapping into investment opportunities that arise from Xerox's research center, the company is expanding its service opportunities, securing new clients, and generating more revenue and earnings.

Today, Xerox's stock price continues to hover around the low teens, and growth has slowed. Burns remains hopeful, citing close to $1 billion in cash and a diversified revenue stream. She is the first to admit that people, even CEOs, make mistakes. Georgetown University's dean of the McDonough School of Business agrees: "I think she has this interesting combination of consulting broadly, listening carefully, being decisive and being accountable for her decisions. By that I mean she's not afraid to a make a mistake and then take accountability for making that mistake."[38] But there is reason for optimism in Burns's leadership: "We see now that the ACS acquisition was probably a very forward-looking, prudent move," noted Deepak Sitaraman, a Credit Suisse analyst.[39] As Xerox seeks to rebuild its investment status, investors wait and watch as Burns seeks out more ways to increase the company's revenue and growth.

Burns's frankness had served her well in her rise through the ranks at Xerox. But when she became CEO, mentors including Vernon E. Jordan Jr., adviser to former president Bill Clinton, and Kenneth Chenault, the chief executive of American Express, gave Burns advice about "patience, perspective, and the importance of building 'followership' across the organization."[40] Confidants warned her that her diction was "too New York, . . . too fast, too informal."[41] Instead, she was encouraged to "avoid the use of $10 words—like . . . 'bespoke.'"[42] She was also advised to modulate her frank and sometimes sharp-tongued style. Burns decided to adapt the advice she was given to fit her style. She decided not to change her words, not to act like she was someone else. After her all, her mother always told her, "Don't get confused when you're rich and famous."[43] Ultimately, her mother's advice won out: she drew on her childhood-bred honesty, pragmatism, and determination and went to work changing the company's office culture to increase productivity, to dispel investors' fears, to find new opportunities for business growth, and to close the company's historic deal with ACS. But she admits that her frankness produces some unique leadership challenges, and she seeks to improve incrementally each day. "I have to be better at saying things when people are ready to listen," she confesses.[44]

When Burns ascended to the top job at Xerox, she garnered an avalanche of media and public attention. Dozens of news stories appeared telling her life story and highlighting the fact that she was the first African American woman to run a Fortune 500 company. Even she was amazed by the fever pitch of publicity: "The accolades that I get for doing absolutely nothing are amazing—I've been named to every list, literally, since I became the C.E.O. . . . What have I done? In the first 30 days, I was named to a list of the most impressive XYZ. The accolades are good for five minutes. . . . The real story is not Ursula Burns. I just happen to be the person standing up at this point representing Xerox."[45] Burns has done what she could to shift the spotlight and to debunk the "savior" mythology that accompanied her rise to the top spot, emphasizing the role of the company and its employees instead.

Burns and her husband, Lloyd Bean, are the parents of two teenage children. Like many high-powered women executives, she has often been asked about her own strategies for balancing work and family. She has been candid about the fact that because Bean is twenty years older, he had retired by the time they had children and was able to provide primary care for them while she traveled the world and ascended the corporate ladder. In a recent interview, she took on the notion that women can "have it all:"

For as long as I have been alive, we [as women] have been discussing this concept of "having it all"—if you work hard enough, you can be anything you want to be; you can take care of yourself, you can run marathons, raise kids, work full time, and be a great wife. But that's not the point. . . . The point is to pick the places you want to be great and that you really want to focus your energies on, and do that, understanding that you're not going to be great at everything. And then relax.[46]

Indeed, Burns has suggested that "women get comfortable with the idea of taking 'your entire life to find balance. You should have balance, on average, over time—not in a day or in a month.'"[47]

So who motivates Burns to practice courageous leadership? Without a doubt, it is her mother. Burns recalled, "My mother was pragmatic, focused and extremely, exceedingly practical, and she was the ultimate self-determining person."[48] Burns's mother showed her how to stay true to herself, even when others asked her to change her entire persona when she became CEO. Instead of buckling, she harnessed the spirit of her mother and became a steadfast, self-determining leader. She negotiated a tough multibillion-dollar acquisition deal, spoke frankly with her employees, calmed testy investors, and secured new lines of revenue for the company. Her leadership has extended far beyond Xerox; in addition to serving on the boards of other companies and community organizations, she also serves on President Barack Obama's economic advisory council.

Perhaps the best advice Burns's mother gave her was when she taught her children that "where you live has nothing to do with who you are. Who you are is about your character, it's about the amount of energy you put into things, it's about how much control you take of your whole life."[49] Burns has spent her life modeling her mother's self-determination and grit. She adopted her mother's leadership style, which was rooted in honesty, industry, determination, and courage. This form of leadership took her all the way to the top of the corporate ladder, making her the first African American woman in American history to lead a multinational, global corporation.

## Notes

1 Cheryl Hall, "CEO Leads Xerox in a New Direction with ACS Deal," *Dallas News*, May 4, 2014, http://www.dallasnews.com/business/columnists/cheryl-hall/20130504-ceo-leads-xerox-in-a-new-direction-with-acs-deal.ece.

2 MilestoneVideoNY, "Mentoring—Anne Mulcahy and Ursula Burns," YouTube, December 1, 2013, http://youtu.be/4Tm8BRfbIZo, video.

3 Betsy Morris, "Ursula Burns," *Fortune* 153, no. 2 (2006): 57.

4 Carol Hymowitz, "Xerox's Ursula Burns on Her Career Path and Changing Company Strategy," *Businessweek*, August 8, 2013, http://www.businessweek.com/articles/2013-08-08/xeroxs-ursula-burns-on-her-career-path-and-changing-company-strategy.

5 "Xerox CEO: 'If You Don't Transform, You're Stuck,'" National Public Radio, May 23, 2012, http://www.npr.org/2012/05/23/153302563/xerox-ceo-if-you-don-t-transform-you-re-stuck.

6 Edward Tenner, "The Mother of All Invention," *Atlantic*, July–August 2010, http://www.theatlantic.com/magazine/archive/2010/07/the-mother-of-all-invention/308123/.

7 David Owen, *Copies in Seconds: Chester Carlson and the Birth of the Xerox Machine* (New York: Simon and Schuster, 2004).

8 Caitlin Deinard and Raymond Friedman, *Black Caucus Groups at Xerox Corporation* (Boston: Harvard Business Publishing, 1990), 2.

9 Ibid., 17–19.

10 Ibid., 3.

11 Ibid.

12 Ibid., 9.

13 Paul Solman, "How Xerox Became a Leader in Diversity—and Why That's Good for Business," *PBS NewsHour*, September 15, 2014, http://www.pbs.org/newshour/making-sense/xerox-employees-arent-carbon-copies/.

14 Nanette Byrnes and Roger O. Crockett, "Ursula Burns: An Historic Succession at Xerox," *Businessweek*, May 28, 2009, http://www.businessweek.com/magazine/content/09_23/b4134018712853.htm.

15 Adam Bryant, "Xerox's New Chief Tries to Redefine Its Culture," *New York Times*, February 20, 2010, http://www.nytimes.com/2010/02/21/business/21xerox.html?pagewanted=all&_r=0.

16 Ibid.

17 Byrnes and Crockett, "Ursula Burns."

18 Bryant, "Xerox's New Chief Tries to Redefine Its Culture."

19 Ibid.

20 Pearl Doherty, "Leading the Way," *Business Strategy Review* 23, no. 1 (2012): 14.

21 Bryant, "Xerox's New Chief Tries to Redefine Its Culture."

22 Doherty, "Leading the Way," 14.

23 MilestoneVideoNY, "Mentoring."

24 Betsy Morris, "The Accidental CEO," *Fortune* 147, no. 13 (2003), http://archive.fortune.com/magazines/fortune/fortune_archive/2003/06/23/344603/index.htm.

25 Ibid.

26  Ibid.
27  Bryant, "Xerox's New Chief Tries to Redefine Its Culture."
28  Ellen McGirt, "Fresh Copy," *Fast Company* 161 (2011), http://www.fastcompany
    .com/1793533/fresh-copy-how-ursula-burns-reinvented-xerox.
29  Geoff Colvin, "Ursula Burns Launches Xerox into the Future," *Fortune*, April 22,
    2010, http://archive.fortune.com/2010/04/22/news/companies/xerox_ursula
    _burns.fortune/index.htm.
30  Morris, "Accidental CEO."
31  Ibid.
32  Ibid.
33  Anne Mulcahy, quoted in ibid.
34  McGirt, "Fresh Copy."
35  Byrnes and Crockett, "Ursula Burns."
36  Colvin, "Ursula Burns Launches Xerox into the Future."
37  Andrew Nusca, "Backstage with Xerox CEO Ursula Burns," *Fortune*, March 24,
    2014, http://fortune.com/2014/03/24/backstage-with-xerox-ceo-ursula-burns/.
38  Lorena O'Neil, "Swapping Out Xerox's Toner," OZY, March 24, 2014, http://one
    .ozy.com/rising-stars-and-provocateurs/ursula-burns-is-taking-xerox-from
    -copies-to-client-services/30486.article.
39  McGirt, "Fresh Copy."
40  Bryant, "Xerox's New Chief Tries to Redefine Its Culture."
41  Ibid.
42  Ibid.
43  Hymowitz, "Xerox's Ursula Burns on Her Career Path."
44  Fortune Magazine, "Fortune Most Powerful Women Summit: Ursula Burns,"
    YouTube, October 15, 2012, http://youtu.be/ob1seSo9a1I, video.
45  Bryant, "Xerox's New Chief Tries to Redefine Its Culture."
46  Fortune Magazine, "Ursula Burns: 'Chill Out a Little Bit,'" YouTube, October 17,
    2013, http://youtu.be/j61upoCGQfc, video.
47  Leslie Kwoh, "Xerox CEO Ursula Burns Has Advice for Ambitious Women," *At
    Work* (blog), *Wall Street Journal*, March 20, 2013, http://blogs.wsj.com/atwork/
    2013/03/20/xerox-ceo-ursula-burns-has-advice-for-ambitious-women/.
48  Bryant, "Xerox's New Chief Tries to Redefine Its Culture."
49  Doherty, "Leading the Way," 15.

## Bibliography

Bryant, Adam. "Xerox's New Chief Tries to Redefine Its Culture." *New York Times*,
    February 20, 2010. http://www.nytimes.com/2010/02/21/business/21xerox
    .html?pagewanted=all&_r=0.
Byrnes, Nanette, and Roger O. Crockett. "Ursula Burns: An Historic Succession at
    Xerox." *Businessweek*, May 28, 2009. http://www.businessweek.com/magazine/
    content/09_23/b4134018712853.htm.
Colvin, Geoff. "Ursula Burns Launches Xerox into the Future." *Fortune*, April 22,
    2010. http://archive.fortune.com/2010/04/22/news/companies/xerox_ursula
    _burns.fortune/index.htm.

Deinard, Caitlin, and Raymond Friedman. *Black Caucus Groups at Xerox Corporation.* Boston: Harvard Business Publishing, 1990.

Doherty, Pearl. "Leading the Way." *Business Strategy Review* 23, no. 1 (2012): 10–16.

Fortune Magazine. "Fortune Most Powerful Women Summit: Ursula Burns." YouTube, October 15, 2012. http://youtu.be/ob1seSo9a1I. Video.

———. "Ursula Burns: 'Chill Out a Little Bit.'" YouTube, October 17, 2013. http://youtu.be/j61upoCGQfc. Video.

Hall, Cheryl. "CEO Leads Xerox in a New Direction with ACS Deal." *Dallas News,* May 4, 2014. http://www.dallasnews.com/business/columnists/cheryl-hall/20130504-ceo-leads-xerox-in-a-new-direction-with-acs-deal.ece.

Hymowitz, Carol. "Xerox's Ursula Burns on Her Career Path and Changing Company Strategy." *Businessweek,* August 8, 2013. http://www.businessweek.com/articles/2013-08-08/xeroxs-ursula-burns-on-her-career-path-and-changing-company-strategy.

Kwoh, Leslie. "Xerox CEO Ursula Burns Has Advice for Ambitious Women." *At Work* (blog), *Wall Street Journal,* March 20, 2013. http://blogs.wsj.com/atwork/2013/03/20/xerox-ceo-ursula-burns-has-advice-for-ambitious-women/.

McGirt, Ellen. "Fresh Copy." *Fast Company* 161 (2011). http://www.fastcompany.com/1793533/fresh-copy-how-ursula-burns-reinvented-xerox.

MilestoneVideoNY. "Mentoring—Anne Mulcahy and Ursula Burns." YouTube, December 1, 2013. http://youtu.be/4Tm8BRfbIZo. Video.

Morris, Betsy. "The Accidental CEO." *Fortune* 147, no. 13 (2003): 58–64.

———. "Ursula Burns." *Fortune* 153, no. 2 (2006). http://archive.fortune.com/magazines/fortune/fortune_archive/2003/06/23/344603/index.htm.

Nusca, Andrew. "Backstage with Xerox CEO Ursula Burns." *Fortune,* March 24, 2014. http://fortune.com/2014/03/24/backstage-with-xerox-ceo-ursula-burns/.

O'Neil, Lorena. "Swapping Out Xerox's Toner." OZY, March 24, 2014. http://one.ozy.com/rising-stars-and-provocateurs/ursula-burns-is-taking-xerox-from-copies-to-client-services/30486.article.

Owen, David. *Copies in Seconds: Chester Carlson and the Birth of the Xerox Machine.* New York: Simon and Schuster, 2004.

Solman, Paul. "How Xerox Became a Leader in Diversity—and Why That's Good for Business." *PBS NewsHour,* September 15, 2014. http://www.pbs.org/newshour/making-sense/xerox-employees-arent-carbon-copies/.

Tenner, Edward. "The Mother of All Invention." *Atlantic,* July–August 2010. http://www.theatlantic.com/magazine/archive/2010/07/the-mother-of-all-invention/308123/.

"Xerox CEO: 'If You Don't Transform, You're Stuck.'" National Public Radio, May 23, 2012. http://www.npr.org/2012/05/23/153302563/xerox-ceo-if-you-don-t-transform-you-re-stuck.

# Alice Waters

## Transforming American Food

### Stina Soderling and Lisa Hetfield

Background

For the past forty-two years, Chez Panisse has been a fixture of the restaurant scene in Berkeley, California, and of the California "foodie" movement. Located in a two-story townhouse, with old wood detailing and surrounded by trees, the restaurant invites guests to sit down to tablecloths and lit candles and to enjoy the multicourse meal specially offered for that night. In one week, dishes range from the unusual (almond gazpacho with cantaloupe) to the familiar (plum tart and raspberry ice cream). With dinner costing eighty-five dollars, Chez Panisse has been accused of being an elitist approach to food, yet founder and owner Alice Waters staunchly defends her model, and, indeed, it has worked so far, lending a legendary status to the restaurant and launching Waters's career as one of the leading figures of the sustainable food movement.

Waters herself has become at least as much of an icon as her restaurant. This is no small feat. Even though home food production is a deeply entrenched "women's task," and even though close to half of all food establishments are owned by women, the restaurant world still has a reputation of being heavily male dominated and a notoriously difficult space for women to enter. Female chefs repeatedly tell stories of discrimination and belittling. As one of the pioneers and leaders of the "food movement" of the past few decades, Waters is a notable exception to this male dominance. In fact, many people have pointed to her as the leader; she has been said to have "single-handedly change[d] what we ate."[1]

Waters is the executive chef, founder, and owner of Chez Panisse. Ever since the restaurant's founding in 1971, Waters has insisted on high-quality food, with cost never being the primary consideration. Though detrimental to the restaurant's budget in the early years, the model has turned out to be a success in the long run.

But Waters is more than a successful chef: she has initiated several programs to increase access to quality food and has inspired others to do the same. Thus, hers is an example of how business leadership can transform into leadership for social change.

## Formative Years

Alice Louise Waters was born on April 28, 1944, and grew up in Chatham, a small township in north-central New Jersey. Up through World War II, the area surrounding Chatham had been mostly farmland. With the lifting of a wartime building ban, however, the area experienced a building boom in the late 1940s, and the area became largely residential. The changes in Chatham were not unique. The period following World War II witnessed rapid changes in agriculture. The United States was moving increasingly to large, consolidated agricultural businesses, with smaller farms being driven into bankruptcy. This change was due largely to the enormous rise in the production and use of synthetic fertilizers and pesticides, most of them a by-product of the war industry.

While living in a place directly impacted by changing food production practices, little Alice was unaware of this shift. As a kid, the young Alice had not yet discovered a passion for food. She stated that her mom was not a good cook, and hence dinner was not something Alice enjoyed a great deal. Food was eaten but not thought about much. The family "never went to restaurants,"[2] as there was not money for such extravagances. Yet food did play a vital part in the family's life, as they grew much of it in their own garden.

It was as an undergraduate that Alice Waters developed her interest in food. Like for so many other young people, college was a formative experience for Waters, who moved to California to attend college, first at the University of California at Santa Barbara, then at the University of California at Berkeley.

Berkeley in the 1960s was a rich environment for a budding social movement leader such as Waters. The sixties has gone down in history as a period of social activism and the growth of vibrant countercultures, and Berkeley was one of its epicenters. Causes taken up by students, faculty, and community members included the peace movement, spurred by US intervention in Vietnam; the earliest signs of the second wave of feminism; the civil rights movement; and the student movement, which advocated for more student influence over universities. The bustle of activity stretched beyond the campus, to the still-existent People's Park and to the nearby cities of Oakland and San Francisco.

Waters participated in several of the movements at Berkeley during her college years; she was involved in women's rights, free speech, and antiwar work and worked on a congressional campaign, for Robert Scheer. Scheer, a peace activist and journalist at *Ramparts* magazine, was in the running for a Democratic nomination. Although he lost the election, he did win in Berkeley.

Food was a personally satisfying part of Waters's life but at this point not part of her activist involvement. Yet, looking back, she sees the importance of "coming together around the table" in social movements such as those of Berkeley in the sixties.[3] This is part of a long tradition in social movement groups: meals provide bodily and mental nourishment and give groups space for organizing. The Black Panther Party ran a successful breakfast program for children for years, to name one prominent example. Spiritual and religious organizations also often incorporate food in their community-building activities, such as church potlucks or the free meals provided at Sikh temples.

Part of the coming together that inspired Waters happened through a project that she herself ran and began in 1967, called Alice's Restaurant.[4] The "restaurant" was run for a newspaper in San Francisco, the *San Francisco Express Times*, where Waters cooked meals for the artists and writers who were working on the paper. Her food in a very direct sense sustained those who were involved in the creation of the paper.

Waters's undergraduate education also provided her with another important location for inspiration: France. Majoring in French cultural studies, Waters participated in a study-abroad program in France in 1964.[5] It was a transformative experience. During her stay in France, she was exposed to French cuisine and food culture, which has influenced her cooking and food-justice work ever since. She was infatuated with the simplicity yet sophistication of the food she encountered, with a focus on quality ingredients; and she loved how meals were central to daily life.

As the name implies, Chez Panisse, named for a character in a 1930s movie trilogy directed by the Frenchman Marcel Pagnol, started as a French restaurant. Over the years, the menu has shifted to incorporate more and more local products and cooking styles, and it is today often referred to as "new Californian"; but the French influence is still evident through dishes such as soufflés[6] and galettes.[7]

The influence of French food culture on Waters stretches far beyond the plate, however. She was enchanted with the relationship she found that many people in France had to food, viewing cooking and eating as simultaneously nourishment, social gathering, and political act. Thus, when "slow food" started in the 1980s, and when the local food movement boomed in France in the 1990s, it is no surprise that Waters was one of the leaders in translating this movement to the American context.

## Becoming a Restaurateur

After graduation, Waters traveled to London to train as a Montessori teacher. She worked as a Montessori teacher in Berkeley for two years, until she realized that cooking was a bigger passion in her life than was her love for teaching children. Together with her friend Lindsey Shere, she opened a restaurant in Berkeley in 1971, which was to become the famous Chez Panisse. With the help of her father, who believed in her so much that he mortgaged his house, she took out a loan for $10,000 to start the bistro. She also enlisted support from her circle of friends, who invested small amounts and became the key staff and partners in the business, which was incorporated as Pagnol et Cie, Inc. Later, Alice wrote in *40 Years of*

*Chez Panisse*, "It wasn't a partnership, it wasn't a corporation, it was really a community—a real community of interest, where everyone was there for exactly the same reasons, and in it to exactly the same depth."[8] This is typical of the way Waters works, drawing on her network of friends, family, and acquaintances who share her values and join in running her various projects.

From the start, Chez Panisse has been a labor of love. Waters cooked what she wanted to cook, spending long hours in the kitchen, with few prospects of ever making a profit. She bought the best ingredients she could find, spending sums of money that could not be recuperated. For the first several years, Chez Panisse lost money, as Waters and her team figured out how to run a restaurant, but the restaurant began to catch on. In 1979, Waters and Paul Prudhomme from Louisiana were invited to cook at an event in New York that presented the best young chefs in America alongside renowned French chefs. This was a high-profile event at Tavern on the Green, and both Waters and Prudhomme were the featured chefs in the *New York Times* report the next day. Alice Waters and Chez Panisse had arrived on the international food scene.

Today, Waters describes herself as "naive" in starting the restaurant, assuming that her friends would now pay for food she had previously given them for free, and she did not think about how now she would be in the kitchen, not at the dining table. A 1999 article stated that "even today Chez Panisse reportedly earns little profit."[9]

Though Chez Panisse no longer operates at a financial loss, money is still not the driving force in how Waters does business. Says Waters, "My real emphasis is on the farmers who are taking care of the land, the farmers who are really thinking about our nourishment."[10] She sources her food locally and has worked with vendors such as the Garden Project at San Francisco County Jail. For Waters, ingredients are at least as, if not more, important than the cooking process.

In the early days, Waters was "looking for taste,"[11] not organic or sustainable ingredients. In fact, when Chez Panisse opened in 1971, organic and local food was still not common in restaurants. In this process, she started working very closely with farmers, establishing long-term agreements with them, so that farmers are growing for the restaurant, providing Chez Panisse with quality ingredients and the farmers with a reliable source of income. Waters recalls, "I was never looking for organic farmers, I was never thinking about big picture sustainability. When I opened up Chez Panisse, I was only thinking about taste. And in doing that, I ended up at the doorstep of many of you."[12] Thus, with time, Chez Panisse has become increasingly dedicated to sustainable food practices.

Chez Panisse is also a business with a social conscience. The restaurant's staff has marched, under the Panisse banner, in antiwar demonstrations during the second Bush administration's invasion of Iraq. Waters has also experimented with improved labor practices, such as chefs working for six months a year, with the rest of the year off with full pay.

On April 1, 1980, Chez Panisse established a second venture (in the same building): a café, less upscale than the restaurant. The café serves pizzas, salads, and other food that was less experimental than what was in the restaurant. The café is still running and has been quite successful.

Waters stopped cooking at Chez Panisse in 1983, when she had her daughter and wanted to have time for other things. Shortly thereafter, in 1984, Waters opened Café Fanny. Named after her daughter, the café could be seen as a way for Alice Waters to integrate the two parts of life she finds so important: food and family. Café Fanny served breakfast, lunch, and coffee. It was, like Chez Panisse, a popular spot for many people but was seen as unnecessarily pricey, even pretentious, by many others. The café closed in 2012 because it was no longer financially viable. In a public letter about the closing, Waters and her colleagues stated that the café had been started in a spirit of "romance and idealism,"[13] two words that well describe most of Waters's work.

Though it took a few years for Chez Panisse to get off the ground, the restaurant, with its focus on sustainability and high quality, has become groundbreaking. The restaurant and Waters herself have gained great fame among those who are interested in food. Waters's work has foreshadowed the food-justice movement that developed in the United States in the 1990s and first decade of the twenty-first century. Food justice is the notion that everyone has the right to healthy, affordable food and that this food should be produced without harm to any part of the world, including to humans. The respect and popularity that Waters has garnered can be seen in the numerous awards she has won, such as the prestigious Lifetime Achievement award from the James Beard Foundation in 2004 and an honorary degree from Princeton University.

As Alice Waters and Chez Panisse became increasingly famous, Waters also became increasingly controversial. For example, she has repeatedly been accused of being elitist, for her insistence on local, organic food, which can be expensive. At close to a hundred dollars, a meal at Chez Panisse is inaccessible to many people. Waters responds to the claim of elitism by stating that everyone should have access to good food and that advocating for that is not elitist. She has called healthy food an "entitlement" for every American. Indeed, one of the principles of one of Waters's projects is that "good food is a right not a privilege."[14]

Yet how does this work in practice? Can everyone really access nutritious, sustainably produced food? Waters argues that free school food—breakfast, lunch, and a snack—is one important way of achieving food equality, and she has been advocating for a tripling of the federal government's budget for school lunches. Currently, the federal budget for school food is around $16 billion, with a total of five billion meals served every year.

Waters also points out that growing high-quality food is very expensive and that farmers should be paid a price that reflects this fact. She acknowledges that Chez Panisse is expensive but says that the food does cost that much to produce. Indeed, for most food in the United States, the price paid by consumers is far below the actual production costs; prices are kept artificially low through government subsidies for certain crops, a legal system in which agricultural producers do not pay for the environmental damage of production and in which wages are far below a living (or even minimum) wage.

As with many public figures, there is also the accusation that Waters does not always live up to her own standards. When Café Fanny closed, workers did not receive their promised severance pay. Critics and former employees expressed anger that Waters did not follow through on a promise to make sure that those who were laid off in the closing got two weeks of pay. Employees were not informed about the closing until the day before the restaurant shut its doors for good.

## Furthering Her Mission

After many years of cooking at Chez Panisse, Alice Waters gradually stepped away from the role of chef. There was so much else she wanted to do. Part of her shift away from the kitchen was in order to spend more time with her family, but she also wanted to expand and deepen her work on food justice. The question was, how should Waters expand her work on creating a different food system, beyond running her restaurant?

The food-related issues facing the world in the 1990s were both different from and similar to when Waters started her involvement in the food movement in the 1960s. Ever since World War II—and to a lesser degree before that—agriculture has grown increasingly industrial and increasingly dependent on outside inputs, and food is being shipped further and further from its origin.

Thus, in the 1990s, food was still a pressing issue. School lunches were lacking in taste and nutrition; industrial agriculture was depleting soil at a rapid pace; many cities in the United States had developed so-called food deserts: neighborhoods where no grocery stores or other sources of fresh food were available. Even though the problems were large, there was also hope, in the shape of a growing food movement, in which Waters was a crucial part.

This food movement had a strong feminist component. For example, Vandana Shiva—who is a leading figure in the food movement—wrote several influential books, including *Ecofeminism* with Maria Mies. Her later books focused on the environment, always with a feminist lens. Shiva brought attention to the damages caused by the global food system, especially monocropping (the practice of planting only one crop in a field, rather than many crops). While the global food supply used to produce hundreds of varieties and species, global monocropping has minimized the variety to only a handful. Shiva also runs an organization, Navdanya, and heavily influenced Waters, who quotes her in a foreword to a book about slow food.

In the late 1980s, the slow food movement was beginning to take off. Started in southern and western Europe (early activities took place in France and Italy), the movement quickly spread. A word play on the term *fast food*, it is indeed a proponent of a slower model of food production and consumption, but the movement has a bigger philosophy: it seeks a food system that is primarily local, that is sustainable, and that prioritizes pleasure in eating.

Alice Waters writes in her foreword to the book *Slow Food: The Case for Taste* that she remembers the 1986 event that served as the starting point of slow food: "I remember when in 1986 Carlo Petrini organized a protest against the building of a McDonald's at the Spanish Steps in Rome. The protesters, whom Carlo armed with bowls of penne, defiantly and deliciously stated their case against the global standardization of the world's food."[15]

Two years later, in 1988, Petrini, who by then had founded Slow Food International, visited California and made it a point to meet Waters and eat at Chez Panisse. The two began a long friendship and collaboration. There was no question that Waters would play a leadership role in the slow food movement, but how would she take what had been a local commitment in the Bay Area to a global scale? How could Waters use her skills, experiences, and values within this burgeoning movement while avoiding the pitfalls?

## Resolution

Collaboration, community, and core values were integral to Alice Waters's approach to food and her restaurant business from the start. Her creative energy and commitment attracted other creative, idealistic people—artists, writers, musicians, filmmakers, architects—who became her "band of friends" and business partners. They worked together, and they celebrated holidays and anniversaries together. As Waters verged on expanding her role as activist, she built her next steps on two strategies that had already worked well for Chez Panisse: collaborating with her friends and connections in the worlds of food and art to stage high-visibility events to link the pleasure of food with political action; and incorporating her ideas and mission into her successful cookbooks. Significantly, she made a third and important strategic move: she developed the Edible Schoolyard as a local transformative project that could be a model for national and global change.

## High-Visibility Events and a Model Project Promote the Cause

The tenth anniversary of Chez Panisse marked the first time that Waters and her colleagues took their community beyond Berkeley to stage a big event. This event, with hundreds of people gathering at the Joseph Phelps Vineyard in Napa Valley to celebrate the success of Chez Panisse, became a model for what was to become a central strategy for Waters's social-change work.

In the mid-1980s, San Francisco was reeling from the devastation of the AIDS epidemic. The artistic and restaurant communities were hit especially hard. Waters joined with others in the food business to envision Aid & Comfort, the San Francisco restaurant benefit for people fighting AIDS. At two large public events in 1987 and 1990, restaurants prepared thousands of box lunches served on the pier, and there was a sit-down dinner for five hundred people. The combination of high-profile people, the best food and entertainment, and passion for a cause helped to change local and national attitudes about AIDS. Waters and her colleagues at Chez Panisse were now mobilizing their significant connections and fame to make a difference in causes they cared about.

Not long after that, Neil Smith, the principal at Martin Luther King Jr. Middle School in Berkeley, challenged Waters to create a school program to nourish and enrich students' lives. When she visited the asphalt-covered schoolyard, she saw its potential as a garden. The idea for the Edible Schoolyard was inspired by the Garden Project at the San Francisco County Jail, founded only a couple of years earlier, in 1992. Through this program, inmates maintain a garden, and the produce is sold to local restaurants. Many inmates express that participation has been deeply meaningful to them, providing both job training and a well-needed refuge from the dreariness of prison life.

Waters thought to herself, if this program works so well for inmates, could it not also work for schoolchildren? Her answer was that, yes, it could. With funding from three generous donors, she began to create the Edible Schoolyard as an education model. It was two years later—at the twenty-fifth anniversary of Chez Panisse—that she made her next significant move to further her community work. She formed a nonprofit foundation, the Chez Panisse Foundation, later renamed Edible Schoolyard. Her goal was to provide universal free lunch for students of every grade in public schools, centered around a hands-on curriculum, incorporating school gardens, kitchen classrooms, and a lunch room where teachers and students cook and eat.

Not only did Waters model the Edible Schoolyard program on the Garden Project, but she also maintains ties to the original Garden Project, sourcing food for Chez Panisse from it. The success of the Garden Project has been one of the motivating factors in the development of gardening programs at several prisons across the country.

In order to do this work, Waters founded the Chez Panisse Foundation, whose mission is to promote sustainable agriculture, specifically through running Edible Garden programs in public schools. She tapped her vast network of friends and the entire Chez Panisse community to raise funds. The thirtieth anniversary of Chez Panisse was celebrated on the Campanile Esplanade of UC Berkeley. It was an outdoor luncheon party for six hundred guests to benefit the Chez Panisse Foundation. Once again, Waters's inventive energy and vast connections came together to create a gathering for a cause, incorporating the best food, wine, live music, and conversation.

In 2000, Waters took Carlo Petrini to see the Edible Schoolyard at the Martin Luther King Jr. Middle School. He understood her vision as a perfect model for Slow Food International to spread all over the world. With Petrini, Waters was instrumental in forming Terra Madre, the worldwide network of food communities that met for the first time in Turin, Italy, and currently has 153 active countries. Now she thought it was time to mobilize for an all-American event to emulate what was happening in Europe. The result was Slow Food Nation '08, another San Francisco extravaganza to bring together organic farmers, food-safety activists, home gardeners, school gardeners, sustainable ranchers, and foodies. Over eighty thousand people attended, and a year later, organizers planted an organic victory garden in front of San Francisco's civic center. Clearly what had begun in the 1970s as a counterculture movement was entering the mainstream, thanks in large part to the leadership of Alice Waters.

Waters's work with healthy, sustainable food has also expanded into institutions of higher learning. Waters's daughter, Fanny Singer, started her college education at Yale University in 2005. Says Waters, "We walked into the dining commons and recognized that smell of reheated steam-table food. So when I met the president of Yale at freshman orientation, I offered to help Yale's dining halls serve real food that was fresh, local, and organic. And I proposed that they start a school garden that would teach the same lessons at Yale that the Edible Schoolyard teaches in Berkeley."[16] This was the beginning of the Yale Sustainable Food Project. The Yale project is still in existence, influencing dining services at the university and even running a farm.

Taking this model abroad, in 2007, Waters redesigned the kitchen program at the American Academy in Rome. She had been planning this project since the previous year, and in February 2007, the new version of dining at the academy became reality. The academy is now home to the Rome Sustainable Food Project (RSFP). In addition to feeding fellows at the academy, the RSFP also has a garden and runs an internship program.

Alice Waters's activism is not limited to educational settings. She is the vice president of Slow Food International, the organization that served as a source of inspiration in her food-justice work. Waters initiated Slow Food Nation, the nonprofit branch of Slow Food USA.

## Cookbooks Unite Food, Pleasure, and Purpose

Alice Waters has written eight cookbooks, beginning in 1982 with *Chez Panisse Menu Cookbook* and continuing to her most recent, *The Art of Simple Food II: Recipes, Flavor and Inspiration from the New*

*Kitchen Garden*, in 2013. From the first, Waters incorporated her ideas about food. In the *Chez Panisse Menu Cookbook*, her opening chapter is called "What I Believe about Cooking." She writes,

> It is unfortunate for the children who will not remember or will never know the taste of real food. They believe that the mass produced, the phony, is the real and genuine, and I worry that they will be deprived of so much pleasure. Communication around the dinner table and the sense of family that comes with it are largely missing from our society. One of my goals at Chez Panisse is to re-establish gastronomic excitement that inspires and encourages conversation and conviviality. Depersonalized and assembly-line fast food may be "convenient" and "time-saving" but it deprives the senses and denies true nourishment.[17]

Alice uses detailed, vivid descriptions of food in her writing, appealing to the senses and linking pleasure to her ideas of hospitality and community. Over the years, she expanded on this style to incorporate more of her political views. Her voice became an essential tool for her social-change work. In fact, as Waters recounts, it was in an interview in which a journalist asked her about her "unusual suppliers" for Chez Panisse that she cited the underused land at the Martin Luther King Jr. Middle School, which she passed every day on her way to work. She said, "Everything wrong with the world is bound up in that place and the way we treat children."[18] After reading that article, Neil Smith, the principal of the school, invited her to visit and help.

It was only fitting that the Edible Schoolyard project would eventually become a book. *The Edible Schoolyard: A Universal Idea* was published in 2008. In Waters's foreword to that book, she again sets out her larger mission in vivid language linking her life work, Chez Panisse, and her goal to transform our food culture. She writes, "The Edible Schoolyard has been evolving for twelve years now, and it has become the most important thing in my life. It has also served as the incubator for the universal idea that I term 'Edible Education'—a hopeful and delicious idea for revitalizing public education."[19]

Early in the morning on March 8, 2013, a fire ravaged Chez Panisse.[20] The question that Waters and her team had to answer was, should the restaurant reopen? This was the second time there had been a fire at Chez Panisse. The first time was March 7, 1982, a much more devastating fire than the one thirty-one years later. In a 1999 interview, Waters's longtime friend David Goines stated, "Alice's vision is extremely clear. She's not concerned with the restaurant. She's concerned with good food. If you were to light a fire and burn the restaurant down, she'd keep going. She's on a mission."[21]

Chez Panisse did indeed reopen, and Waters is continuing her work, serving food and transformative ideas—and showing no signs of stopping anytime soon.

## Notes

1  Leslie Crawford, "Alice Waters," *Salon*, November 16, 1999, http://www.salon.com/1999/11/16/waters_2.

2  "Alice Waters: 40 Years of Sustainable Food," NPR, August 22, 2011, http://www.npr.org/2011/08/22/139707078/alice-waters-40-years-of-sustainable-food.

3  Ibid.

4  John Whiting, "The Green Gourmets: The Evolution of Chez Panisse," John Whiting's website, 2002, http://www.whitings-writings.com/essays/chez_panisse.htm.

5  Ibid.

6  A soufflé is "a light dish, either sweet or savoury, made by mixing materials with white of egg beaten up to a froth, and heating the mixture in an oven until it puffs up." *Oxford English Dictionary*, s.v. "soufflé," http://www.oed.com/view/Entry/185066?rskey=cctq1h&result=2#eid.

7  A galette is "a broad thin cake of bread or pastry." *Oxford English Dictionary*, s.v. "galette," http://www.oed.com/view/Entry/76206?redirectedFrom=galette#eid.

8  Alice Waters, *40 Years of Chez Panisse: The Power of Gathering* (New York: Clarkson Potter, 2011), 46.

9  Crawford, "Alice Waters."

10  "Alice Waters: 40 Years of Sustainable Food."

11  Ibid.

12  Stuart Leavenworth, "After 37 Years, Alice Waters Still Searches for a 'Slow Food' Life." *Sacramento Bee*, May 28, 2009. http://www.sacbee.com/static/weblogs/the_chef_apprentice/2009/05/after-37-years-alice-waters-st.html/022626.html.

13  Tracey Taylor, "Alice Waters' Café Fanny in West Berkeley to Close," *Berkeleyside*, March 8, 2012, http://www.berkeleyside.com/2012/03/08/alice-waters-cafe-fanny-in-west-berkeley-to-close/.

14 Alice Waters, *Edible Schoolyard: A Universal Idea* (San Francisco: Chronicle Books, 2008), 43.

15 Alice Waters, foreword to *Slow Food: The Case for Taste*, by Carlo Petrini (New York: Columbia University Press, 2004), ix.

16 Waters, *40 Years of Chez Panisse*, 223.

17 Alice Waters, "What I Believe about Cooking," in *Chez Panisse Menu Cookbook* (New York: Random House, 1982), 2.

18 Waters, *Edible Schoolyard*, 10.

19 Ibid., 6.

20 Tracey Taylor, "Fire at Chez Panisse Damages Front of Restaurant," *Berkeleyside*, March 8, 2013, http://www.berkeleyside.com/2013/03/08/fire-at-chez -panisse-damages-front-of-restaurant/.

21 Crawford, "Alice Waters."

## Bibliography

"Alice Waters: 40 Years of Sustainable Food." NPR, August 22, 2011. http://www.npr .org/2011/08/22/139707078/alice-waters-40-years-of-sustainable-food.

Crawford, Leslie. "Alice Waters." *Salon*, November 16, 1999. http://www.salon.com/ 1999/11/16/waters_2/.

Leavenworth, Stuart. "After 37 Years, Alice Waters Still Searches for a 'Slow Food' Life." *Sacramento Bee*, May 28, 2009. http://www.sacbee.com/static/weblogs/the _chef_apprentice/2009/05/after-37-years-alice-waters-st.html/022626.html.

Miles, Maria, and Vandana Shiva. *Ecofeminism*. London: Zed Books, 1993.

Petrini, Carlo. *Slow Food: The Case for Taste*. New York: Columbia University Press, 2004.

Taylor, Tracey. "Alice Waters' Café Fanny in West Berkeley to Close." *Berkeleyside*, March 8, 2012. http://www.berkeleyside.com/2012/03/08/alice-waters-cafe -fanny-in-west-berkeley-to-close/.

———. "Fire at Chez Panisse Damages Front of Restaurant." *Berkeleyside*, March 8, 2013. http://www.berkeleyside.com/2013/03/08/fire-at-chez-panisse-damages -front-of-restaurant/.

Waters, Alice. *The Art of Simple Food II*. New York: Clarkson Potter, 2013.

———. *Chez Panisse Menu Cookbook*. New York: Random House, 1982.

———. *Edible Schoolyard: A Universal Idea*. San Francisco: Chronicle Books, 2008.

———. Foreword to *Slow Food: The Case for Taste*, by Carlo Petrini. New York: Columbia University Press, 2004.

———. *40 Years of Chez Panisse: The Power of Gathering*. New York: Clarkson Potter, 2011.

———. "What I Believe about Cooking." In *Chez Panisse Menu Cookbook*. New York: Random House, 1982.

Whiting, John. "The Green Gourmets: The Evolution of Chez Panisse." John Whiting's website, 2002. http://www.whitings-writings.com/essays/chez_panisse .htm.

# Avid Modjtabai

## Leading Change at Wells Fargo

**Amanda Roberti and Dana M. Britton**

## Background

Imagine yourself an immigrant, having come to the United States at the age of seventeen, now heading up consumer lending at Wells Fargo, one of the four largest banks in the United States. This is Avid Modjtabai's journey. She is currently responsible for over sixty thousand employees and team members and customers in more than thirty-three million households. Having risen through the ranks at Wells Fargo, she was chosen to lead the company's transition to online banking at a time when the idea of moving and managing money through the Internet seemed unthinkable, and the technology did not yet exist to make it possible on a mass scale. Then, when Wells Fargo acquired Wachovia, in what Modjtabai describes as "the most impactful transition in the 160-year history of the company,"[1] she was called on to meet the challenge of integrating the two companies' technical operations and teams. How would Modjtabai's strong sense of Wells Fargo's culture guide her choice of strategies in the transition to online banking? How would her emphasis on collaborative leadership help her to build a team from two diverse companies? Ultimately, what leadership strategies were fundamental to her success?

### Early Life and Education

In 1979, at the height of the Iranian Revolution, seventeen-year-old high school senior Avid Modjtabai left Iran for the United States. Modjtabai had always wanted to attend college in the United

States, and her parents encouraged that dream. However, due to political instability in Iran, she found herself starting her trajectory a bit earlier than expected. But that was perfectly fine with Modjtabai; education was always a focus in her family, but more than that, the value of education was something that had been instilled in her early on. She explains, "My parents were very focused on education for all four of their children. My father's a doctor, my grandfather was a doctor. Actually my great-great-great-grandfather started the first college in Tehran, so education was always a big part of our family. And I think from my parents' perspective, there was an emphasis that you need to be educated, you need to be independent. So it was assumed. It was there. It was part of the culture of our family." Her mother, who did not have a career outside the home, also emphasized the value of education and independence for her daughters. The family was secular, and they had traveled widely during Modjtabai's childhood. This emphasis on education and a global perspective gave Modjtabai the openness and flexibility that allowed her to take on increasing responsibilities in her career.

Upon coming to the United States, Modjtabai settled in Boston to finish her last year of high school near one of her sisters. Her two older sisters, who had gone to college in the United States, had returned to Iran before she left, and her parents were also living there. Modjtabai was focused on her schooling, however. She also felt that she could continue her education abroad and return to Iran: "So it wasn't like I'm packing my bags to leave my country forever." After graduating high school, Modjtabai enrolled in Boston University. She transferred after only a year to Stanford, however:

> When I came to Stanford, it was actually the first time I had been in California. As the situation in Iran was progressively getting more challenging, I started thinking even more seriously around making sure that I'm studying something that would be employable [*laughs*] and where there would be more career opportunities. I recall that my older sister said, "You have to go look at Stanford, because if you don't, and two years from now if you go visit, you may say, 'I had

the option to come here, and I didn't.' You may regret it." So I actually came over for a week, and I fell in love with it.

Ultimately, she decided to major in industrial engineering, which she found "really interesting, very data-driven, [and all about] problem solving." Though she was one of few women in her field at the time, she says she thought little about this: "When I was at school, it wasn't like, 'Wow, I'm one of a few women.' It was just fact based; it was what it was. And I really didn't focus on it."

During Modjtabai's third year at Stanford, a professor connected her with an offer to work for an investment fund. Lured by the learning opportunity, as well as permanent residency benefits— the company was willing to sponsor her on a work visa—Modjtabai took the position. At this point, she had accumulated enough credits to graduate with her bachelor's degree. So a recently graduated Modjtabai took a job in the financial industry. From that point forward, she did not practice engineering, at least in the sense of working in the profession. She found that she enjoyed putting her technical skills to work in finance, however, and it paid off. After three years in the industry, she had developed an interest in business and decided to pursue an MBA.

Modjtabai was admitted to Columbia Business School and in 1986 returned to the East Coast to attend Columbia and to be close to her sisters, two of whom had recently moved back to New York. During her first year at Columbia, Modjtabai began to get a taste of the banking industry by working as an investment banker at First Boston. Of that time, she explains, "It was a very enriching experience. But one of the things that I clearly learned from that experience was that the culture of a place is really important, and it needs to be a good fit with you personally." Finding that investment banking was "too individual achievement oriented," Modjtabai got into consulting, joining McKinsey in 1988. She felt that consulting offered her more of the complex situations she really enjoyed tackling and was "intellectually extremely simulating." Modjtabai worked for the firm for three years in New York. She transferred within the company to San Francisco to be with her new husband, but after a year and a half, she decided that work-life balance was a priority and decided to look for a new position elsewhere.

## Wells Fargo

Modjtabai looked at several companies but ultimately took a job at Wells Fargo in 1994. She had learned during her early career that the culture of a company mattered to her, and she felt that Wells Fargo was a good fit:

> What really impressed me with Wells was its people, its culture, the legacy, the importance of stability. It's a company that's been around 162 years, and it's a company that intends to be around for a very long time. So it's making decisions that are very long term. There is a lot of focus around vision and values, around focusing on the customer, doing the right thing for the customer, growing in a disciplined way. It's a culture that's about caring. One of our favorite sayings is, "We don't care how much you know until we know how much you care."

Within six months, Modjtabai rose from an internal strategy position to a position as product manager for savings and investments. She stayed in this position for two years until her son was born and decided to go "on a quote-unquote part-time schedule, although that part-time was more like a fifty- to sixty-hour workweek." Despite the demanding hours, Modjtabai valued the flexibility at Wells Fargo that allowed her to pick her son up from preschool and spend time with him during his early years.

By the late 1990s, when Modjtabai's son was in kindergarten, she was offered an opportunity to work on a new initiative. Wells Fargo was setting its sights on burgeoning technological advances in banking. Online services at that time were still quite limited, but leaders at the company understood that this would be the wave of the future. She explains, "Wells Fargo was the first bank to offer Internet banking. By 1998, we had about 125,000–150,000 online banking customers and provided access to checking accounts online. We also had a website that provided information about the company. But that was the full extent of what we offered through the Internet. By then, we had the conviction and the belief that this is going to be a significantly bigger part of our customers' daily lives and more important to their experiences." Being part of a team that would revolutionize the way customers do their banking was an exciting prospect for Modjtabai. At that time, the only people using online banking were already at the forefront of technology as a part of everyday life: "Internet banking at that time was for early adopters. It was more the technologists, the people who were comfortable with PCs, a lot of what we called remote customers, customers who didn't walk into our stores." The online banking customers at that time had "view-only" capabilities; they were able to view their account balances remotely. The bank had not yet developed the ability to manage multiple accounts, make transfers between accounts, or move money. Fully realizing the potential of online banking would mean extending those services to all of its customers, from those with small accounts to large corporations. Modjtabai's team would have to figure out a way to make Internet banking accessible, likeable, and part of people's lives—something they could not imagine living without.

Modjtabai joined the leadership team of the Internet Services Group without even a clear idea of how they would approach their vision of what Internet banking should be. No bank of Wells Fargo's scale had ever created an Internet banking platform before, so there were no prescriptions about how it should be done. Debate about the direction the company should take ranged over a variety of options. As the bank was highly decentralized into lines of business, one option was that each of the lines of business would build its own platform. Modjtabai describes the discussion at the time: "We were committed to build Internet banking capabilities. Some of our lines of business wanted to build their own sites and capabilities. As a company across the board, we believed that Internet banking played an important role, so there were questions related to whether we wanted to have each line of business build their own capabilities." Other banks had spun off their Internet services with great profitability at the time of the Internet bubble in the US economy in the late 1990s. Modjtabai remembers, "All the valuations for the Internet companies were very high. We had consultants and investment bankers come in and say, 'Well, if you spin off your Internet platform, you're going to get this [very high] valuation, and you should run your Internet banking as a separate business.' Bank of America and US Bank had gone that way; there were many Internet-only banks at the time." Ultimately, Modjtabai and her team rejected all of these options.

Instead, they developed a vision of Wells Fargo's Internet platform as one part of a unified whole, with the customer experience seamlessly integrated in physical and virtual space:

> We had the belief that we are focused on our customers. What makes us unique and different than an Internet-only bank or a physical-only bank is the fact that we could integrate all of those capabilities together. That's going to be our competitive advantage. We don't want to think of our customers, they're Internet only or store only. There are some things that customers want to do online, but then there are other things that they want to do by walking into a store. When they want to open a checking account, when there's an issue that they need to resolve, they want to see someone. Even if they're not walking to our stores, seeing our stores in the corner of their neighborhood gives them comfort, that "if I need something, I could walk there." So we had this belief that it's an integrated model. We wanted to provide the choice to the customers to use all of our channels, and how we are going to be different is by integrating them more effectively. As they go from one to the other, they could easily move around and navigate the organization.

This was a novel concept and one that would create a bank that was remarkably different, at least in form, from the Wells Fargo that had been operating since its beginnings 160 years before. Wells Fargo's vision, however, drew on the cultural values that drew Modjtabai to the company in the first place; she sought first and foremost to see Internet banking from the perspective of the customer.

The second question was one of how Internet banking could be profitable and produce a return on Wells Fargo's initial investment. Again, Modjtabai and her team turned to the value of the customer experience and the value that the Internet platform could add: "We started looking at the data in a way that we could make the economic case. I remember at the time, Clyde Ostler was running the group. I joined Clyde in a few very senior operating-committee-level discussions and off-sites where we presented the data and the analytics. We were able to show that once customers are online, they become a lot more profitable. They would hold more products with us; they would stay with us longer. So we put that issue to bed early on." Customer loyalty and, by extension, profitability became key drivers in the argument about the case for the move to online banking. Online, the bank could offer more of its products, and the ease with which customers could manage their (now multiple) accounts would, Modjtabai's team believed, retain them longer as customers.

The final decision was the form the team and the platform were to take. Rejecting calls for a piecemeal approach in which each of the bank's lines of business would develop its own Internet banking platforms, Wells Fargo opted for a centralized group that would develop one platform for the entire company. In making this decision, Modjtabai broke with the practice of decentralized control that had characterized Wells Fargo throughout its history. She had the support of the senior leadership, however:

> I think kudos go to our most senior leadership, Dick Kovacevich, our CEO at the time, and John Stumpf. We made the case to Dick and John, and they fully supported it. We made the case that this is a space where we don't have 162 years of legacy. Here we started with a clean slate, and we have the opportunity to do it right. And if we let the current organization structure define the experience for our customers, we've missed a huge opportunity. So if we say, "Mortgage reports here and card reports here and deposit reports here and small business reports here: each one of you own all aspects of your business, and you do this, too," we're going to basically create all these disjointed experiences for our customers. But instead we will say, "This is one Wells Fargo experience from a customer perspective." When they come to WellsFargo.com, it's one company. It's one store. We want to create an experience that says that. And John and Dick absolutely supported that vision.

Modjtabai and her manager at the time, Clyde Ostler, understood that the move to an Internet platform would require a new structure, but in making the customer experience central, they also wanted to honor the values that had initially drawn her to the company. Their vision reflected that, and they had support from the top.

The process to build the Internet platform started with the formation of a specialized, stand-alone team within the company. To accomplish such a dramatic, company-wide transformation, Modjtabai and the team needed not only the strong support of senior leadership but also the support of the leaders of the various lines of business throughout Wells Fargo. She gained this support by adopting a transparent, collaborative style in communicating her vision and strategy:

> I believe it is critical to be very close to my business partners and be very engaged with them and to make sure that there's a lot of transparency. We were equal partners at the table; there's no preferred status. They bring the business expertise, we bring the channel expertise—how do we work together? I had a monthly letter that I sent to all my business partners, was available, would go out and meet with them on a regular basis. There was collaboration and partnership. There were issues that would be coming up, but we would address them through the normal course of working together, which helped not having anything become a big block that would stop you from moving forward.

Instead of being the kind of leader who waited for problems to arise to deal with them, Modjtabai's proactive, flexible, creative, and transparent approach allowed her to prevent problems from arising in the first place—something that helped build support for her vision and strategy.

By 2005, the move to online banking was well under way. Modjtabai left the Internet Services Group to serve as human resources director for Wells Fargo, a position she held for two years. In 2007, the head of technology for the company left, and she was asked to lead the Technology Information Group. As she stepped into that role, the United States began to feel the effects of the worst global financial crisis since the Great Depression. The stock market (as measured by the Dow Jones Industrial Average) lost more than half its value in one year, dropping from more than fourteen thousand points in October 2007 to sixty-six hundred points in 2008. Due largely to losses around subprime lending, several major US banks failed outright. Some, like Wells Fargo, received substantial government assistance.[2] Others became takeover targets. Wachovia, then the fourth-largest bank holding company in the United States, was one of the latter.

On October 3, 2008, Wells Fargo officials announced that they were acquiring Wachovia. Like Wells Fargo, Wachovia was a company with a long historical legacy (it had been founded in 1879), a strong company culture, and diversified banking operations in the areas of personal banking, asset management, wealth management, and corporate and investment banking products and services. It had suffered heavy losses during the financial crisis, and the federal government forced its sale; ultimately, Wells Fargo emerged as the successful buyer.

The acquisition added another level of complexity to the task faced by Modjtabai and her technology group; she was now responsible for online banking for a company that had the largest branch network in the United States. Modjtabai faced several new challenges. She had to integrate the two institutions into a single online platform, bring new talent and stakeholders to the table, and at the same time honor what she saw as the customer-centered culture of Wells Fargo and her own vision.

## Resolution

Modjtabai clearly understood the scale of the challenge she now faced. The changes involved in the acquisition of Wachovia were revolutionary for Wells Fargo. She notes, "Of any transformation that our company has gone through over the last 160 years, this is the most impactful transformation. We're going from a regional bank to a national bank. We're going from West Coast only to nationwide. We're going from three thousand stores to six thousand stores.

We're going from nothing in brokerage to being the third-largest retail brokerage firm. Wachovia's going from little presence in cards to a combined card business, a large mortgage business." All of these lines of business ultimately had to be integrated and supported by a single technology organization for which she was responsible. The scale of the task was significant, as the company would now combine a large number of new branches all over the country.

Modjtabai began (re)building her technology team and driving the integration in this radically different environment. There were three key elements of her strategy. The first was to make employees of Wachovia feel like they were part of the team. The acquisition of Wachovia by Wells Fargo took place during the financial crisis, and the Wachovia employees faced considerable uncertainty about their futures and had no idea how or if they would be integrated into the structure of Wells Fargo. She remembers an early meeting with her Wachovia counterpart in Charlotte, where the company had been headquartered: "The first visit I went to Charlotte, I remember I went to a meeting with my counterpart there, and in the middle of the meeting, he said, 'Well my direct reports are going to be here to meet with you.' And then they all came and stood by the wall. No one came to the table. [And I said], 'No, come to the table [*laughs*]. We're the same team.'" Modjtabai initially spent time getting to know the talent available at Wachovia and built a structure that integrated people from both companies: "I spent a lot of time at the very front end to meet two, three, four levels down in the technology and operations organizations to get to know the people. I put a lot of thought into the structure. And we ended up with a structure within technology and operations that was 50 percent Wells Fargo, 50 percent legacy Wachovia at all levels, including the leadership.'" The resulting structure fully integrated talent from both companies. This intentional team building helped to assuage the concerns of the (former) Wachovia employees that they would be excluded from the process of bringing the new, united company together within a single, integrated technology organization.

The second element of Modjtabai's strategy involved building a shared culture. She understood the importance of vision and values in motivating and uniting her team. Wachovia also had a strong culture, and integrating the team was crucial to her success. She set about building a culture carefully:

> Throughout the integration, we actually spent a lot of time in building a common culture. At the company level, we had a team that said, "Let's think about the key cultural attributes of each organization, and let's decide, where do we want to be as a combined company, and how are we going to be moving there?" And we kept calling ourselves out when we weren't doing it the right way. This role allowed me to focus on the culture of an organization and what kind of culture you need to create so that you can bring in the talent that you need to bring in. Paying a lot of attention to the culture, how we build a work environment that would attract talent is a very important lever in how you lead a team and how you drive success.

Ultimately, Modjtabai's strategy of open communication and creating a shared vision and culture within the technology and operations team was fruitful. Under difficult circumstances, she was able to form a highly motivated team from two formerly disparate companies.

Modjtabai did not leave motivation to chance, however. The third element of her strategy relied on building alignment and recognizing those efforts across the team. She recognized that as a leader, she had to set priorities, create alignment, and celebrate success. As her team reached important milestones, she made sure they were recognized: "We have all the formal mechanisms. We have our annual recognition trips; we have our recognition programs. Our recognition is tied to our shared goals. So team members who exhibit or help us make progress against those goals [should be recognized]. Frankly, the most powerful thing is to pick up the phone and talk to people or send them an email or send them a card, assuring them that what they've done is visible, it's seen as making an impact." Ultimately, all three elements proved to be crucial to her success. She built a high-performing team that was motivated to accomplish a transition of the scale required in a company that had essentially doubled in size.

Modjtabai describes the move to create a new technology and operations organization as a journey. First, she built a team with a shared vision and culture. Then she forged partnerships within the company across the different lines of business to understand the needs of those groups. Then her team set about meeting those needs. As she built out this new team, her earlier work in helping begin the journey to an Internet banking platform also continued to deliver results for Wells Fargo. Wells Fargo has been named "Best Consumer Internet Bank in the US," by *Global Finance* magazine on numerous occasions, most recently in 2013. Through Modjtabai's efforts and leadership, she ensured that Wells Fargo's legacy would survive and flourish in the Internet age.

Modjtabai left the Technology Information Group (now known as the Technology Operations Group) in 2009 to take a position as senior executive vice president and head of the Consumer Lending Group, the role in which she currently serves. In this capacity, she is in charge of home lending for the country's biggest originator and servicer of mortgages, as well as consumer credit solutions and indirect auto lending. In 2014, she was ranked number six on the *American Banker* list of the twenty-five most powerful women in banking.[3] Looking back, she notes that her trajectory in the company was not always upward, however:

> I took a lot of roles that were not necessarily moving into a bigger place. For example, when I came to the company in the corporate strategy role, I was two down from our CEO and president. And then I became a group product manager that was probably six down in the organization. But that wasn't the criteria. I talk to a lot of people who'd say, "Well why would I want to take this role? I won't be able to go to this meeting," or "I'm going to be one level down from my current role." But I thought, "Well, you want to take it because it's a bigger role. You're going to learn a lot more. You're going to have a big impact. You personally are going to grow." So for me, being in place or making decisions that would give me opportunities to make a difference, to learn, and to have fun have always been the key guiding principles.

In each position she took and each move she made—both lateral and vertical—Modjtabai saw opportunities for learning, focusing on potential for growth, and being challenged. Hierarchy was less important to her than experience.

As a woman, Modjtabai is a rarity at this level in banking—or in fact in any large corporation. The proportion of women who hold positions as corporate officers in Fortune 500 companies is less than 15 percent.[4] In telling her story, Modjtabai herself does not describe particular instances of gender discrimination she experienced. She views her own leadership at Wells Fargo as mostly gender neutral; as she says, "I don't think there's any point that if a man had been in my position, he would have made a different decision than I would have." But when asked to reflect on women's leadership in general, she takes a somewhat different tack:

> I actually do think that gender may play a role. I think maybe for women there is more of looking at 360-degree views—not just look-ing at the decision or the impact to the customer but having more things under consideration. But even that, I don't know—I've never been a man making a decision [*laughs*]. But maybe for women it's the inclusiveness, it's how you listen, who you bring to the table. It's taking the time to build those one-on-one relationships, bring empathy to the table. So it's more the EQ elements, I would guess. In my own journey, my early years were all around the IQ pieces. It was getting to the right answer and the data and the analysis. But as I moved up the organization and as I had different experi-ences, I think for me personally, I became more focused on the importance of the softer aspects of how you lead and how you build high-performing teams. Because frankly, as you move up the orga-nization, I don't think it's a male or female issue. You have to lead through others. It's more around how you influence sixty thousand people. You need to pay a lot of attention to how you communicate to your team, how you connect them to the bigger purpose—how you set the example and be a role model around what your expecta-tions are from the cultural norms in the organization.

In thinking about her transition to high-level leadership, Modjta-bai makes a key distinction between IQ, which she sees as the basic technical knowledge one needs to do one's work and be successful, and EQ, which is essentially emotional intelligence. She sees the latter as vital if one is to assume leadership at the scale of a corporation the size of Wells Fargo and suggests that women may draw on this kind of intelligence more readily than men do. Indeed, this reliance on EQ is very much a part of her story of success; it is in her emphasis on building a shared culture, building alignment, recognizing success, communicating with stakeholders, understanding the customer experience, and putting forward a clear vision for change.[5]

In the transition to online banking at Wells Fargo, Avid Modjtabai's openness to learning and her collaborative and transparent leadership style enabled her to assemble and manage the team of experts who would successfully launch the first Internet banking platform. Her commitment to building a common culture that drew on the original values of the company convinced Wells Fargo leadership that a revolutionary way of banking and customer service was the wave of the future. Ultimately, her efforts were realized in a customer-centered Internet service unlike any that Wells Fargo, Wachovia, or any other bank had attempted before.

## Notes

1 All direct quotes from Modjtabai are taken from a conversation between her and Lisa Hetfield on July 17, 2014. The editors are grateful to Modjtabai for her comments on an earlier draft of this case study.

2 This assistance took the form of a sale of Wells Fargo stock to the US Treasury. Wells Fargo redeemed the stock in 2009, paying back the value plus $1.441 billion in dividends.

3 "The 25 Most Powerful Women in Banking: No. 5: Avid Modjtabai, Wells Fargo," *American Banker*, September 18, 2013, http://www.americanbanker.com/magazine/123_10/the-25-most-powerful-women-in-banking-avid-modjtabai-wells-fargo-1062161-1.html.

4 Catalyst, "2013 Catalyst Census: Fortune 500 Women Executive Officers and Top Earners," December 10, 2013, http://www.catalyst.org/knowledge/2013-catalyst-census-fortune-500-women-executive-officers-and-top-earners.

5 The research literature suggests that women typically have higher scores on many measures of emotional intelligence than men do. However, other research suggests that it may be that women develop these qualities because others expect these capabilities from them but not from men. For example, see Esther Lopez-Zafra and Leire Gartzia, "Perceptions of Gender Differences in Self-Report Measures of Emotional Intelligence," *Sex Roles* 70 (2014): 479–495.

## Bibliography

Catalyst. "2013 Catalyst Census: Fortune 500 Women Executive Officers and Top Earners." December 10, 2013. http://www.catalyst.org/knowledge/2013-catalyst-census-fortune-500-women-executive-officers-and-top-earners.

Lopez-Zafra, Esther, and Leire Gartzia. "Perceptions of Gender Differences in Self-Report Measures of Emotional Intelligence." *Sex Roles* 70 (2014): 479–495.

"25 Most Powerful Women in Banking, The: No. 5: Avid Modjtabai, Wells Fargo." *American Banker*, September 18, 2013. http://www.americanbanker.com/magazine/123_10/the-25-most-powerful-women-in-banking-avid-modjtabai-wells-fargo-1062161-1.html.

# Martha Stewart

## The Rise, Fall, and Comeback of a Brand

### Carolina Alonso Bejarano and Lisa Hetfield

## Background

On December 27, 2001, a chartered private jet landed in San Antonio, Texas, to refuel before heading on to San Jose del Cabo, Mexico. In the aircraft was Martha Stewart, the celebrity designer of home decorating supplies and entertainment needs, who, after discovering a missed call on her cell phone from someone at her brokerage firm, proceeded to return the call. It was 1:41 p.m., Eastern Standard Time. Two minutes later, at 1:43 p.m., Stewart's trading assistant at Merrill Lynch, Douglas Faneuil, executed a sell order that she placed for her entire holding of ImClone shares.[1]

This ostensibly harmless transaction—which, considering the size of other activity in Stewart's portfolio, was rather insignificant—nevertheless was the beginning of what turned into a nightmarish era both for Martha Stewart Living Omnimedia, the company she founded and still heads, and for Stewart personally. Because of her now-infamous phone call, Stewart was publicly accused of insider trading. The share price in her company dropped dramatically; her award-winning television show was canceled; advertising revenues in her magazine plunged; and many of her corporate officers resigned. All this took place while Stewart was tried and convicted on four counts of obstruction of justice and lying to investigators.

In an age when market collapse and increasing unemployment were a matter of daily news and with public tolerance for white-collar misconduct at an all-time low, how can a brand name and corporate fortune built around the image of a living person survive the scandal of that person's perceived disregard for the law? What follows is the story of the rise and fall of Martha Stewart and of the decisions she made to restore her name and that of her company.

## From Martha Kostyra to Martha Stewart Inc.

Martha Kostyra was born in Jersey City, New Jersey, on August 14, 1941. The granddaughter of Polish immigrants and the second of six children, Martha developed a passion for helping with the household chores during her early years. She learned the basics of cooking, canning, and sewing from her mother, a teacher and homemaker; and she learned gardening as a young child from her father, a pharmaceutical salesman and passionate gardener who liked to work with her in the family's little, but neat, backyard.

When Stewart (then Kostyra) was a teenager going to Nutley High School in New Jersey, where she was a member of the Honor Society and active in her school's Art Committee, she modeled ready-to-wear in New York City at the Bonwit Teller department store on Fifth Avenue. After graduating high school in the summer of 1959, she decided to attend Barnard College in New York and pursue an art history degree. During her first year at Barnard, she met Andy Stewart, a Yale Law School student whom she married in July 1961 and divorced in 1990. In 1962, Martha gave birth to her daughter, Alexis, her only child.

In 1968, Stewart took a brokerage course at the New York Institute of Finance, and later that year, she was licensed as a member of the New York Stock Exchange. She joined the firm Perlberg, Monness, Williams and Sidel, and within two years, she was among its top sales representatives. In 1973, Martha left her job to move to Connecticut with her family. After a few years of suburban life, Stewart was keen to get back into business, and in 1976, she partnered with a friend and formed her first company: An Uncatered Affair. Stewart's collaboration with her friend lasted less than six months, and the partnership was quickly dissolved, ostensibly due to Stewart's excessive perfectionism and overbearing personality.[2]

An Uncatered Affair was the first of many catering-related businesses that culminated with the 1980 birth of Martha Stewart Inc. and the publishing of her first book: *Entertaining*. Published in 1982 and sold at thirty-five dollars, *Entertaining* was one of the most expensive cookbooks on the market. But neither its price nor the later-proven charges of plagiarism discouraged the book's buyers. Its first printing of twenty-five thousand copies sold out within a month, and *Entertaining* became Stewart's first best-seller. The book took what at the time were distinctive and comparatively small media niches—cooking, baking, horticulture, entertaining, crafts, and holidays—and pooled them into one category: "Lifestyle." Building on the success of *Entertaining*, Stewart created a company that framed economic consumption as more than the mere acquisition of goods; she turned her products into an expression of the buyer's personal taste, style, and identity. By 1985, the *Wall Street Journal* nicknamed Martha Stewart "America's goddess of graciousness,"[3] and in 1988, *Fortune* included her in their prestigious list of the "50 Most Powerful Women."[4] As Stewart herself said to staff assistants, "Remember, I'm not Martha Stewart the person anymore. I'm Martha Stewart the lifestyle."[5]

In 1987, Stewart signed a contract with Kmart to create and oversee the manufacture of a line of bedding and bath products. In return, Kmart paid royalties on all Martha Stewart–branded products. By 1990, Martha Stewart's line accounted for 3 percent of the company's revenue and $1 billion in sales. Stewart published the pilot issue of the magazine that was to become her signature product, *Martha Stewart Living*, in 1991 under the patronage of Time Warner. Stewart's lifestyle empire soon grew to include two magazines, a cable-television show, a syndicated newspaper column, a series of how-to books, a radio show, and $763 million in annual retail sales for Martha Stewart Inc. by 1997.

With *Martha Stewart Living*, aspects of Stewart's personal life became part of the product that her company offered to its consumers. For instance, for the first fifteen years of *Martha Stewart Living*, Stewart opened and ended each issue with two columns of her own: "Letter from Martha," which embodied and gave meaning to her business and its products, and her "Remembering" column, which offered her personal reflections on her life, society, and style. Through her two columns, Stewart made her readers feel "at home" with her; they knew her childhood stories, her sadness and happiness, her disappointments, her battles: she was one of them.

Stewart's "Letter" was innovative in its upscale look and its informed presentation of the business. Stewart knew that, compared to the readers of other women's magazines, her readership was older, better educated, higher earning, and often professional or managerial. This is why she offered insights on her business in her "Letter," giving her customers a window into her approach to management, her leadership, and key decisions she made on a daily basis. In contrast to the more professional tone of her "Letter," Stewart's "Remembering" presented a more spontaneous, personal, and evocative side of her. Here, she ruminated on mostly personal matters, a sentimental recollection of moments from her family and childhood. Consequently, when people saw Stewart's company, they saw Martha Stewart.

## The Rise and Fall of Martha Stewart Living Omnimedia

In 1997, seven years after the start-up of *Martha Stewart Living*, Stewart purchased her magazine from Time Warner for a reported $75 million. This move boosted the media's coverage of her business, overriding earlier critiques of her reported perfectionism, caustic personality, and sometimes-despotic management style. Within two years, on October 19, 1999, *Martha Stewart Living* went public, and Martha Stewart Living Omnimedia (MSLO) was born. Standing on the balcony of the New York Stock Exchange watching the main trading floor, Stewart witnessed her net worth skyrocket from $614.7 million to $1.27 billion in an instant. This initiated an upward trajectory for the company, as MSLO expanded to television and radio shows, a syndicated newspaper column, an extensive line of books and other publications, and a successful Kmart product line.

Martha Stewart Living Omnimedia became a commanding designer of "how-to" content and related goods. By 2001, the year of the disastrous San Antonio cell-phone call, the company had a total revenue of $295.7 million for the year. The business encompassed multiple business avenues, including four magazines, an Emmy Award–winning television program, a weekly piece on *CBS*

*This Morning,* thirty-four book titles that together had sold more than ten million copies, a weekly "Ask Martha" newspaper column syndicated in more than 230 newspapers, a radio show airing on more than 330 stations throughout the United States, and a website (marthastewart.com) with more than 1.7 million registered users.

On December 27, 2001, everything changed when Martha Stewart sold her 3,928 shares in the pharmaceutical company ImClone, on the eve of a critical Food and Drug Administration (FDA) ruling on the company's new cancer drug, Erbitux. Only one day after Stewart sold her stock, the FDA announced its rejection of Erbitux, causing ImClone shares to plunge. Less than six months after that, in early June 2002, news broke of an investigation into Stewart's ImClone trade. The *New York Times* and the *Washington Post* published stories addressing the circumstances of Stewart's share sale; immediately after this, public accusations of insider trading arose.

On June 12, 2002, Stewart released a statement contending that the sale was the result of a $60 stop-loss order she had placed in November 2001 with the Merrill Lynch broker Peter Bacanovic. The press responded by asking why her stock was not sold immediately when the share price dropped below $60 to $59.98, at 11:07 a.m. the morning before the phone call. At about the same time, information emerged regarding sales of $79 million worth of MSLO stock by both Stewart and her associates, transactions that took place before information about Stewart's investigation was made public. Martha Stewart never addressed or explained these issues. MSLO shares began a steady fall and closed on June 25, 2002, at $13.60 per share, an all-time low since the company went public in 1999.

MSLO stock continued to plunge dramatically. By July 2002, it had lost $300 million in market valuation. In September of that year, the House of Representatives asked the Department of Justice to investigate Stewart for insider trading. Nine months later, on June 4, 2003, Martha Stewart was indicted on charges of obstructing justice and securities fraud related to the sale of ImClone stock. The day after her indictment, she took out a $79,000 full-page ad in *USA Today* and the *New York Times*—titled "An Open Letter from Martha Stewart" and addressed "To My Friends and Loyal Supporters"—in which she asserted her innocence. Stewart wrote, "After more than a year, the government has decided to bring charges against me for matters that are personal and entirely unrelated to the business of Martha Stewart Living Omnimedia. I want you to know that I am innocent—and that I will fight to clear my name."[6]

Despite Stewart's claims of innocence and her attempts to distinguish between her personal life and her company, MSLO stock prices continued to suffer. In the aftermath of the scandal, ad revenue dropped 54 percent, and *Martha Stewart Living* lost 22 percent of its subscribers. By spring 2003, the MSLO stock flirted with the $7 mark, a loss of more than two-thirds of its value in comparison to the previous spring. Press reports calculated Stewart's personal losses from failed marketing projects, decreasing magazine profits, the cancellation of her CBS television *Morning Show* segment, and her plummeting company shares at more than $400 million.

The period leading up to the trial and the trial itself attracted enormous press attention. Stewart, who was famous for her accomplishments and for being the embodiment of style and good taste, was also known for her imperious behavior. She had been variously depicted as "harsh" and "rude."[7] Christopher Byron and Jerry Oppenheimer had written scathing biographies of her, with damaging stories about her character. During the trial, the government's key witness, Douglas Faneuil, the Merrill Lynch assistant who had made the fateful call to Stewart, testified about his various communications with Stewart. He described rude, sometimes harsh treatment by her. Once, when his boss, Peter Bacanovic, had the nerve to put Stewart on hold, she launched into a tirade against Faneuil, including telling him that she was "going to leave Merrill Lynch unless the hold music was changed."[8] Stewart's reputation as a difficult person and the state of New York's previous charge against Stewart for lying about the location of her residence to avoid taxes may have been the reasons she was not called to testify. In any case, the jury of eight women and four men made their decision without hearing from the defendant.[9]

Martha Stewart was convicted of obstruction of justice on March 15, 2004. She wrote her last "Letter from Martha" in the May issue of her magazine, where she made a point of reaching out to her followers and thanked everyone: "readers, advertisers, business partners, family, friends, staff—for the outpouring of affection and support that you have shown me recently, just as you have consistently done for nearly two years." She also made an apology: "for the upset that my personal legal troubles have caused for all of you."[10] Two months later, on July 16, she was given the most lenient sentence possible: five months in a minimum-security prison. Moments later, on the courthouse steps, Stewart gave a statement to the press comparing her situation to that of Nelson Mandela—South Africa's persecuted antiapartheid hero—saying that "many, many good people have gone to prison" and closing her statement with a short sales pitch. "Perhaps all of you out there can continue to show your support by subscribing to our magazine, by buying our products, by encouraging our advertisers to come back in full force to our magazines." She paused and added, "And I'll be back. I will be back."[11]

The indictment, the guilty verdict, and Stewart's jail term seriously jeopardized not only her credibility but also her future as a director of a publicly traded firm in the United States. The company's value, which following the initial public offering (IPO) in 1999 rose to a peak of more than $2 billion, lurched to $539 million following her conviction. What was worse, according to a survey conducted by the marketing firm Brand Keys, after the verdict was announced, consumers viewed the Martha Stewart brand even more negatively than they viewed the Enron Corporation. In the words of Morris L. Reid, the managing director of marketing consultancy Westin Rinehart, "I think the brand as we know it is dead."[12] Martha Stewart, on the brink of losing everything she worked for, needed to formulate a strategy to regain her credibility and that of her business.

## Resolution

At the midpoint of Martha Stewart's prison sentence, the stock of her company had not merely rebounded; it was 50 percent higher than before anybody had heard of her ImClone stock and the ill-fated cell-phone call. Furthermore, upon her release from prison, ad revenue at her magazines picked up, and the share price of MSLO neared an all-time high. Stewart is an example of a CEO who got her story out. What accounted for this success, and what strategies, programs, and methods did Stewart use to reach out to employees, shareholders, and consumers in order to restore her reputation and that of her brand?

Stewart carefully orchestrated a multitiered campaign to restore her reputation. After she was indicted for obstruction of justice in the federal government's insider-trading investigation of ImClone stock, she immediately left her position as chairwoman and CEO of her company (but continued on in a newly appointed position as creative director). Stewart stopped writing her signature "Letter" and "Remembering" columns in *Martha Stewart Living*, but she continued to communicate with her followers not only through the magazine but through other outlets as well.

Besides the full-page advertisement in *USA Today* and the *New York Times* discussed earlier, Stewart also published her "Open Letter from Martha Stewart" on her newly launched website, marthatalks.com. Reading her "Open Letter," one realizes that Stewart understood that when a hero missteps, she has to reconcile two conflicting images of her persona—the larger-than-life presence she once commanded and her new fallen state. In her letter, Stewart made sure people heard her side of the story. She denied any charges of insider trading, but she also hammered home the untrustworthiness of the three key witnesses on whom the federal government based its case. Finally, she very proactively invited others to continue to believe in her strength: "This is not an end to anything, but a kind of fresh start, I believe."[13]

Stewart's reach was broad and effective; media analysts reported of marthatalks.com that "on the front page, Stewart thanks her audience for its support, mentioning the more than 9 million hits and nearly 50,000 visitors that the site logged in just a few days."[14] Additionally, Stewart's "Open Letter" was supported by a statement that her attorneys, Robert G. Morvillo and John J. Tigue Jr., posted on her website inviting the media to investigate why it took the government six months to file charges against her: "Is it because she is a woman who has successfully competed in a man's business world by virtue of her talent, hard work, and demanding standards?"[15] With this move, Stewart and her legal advisers successfully portrayed her as a David struggling to survive an attack from both the media and the government. The more she got her version of the story out, the more loyal her supporters became.

Two months after Stewart's sentencing, on September 15, 2004, she announced that she would serve her time as soon as possible due to her "intense desire and need to put this nightmare behind."[16] With the announcement, MSLO shares went up 12 percent, indicating investors' approval of her decision. During her incarceration, Stewart continued to communicate with her followers through her new website. Following the formula she had used in her "Letters" and "Remembering" columns, her messages were straightforward and honest, and she combined positive and negative feelings about her experience but usually ended with optimism and strength. Take, for example, her Thanksgiving entry:

*Dear Friends,*

*As the Thanksgiving holiday approaches, I want to extend my deepest thanks and appreciation for the steadfast support I continue to receive from so many of you. I am told this web page has logged nearly 8 million hits since I began serving my sentence last month, and that supporters have sent more than 15,000 emails. I have also received thousands of letters. I cherish them all. . . . I want you to know that I am well. As you would expect, the loss of freedom and the lack of privacy are extremely difficult. But I am safe, fit and healthy, and I am pleased to report that, contrary to rumors you might have heard, my daily interactions with the staff and fellow inmates here at Alderson are marked by fair treatment and mutual respect. . . . I am in good spirits and making the best of this difficult situation. Visits from my friends, family and colleagues— together with your goodwill and best wishes—will get me through this chapter in my life. For this friendship and support, I am very grateful this Thanksgiving.[17]*

Stewart completed her jail term on March 4, 2005. Immediately after her release, she went back to her position as creative director of her company. MSLO celebrated her return by featuring her photo on the next cover of the *Martha Stewart Living* with the words

"Welcome Back Martha." Although she never wrote another "Letter" or "Remembering" column, she created a different column, "From My Home to Yours," which she still writes regularly.

In September 2005, Stewart began hosting a new daytime talk show, *Martha*, nominated for several Emmy awards (and canceled in 2012), which blended celebrity guests with segments on cooking, gardening, and interior design. In 2006, she continued to expand the reach of MSLO into new territory, producing a new magazine (now an online publication), *Blueprint: Design Your Life*, targeted at women in their thirties who want to live in style while on a budget. Also in 2006, one of the company's undertakings in the realm of brand expansion was the building of "Martha-branded" communities, in association with the home-building company KB Homes. The project started in Raleigh, North Carolina, but "Martha Homes" can now be found in nine states across the United States. With plans to build Martha-inspired houses and assorted products in new communities around the country, this venture's corner stone is Stewart's status and lifestyle as a domestic guru, as the houses are inspired by Stewart's own three homes in New York, Maine, and Connecticut. By May 2006, less than a year after her release from prison, the media nicknamed Martha Stewart "the comeback queen."[18]

This brief account of Stewart's founding and development of her influential magazine and enduring business enterprise reveals a very important aspect of her charismatic leadership. Not only was it important to be driven and have a clear and particular business mission, but also by reaching out to her followers and sharing both her vision for her company and her feelings about it, once she found herself in trouble, Stewart was able to bank on her relationship with her followers and turn her circumstances around. In the case of Martha Stewart, there was never a clear divide between her public and personal life, and this is a key element of her leadership.

This case reveals another strategy employed by Stewart: the adamant denial of her guilt. She never took responsibility for her actions on that Texan afternoon when she made the infamous phone call to her trading assistant or for her subsequent lying to investigators about a preexisting order to sell ImClone stock when the price reached $60 per share. On the contrary, she had maintained her innocence. When she learned that she was given a very short prison term, she decided, guilty or not, to move on quickly and take the fall instead of dragging the issue through an appeal. She separated herself from the company as quickly as possible; and even in prison, she found a way (different from before) to stay in touch with loyal fans and continued to deny her responsibility despite conviction and evidence. She offered an account of her situation that placed the blame elsewhere (she was prosecuted for being a woman in a man's world) and presented herself as a victim who was marching on despite the circumstances.

Both Martha Stewart and her business have endured change over time; some of it was planned and successful, whereas some of it was not, but in both cases, Stewart maintained a sense of positive momentum, of moving forward, and of persisting under difficulty, often through the use of positive communication and affirmative language. And this has not changed. For instance, in a *New York Times* article on MSLO's 2013 losses of $3 million across the company (including *Martha Stewart Living*—which had a 35 percent decline in newsstand sales that year), Stewart explained her company's new strategy to boost profits while remaining the positive and charismatic leader she has been thus far: "I don't want to retire," she said to the *Times*. "We're trying to help figure it out. I don't think it's anything to run away from. I'm not banging my head against a stone wall here."[19] Regardless of one's view of Stewart, hers is a definitive story of resilience and determination in the face of career disaster.

## Notes

1 Constance L. Hays and Patrick McGeehan, "The Media Business: Advertising; Stewart Broker Handled Shares for Her Friends," *New York Times*, July 3, 2002, http://www.nytimes.com/2002/07/03/business/the-media-business-advertising-stewart-broker-handled-shares-for-her-friends.html.

2 Christopher Byron, *Martha, Inc.: The Incredible Story of Martha Stewart Living Omnimedia* (New York: Wiley, 2002), 21–47.

3 Ross Z. Chesnoff, "America's 'Goddess of Graciousness,'" *Wall Street Journal*, March 11, 1985.

4   "50 Most Powerful Women," *Fortune*, October 1988.
5   Ibid., 68.
6   Reprinted in Susan Fournier, "Martha Stewart and the ImClone Scandal," Tuck School of Business at Dartmouth, Teaching Case No. 1-0083, http:// mba.tuck.dartmouth.edu/pdf/2004-1-0083.pdf.
7   Jeffrey Toobin, "A Bad Thing," *New Yorker*, March 22, 2004.
8   Ibid.
9   Reprinted in Susan Fournier, "Martha Stewart and the ImClone Scandal," Tuck School of Business at Dartmouth, Teaching Case No. 1-0083, http://mba .tuck.dartmouth.edu/pdf/2004-1-0083.pdf, 13–15.
10  Martha Stewart, "A Letter from Martha," *Martha Stewart Living*, May 2004, 6.
11  Krysten Crawford, "Martha: I Cheated No One," CNN Money, July 20, 2004, http://money.cnn.com/2004/07/16/news/newsmakers/martha_sentencing/.
12  Nathan Irwin, "For the Stewart Brand, an Uncertain Future," *Washington Post*, March 8, 2004.
13  Martha Stewart, "An Open Letter from Martha Stewart," Martha Talks, March 2004, http://www.marthatalks.com.
14  Jeffrey A. Sonnenfeld and Andrew J. Ward, "Firing Back: How Great Leaders Rebound after Career Disasters," *Harvard Business Review*, January 1, 2007, 56.
15  Ibid.
16  Krysten Crawford, "Martha Ready to Do Time," *Fortune*, September 15, 2004.
17  Martha Stewart, "Thanksgiving," Martha Talks, November 2005, http://www .marthatalks.com.
18  Oliver Burkeman, "Comeback Queen: Martha Stewart's Next Lifestyle Launch," *Guardian*, May 1, 2006, http://www.theguardian.com/world/2006/may/02/usa .oliverburkeman.
19  Christine Haughney, "Under Pressure, Stewart Shifts Company's Focus," *New York Times*, June 16, 2013, http://www.nytimes.com/2013/06/17/business/ media/under-pressure-stewart-shifts-companys-focus.html?_r=0.

## Bibliography

Burkeman, Oliver. "Comeback Queen: Martha Stewart's Next Lifestyle Launch." *Guardian*, May 1, 2006. http://www.theguardian.com/world/2006/may/02/usa .oliverburkeman.

Byron, Christopher. *Martha, Inc.: The Incredible Story of Martha Stewart Living Omni-media*. New York: Wiley, 2002.

Chesnoff, Ross Z. "America's 'Goddess of Graciousness.'" *Wall Street Journal*, March 11, 1985.

Crawford, Krysten. "Martha: I Cheated No One." CNN Money, July 20, 2004. http://money.cnn.com/2004/07/16/news/newsmakers/martha_sentencing/.

———. "Martha Ready to Do Time." *Fortune*, September 15, 2004.

"50 Most Powerful Women." *Fortune*, October 1988.

Fournier, Susan. "Martha Stewart and the ImClone Scandal." Tuck School of Business at Dartmouth, Teaching Case No. 1-0083. http://mba.tuck.dartmouth.edu/pdf/2004-1-0083.pdf.

Haughney, Christine. "Under Pressure, Stewart Shifts Company's Focus." *New York Times*, June 16 2013. http://www.nytimes.com/2013/06/17/business/media/under-pressure-stewart-shifts-companys-focus.html?_r=0.

Hays, Constance L., and Patrick McGeehan. "The Media Business: Advertising; Stewart Broker Handled Shares for Her Friends." *New York Times*, July 3, 2002. http://www.nytimes.com/2002/07/03/business/the-media-business-advertising-stewart-broker-handled-shares-for-her-friends.html.

Irwin, Nathan. "For the Stewart Brand, an Uncertain Future." *Washington Post*, March 8, 2004.

Sonnenfeld, Jeffrey A., and Andrew J. Ward. "Firing Back: How Great Leaders Rebound after Career Disasters." *Harvard Business Review*, January 1, 2007, 56.

Stewart, Martha. "A Letter from Martha." *Martha Stewart Living*, May 2004, 6.

———. "An Open Letter from Martha Stewart." Martha Talks, March 2004. http://www.marthatalks.com.

———. "Thanksgiving." Martha Talks, November 2005. http://www.marthatalks.com.

Toobin, Jeffrey. "A Bad Thing." *New Yorker*, March 22, 2004.

# Barbara Krumsiek

## Putting Social Responsibility on the Investment Agenda

### Crystal Bedley and Lisa Hetfield

## Background

In May 2014, when Barbara Krumsiek announced her retirement, as president and chief executive officer of Calvert Investments Inc.—a socially responsible investing mutual fund firm—her leadership accomplishments were well known and widely celebrated in the financial services arena. As the visionary behind the Calvert Women's Principles and the architect of their global dissemination, Krumsiek had demonstrated how her mathematics background, her analytical and problem-solving skills, and her keen desire to help people led to her pivotal role in transforming the ways companies think about diversity and business success. Along with the announcement of her stepping down from the CEO position, while continuing as Calvert board chair, came her appointment as the first chairwoman of a newly created Calvert Institute. The institute is designed to "promote the growth of sustainable and responsible investing (SRI) through research, advocacy and fostering innovation in the field of sustainable investing."[1] The mathematics major and would-be PhD turned corporate executive would continue her work to transform the business world to create environments that work for all people and promote better communities.

Barbara Krumsiek's belief in herself and in women's abilities dates back to her childhood. Growing up in Queens, New York, Krumsiek first developed her leadership skills and early interest in business as a Girl Scout. In her troop, she thrived when taking the lead, whether by starting a campfire or vying to win a top-seller award for the famous Girl Scout cookies. She liked math and recalls, "I remember as a young teenager, my parents lived in a neighborhood in Queens. At Christmas, we would always go next door to the couple who were Russian immigrants to say 'Merry Christmas.' I remember the husband asking each of us what we wanted to do—what our favorite subjects were and what we were studying. I said I loved math. He said, 'Oh, girls, women don't do math.' I remember being—whatever I was—thirteen or something, thinking very calmly to myself, 'He doesn't know what he's talking about.'"[2]

Krumsiek honed her leadership skills and developed her confidence at Hunter College High School, a selective public school for intellectually talented students. At the time, Hunter High was an all-girls school. Krumsiek graduated with a bachelor's degree in mathematics, Phi Beta Kappa with honors, from Douglass College in 1974. Douglass was the women's college at Rutgers University. Having finished her undergraduate work in three and a half years, Krumsiek was a first-generation college graduate who was paying her own way with some help from her parents. As she tells it, "So here I was in January, and knowing I wanted to go to graduate school and having applied for PhD programs in mathematics, but knowing I had six months before I would have to begin and a few months before I'd hear from schools. I wanted to work, and I didn't have much money; so I decided I would like to find a job that used my math background, rather than a waitressing job."[3]

Krumsiek landed a full-time job with Equitable Capital Management Corporation (subsequently acquired by Alliance Capital Management LP, now AllianceBernstein LP) and was assigned to work for the chief investment officer. At the time, she knew nothing about investments. She had only maintained a passbook savings account, and her parents were still paying bills with money orders. But Krumsiek was intrigued by the position because she could use her math skills to help solve business problems and to help people, ordinary people, to invest. When Krumsiek got her acceptance into a PhD program in applied math at John's Hopkins, where she was given a full scholarship, she decided to delay it a year to continue her work at Alliance Capital. But at the end of that year, she realized that she did not want to leave, because she loved what she was doing. She spent the next twenty-three years at Alliance Capital working her way up to managing director, while earning a master's degree in mathematics from New York University at night and working full-time during the day. She is the first person to tell you that she could never have predicted her career path, and yet she has become one of the most prominent leaders in mutual funds and investment management.

For most of the 1980s, Barbara Krumsiek thrived in what she now calls the "meritocracy phase" of her career. It was a time when goals and objectives were clear and assessments were based on meeting those measureable and time-limited goals. She noticed that she was one of a few women to hold a senior position in investment management. Krumsiek had heard about the "leaky pipeline" that prevented many women from ascending the professional ranks, but she personally had advanced through the ranks through a combination of talent and hard work. The pipeline serves as a metaphor for women who leave science, engineering, mathematics, and technology (STEM) jobs at all career stages. During that period, it was understood that addressing women's underrepresentation in business took the form of individual women changing their behavior to improve their chances for being hired and promoted. There was not the sense that, as a group, women were disadvantaged in the workplace. The popular opinion of the time, which Krumsiek exemplified, was that one's qualifications determined his or her ability to ascend the corporate ladder. Krumsiek had quickly adapted to the corporate environment at Alliance Capital, where she was an operations research analyst before being promoted to management seven years later. Her worldview, that career advancement is a result of one's commitment and achievements, remained unchallenged until the birth of her first child, when she personally experienced how gender discrimination shapes professional opportunities.

## A Time of Change for Women in Careers

The 1980s were a pivotal time for women in the workplace. According to the Pew Research Center, 50 percent of women ages of sixteen and older were in the labor force, and the numbers were increasing. The doors to elite universities and professional schools were opening up to women. Yet women did not advance in corporations at the same rate as their male counterparts. While the first interventions to address gender inequity in the workplace focused on strategies for individual women, there was a growing awareness that women's underrepresentation in leadership stemmed from systemic problems. The expression "the glass ceiling" first appeared in a *Wall Street Journal* article in 1986. This article talked about the "puzzling new phenomenon" of an invisible and impenetrable barrier between women and the executive suite. The phrase caught on, and business leaders, journalists, and scholars began to write about the glass ceiling to describe the set of unseen yet structural barriers that women confronted in business as they sought to advance to higher levels of authority.

In 1987, A. M. Morrison and others published a book titled *Breaking the Glass Ceiling: Can Women Reach the Top of America's Largest Corporations?* The book looked at the persistent failure of women to climb as far up the corporate ladder as might be expected given their qualifications and representation in the working population as a whole. The glass ceiling was revealed to be not simply a barrier to individuals but a barrier applied to women as a group, keeping them from advancing simply because they are women.[4]

The Federal Glass Ceiling Commission was created as part of Title II of the Civil Rights Act of 1991 and conducted its work from 1991 to 1996. In 1995, the commission issued its fact-finding report *Good for Business: Making Full Use of the Nation's Human Capital*. The report identified societal, company internal, cultural, corporate climate, and pipeline barriers contributing to "the glass ceiling" phenomenon.

Women's initiatives and leadership programs in the business world began to expand after the Glass Ceiling Commission's report, which specifically identified eleven pipeline barriers to women's and minorities' advancement, including lack of management training, lack of opportunities for career development, and lack of opportunities for training tailored to the individual. The report called for leadership and career-development programs that focused on long-term goals of advancing potential leaders. As a result of the commission's work, companies faced increased scrutiny to address these barriers.

It was not until 1988, when Krumsiek became pregnant with her first child that she had a wake-up call about the barriers to women's advancement. Excited to discuss her work plan for her return from maternity leave, Krumsiek met with her supervisor. He informed her that his wife said that women who loved their children stayed home to raise them. At first, Krumsiek assumed her supervisor was joking and laughed. But he was not laughing. At that point, she entered that phase of her career she often refers to as "The Messy Middle," that vulnerable time between the "Meritocracy" and "Leadership" phases. When she returned to work, she discovered that she had less managerial oversight since part of the department she led had been moved in her absence. Although she continued to meet and exceed her goals, she did not get the expected promotions. Always confident, Krumsiek for the first time in her career experienced self-doubt and confusion, wondering if her supervisor had lost confidence in her priorities.

Rather than Krumsiek acquiescing to the new conditions she encountered, she made two strategic changes: she hired a personal coach, and she joined several women's organizations to find support and engage with other women in similar circumstances. Through her participation in the Financial Women's Association and the Women's Economic Roundtable, Krumsiek reexamined what she had previously believed about the way corporations worked and realized that gender inequality was not about her supervisor's biased actions or the changes a woman should make to conform to corporate life. Instead, she saw that gender inequality resulted from structures and underlying assumptions that penalize women who want to have a family and a career, especially in male-dominated arenas such as banking and finance. This understanding of structural inequalities became even more apparent when Krumsiek transitioned out of her position as managing director at Alliance Capital. Little did she know at the time that this perspective, combined with a new leadership role, would serve as the foundation for a shift in consciousness among business leaders about the connection between successful business organizations and diversity practices. Krumsiek was about to show the business world that it was time to move beyond changing the woman or fixing the leaky pipeline. The time had come to focus on how championing diversity enhances a company's value and its bottom line.

## From the Messy Middle to the Leadership Phase

During the 1990s, Krumsiek had developed a reputation as being a highly effective investment manager as well as a committed advocate for women's empowerment, while being adept at leveraging business practices to help people. This reputation led to an offer to become the chief executive officer of the Calvert Group, a socially responsible investment-management firm. When Krumsiek resigned from her position at Alliance Capital in 1997 (two years after the report on the glass ceiling) to accept the CEO position at Calvert, it was clear to her that top executives had different expectations about men and women in business—including making the assumption that men are more ambitious. Surprised by her departure, the CEO of Alliance Capital remarked that he would have made her the president of something if he had known she wanted to be a president. The implication was clear: top women were not perceived to be as ambitious as their male counterparts. For Krumsiek, whose analytical talent and mathematical ability had always defined her sense of who she was, this perception was a revelation.

As president, CEO, and chair of Calvert, Krumsiek oversaw $13.5 billion in assets across forty-four portfolios, including award-winning fixed-income portfolios, and a full family of equities funds and nationally recognized sustainable and responsible mutual funds. Clients include, but are not limited to, individual and institutional investors, workplace retirement plans, endowments, and foundations. Headquartered in Bethesda, Maryland, Calvert is considered not only a leader in sustainable investments and mutual funds but, under Krumsiek's leadership, also a trailblazer in championing women's rights in business. Krumsiek's approach to leadership at Calvert is grounded in her belief that "there's no reason why a company can't both be a successful business actor and a successful actor in society."[5] Relying on the firm's strength in researching and assessing companies to understand their strengths and weaknesses, Krumsiek jumped to the forefront of developing clear measures of the links between sound business practices in diversity and bottom-line success. Her work at Calvert has ushered in a new argument for empowering women—the business case for diversity. Simply put, businesses that focus on enhancing diversity will thrive, and Calvert was becoming an exemplary case.

A frequent mention on *Working Mother* magazine's list of "100 Best Companies for Working Mothers" in the 1990s,[6] Calvert prides itself on promoting work-life balance through programs allowing a number of employees to telecommute, compress workweeks, job share, or work on flex time. Calvert's commitment to diversity is demonstrated through policies of actively hiring and promoting women and minorities, and currently the company workforce has 33 percent minority representation. In addition to its commitment to diversity, Calvert is working to reduce its carbon footprint, and it hosts an extensive community-outreach program, Calvert Community Partners. Calvert Community Partners encourages employees to engage in a wide range of community-service activities such as working in soup kitchens, volunteering in schools, and cleaning up the environment. Through the program, employees are given one paid volunteer day each month so that they can contribute to their communities in meaningful ways.

The values of maintaining and enhancing diversity, community outreach, and work-life balance exemplified by Calvert extend to its investment practices, which are neatly summed up in the slogan "Investing with Calvert Means Investing in Women." At Calvert, including women within the investment framework is an integral part of the company's success. This is accomplished through helping financial advisers better meet the needs of their female clients, including gender diversity in corporate valuation, leveraging the shareholder voice to push companies to think differently about women, and providing global leadership on investment topics that matter to women.[7] Calvert analyzes and reports on S&P 100 companies across ten key diversity indicators including equal employment opportunity policies, scope of diversity initiatives, family-friendly benefits, the representation of women and minorities on a company's board of directors, and the representation of women and minorities within a company's five highest-paid positions.

Despite recent progress, the playing field for men and women in business is still unequal in many areas in the United States and abroad. One area of inequality is pay. In the United States, women who work full-time have average earnings that are seventy-seven cents to every dollar earned by men.[8] A 2012 report by the American Association of University Women found that even when men and women held jobs in the same occupation, had the same college majors, and worked the same number of hours, the wage gap shrunk but did not disappear.[9] The differences in income between men and women can be explained in part by another trend, namely, the representation of men and women in leadership and management positions. In 2014, women held only 4.8 percent of S&P 500 CEO positions.[10] International companies including Nintendo, Sketchers, Samsung, and Toyota have no women on their boards of directors, according to findings of the risk-assessment firm GMI Ratings. In fact, more than 40 percent of the world's four thousand largest companies do not have a female member on their boards. Of these four thousand companies, only eighty, or 2 percent, have boards that are chaired by women.[11]

Research on diversity and corporate success shows that there is a business case to be made for promoting gender equity. A Thomson Reuters study reveals that companies with no women on their boards underperform when compared to companies with women on their boards.[12] The Australian government's Workplace Gender Equality Agency argues that businesses that promote gender equality tend to attract the best employees, have reduced staff turnovers, have better financial outcomes, have greater access to targeted markets, and have enhanced reputations.[13] One study of 353 companies showed that companies with a greater representation of women on the top management team experienced a 35 percent higher return on equity and 34 percent higher total return to shareholders.[14] Corporate success as a result of greater gender equity is also evidenced through better decision making regarding complex issues while also minimizing risk.[15]

Beyond gender inequality in wages and representation in leadership positions, there are also gender differences in work-life balance. On the one hand, men spend more time doing paid work than women do in developed nations, according to the Organization for Economic Cooperation and Development. On the other hand, women spend more time doing unpaid work, such as cleaning and child care. Across these developed nations—which include the United States, Japan, Canada, Germany, South Africa, France, and India, to name a few—working mothers devote about 50 percent more work time to child care than do fathers who do not work.[16] It comes as no surprise then that 70 percent of men and women in the United States report some tension between work and their home responsibilities.[17]

Clearly, challenges to gender equity in male-dominated fields persist. As Krumsiek continued to observe these challenges, she repeatedly asked herself, "Why isn't more progress being made toward gender equality? What barriers are preventing women from succeeding?" After all, by 2004, it had been almost ten years since the report from the Glass Ceiling Commission. How could progress be assessed more effectively? Did businesses have the right assessment tools? As CEO of Calvert, Krumsiek was ideally positioned to influence business practices and to promote the business case for diversity. Given that Calvert already monitored diversity in major corporations to better serve its clients, it seemed like the ideal home for the development of a code of corporate conduct focusing on gender equality and women's empowerment. How could Krumsiek translate Calvert's success and knowledge into best practices across the sector and beyond? Working with her team, which included Calvert analysts and members of Calvert's Fund Advisory Council, she realized that companies did not have the tools to assess progress. Yet an even greater challenge would be developing a strategy for global adoption of these assessments and their related benchmarks. How would Krumsiek encourage other CEOs to buy into her vision that businesses will experience greater success when they explicitly focus on enhancing and measuring diversity?

## Resolution

Barbara Krumsiek's story is a case study about how a visionary corporate leader moved beyond her organization to lead business transformation on a national and global scale. She used three key strategies to effect this change: (1) to make the business case for a set of principles based on research and data analysis; (2) to align the new principles with the United Nations Millennium Declaration to place the goals within a larger framework; and (3) to eventually turn over the Calvert tools to the United Nations for global dissemination. At her core, Krumsiek is a mathematician and a problem solver who understands the importance of research and data analysis. As a leader, she has a strong commitment to corporate responsibility and a clear vision for empowering corporations to create work environments that work for both women and men and to work with governments and nongovernment organizations to address complex social problems.

In 2004, Krumsiek spearheaded the development of the Calvert Women's Principles. The first step in developing the Women's Principles involved identifying which gender-equity issues to tackle and then to create the benchmarks that would allow companies to determine their progress on addressing these issues. The purpose of the Calvert Women's Principles Initiative is to provide companies and other organizations seeking to improve conditions and opportunities for women with a comprehensive framework for accomplishing these aspirational standards. Importantly, the Calvert Women's Principles are the first global code of conduct for corporations.

Building on the United Nation's Millennium Declaration committing countries to promote gender equity and women's empowerment as a means of combating poverty, the Calvert Women's Principles focus explicitly on how business corporations can address gender inequality and women's employment, while at the same time providing benchmarks for assessing progress on these fronts. The Calvert Women's Principles assert that "there is a strong business case for promoting women's economic development, entrepreneurship and enterprise. As a result of gender inequities, women remain—to some degree in all parts of the globe—an untapped economic resource and an under-utilized economic asset."[18] An underlying assumption of the principles is that corporations will play a critical role in addressing gender inequality primarily by providing employment opportunities, while acknowledging that corporations cannot tackle such a complex social problem on their own. It is essential that governments, foundations, corporations, and non-government organizations work together to provide educational and economic opportunities worldwide. In addition, the Calvert Women's Principles Initiative continues to support and disseminate research on the business case for gender equity.

## Partnership with the United Nations

Krumsiek's solution for broadscale adoption of the Women's Principles emerged from a partnership with the United Nations. In the planning stages of the Women's Principles, a Calvert analyst suggested sending an invitation to the US representative for the United Nations Development Fund for Women (UNIFEM), who became instrumental in shaping the principles. Impressed by Krumsiek's vision of a corporate commitment to making the workplace work for women at all levels, UNIFEM wanted to facilitate the global reach of the Women's Principles Initiative. Ultimately, Krumsiek decided that the best strategy for partnering with the United Nations was by selling the Women's Principles to the United Nations for the hefty sum of one dollar. In essence, Krumsiek knew that donating the Calvert Women's Principles to the United Nations would have a global impact that Calvert could not accomplish alone.

The Calvert Women's Principles focus on seven areas intended to promote gender equality and women's empowerment: (1) Employment and Compensation, (2) Work-Life Balance and Career Development, (3) Health, Safety, and Freedom from Violence, (4) Management and Governance, (5) Business, Supply Chain, and Marketing Practices, (6) Civic and Community Engagement, (7) Transparency and Accountability.

In order to address employment and compensation, the Women's Principles advocate for corporations to implement employment policies and practices that eliminate gender discrimination in recruitment, hiring, pay, and promotion. To accomplish this principle, companies should strive to pay a living wage to all women, recruit and retain women from traditionally underrepresented groups (such as African Americans, Hispanics, and members of the lesbian, gay, bisexual, and transgendered communities), and prohibit discrimination based on marital, parental, or reproductive status when making decisions about employment and promotion, including providing job security and opportunities for advancement that allow for interruptions in work for family-related responsibilities.

To promote policies and practices that support work-life balance and career development, companies should engage in activities such as supporting access to child care by either offering child care at the company or providing information and resources on local child-care services; providing equal access and opportunities for employees to participate in literacy, education, certified vocational, and information technology training; and providing professional development opportunities that include both formal and informal networking and mentoring programs.

Some of the indicators important to securing the health, safety, and well-being of women workers include providing and promoting company policies and programs that address domestic violence, ensuring the safety of women employees while in the workplace but also when traveling to and from work, and providing equitable health services and insurance to all employees.

To promote equal representation of women and men in the management and governance of corporations, these corporations should proactively recruit and appoint women to managerial positions and the board of directors; include gender equity as a factor in performance measures, strategic planning, and budget decisions; and ensure that women participate in decision making at all levels and in all areas of the corporation.

Improving business, supply-chain, and marketing practices can occur by maintaining ethical marketing standards, which exclude gender or sexual exploitation in marketing and advertising campaigns and promote respecting the dignity of all women. Other indicators to achieve this principle include encouraging and supporting women's entrepreneurship by entering into business relationships and working with these businesses to arrange fair credit and lending terms.

In order to enhance equitable participation in civic life and community engagement, companies should encourage philanthropic foundations associated with the company to donate funds to causes that support the Calvert Women's Principles, to encourage women and girls to enter nontraditional fields by providing accessible career information and training programs designed specifically for them, to work with the community where the company does business to eliminate gender discrimination while also supporting women's organizations and community groups that are working to advance women, and to respect female employees' rights to participate in legal, civic, and political affairs, such as providing time off to vote.

Finally, after establishing policies and practices that support gender equity and women's empowerment, companies must make these policies and practices transparent and hold themselves accountable to the principles. This can be accomplished by making their policies and practices public and then monitoring and enforcing these policies. Strategies to promote transparency and accountability include for CEOs to publicize their commitment to the principles and prominently display them in the workplace, making sure employees have access to them. Companies should also establish benchmarks to measure progress and report on the results, as well as conduct periodic self-evaluations through data collection and analysis to determine how much progress has been made toward achieving the principles.

### From Coffee to Computers

Starbucks and Dell became the first global corporations to speak on behalf of the Calvert Women's Principles at their launch in 2004. In 2008, Calvert partnered with the city of San Francisco's Department on the Status of Women and Verité (a consulting and research organization focused on fair labor) to launch the Gender Equity Principles (GEP), which are based on the Calvert Women's Principles. GEP's website provides a one-stop shop for companies looking to implement and promote the principles by providing assessment tools and resources. In 2013, GEP launched the Gender Equality Challenge, a program that aligns with the seven core principles and through which companies can share their models for enhancing gender equality. Company programs ranging from Twitter's and eBay's career development for women to Levi Strauss & Co.'s health program to AT&T's community-engagement program are featured and recognized by the city and county of San Francisco as upholding the core principles.

In 2010, the United Nations adapted the Calvert Women's Principles to create the Women's Empowerment Principles, which are designed to empower women in the workplace, marketplace, and community, especially in emerging economies. A major goal of the Women's Empowerment Principles is to identify best practices for promoting gender equality and women's empowerment. A CEO Statement of Support indicating that companies would uphold the Women's Empowerment Principles launched the same year. To date, over 770 companies have made the commitment to lead on gender equality and women's empowerment and to encourage fellow business leaders to do the same. These companies span multiple industries and include global corporations such as Coca-Cola and Kellogg. The success of the Women's Empowerment Principles shows how Krumsiek's visionary leadership has quickly effected change on a global scale, demonstrating that corporations see gender equality as making good business sense.

Barbara Krumsiek may not have been able to predict which obstacles she would encounter on her career path. Yet, by overcoming these obstacles herself and by applying her analytic skills to the burning questions of "Why aren't working women there yet?" and "How do you take a culture and environment and make it work for all genders?" she developed powerful tools for increasing women's participation and representation in business. Her efforts to reform corporate policies and cultures, beginning with Calvert, have flourished to make a global impact that is gaining momentum. Her work shows that investing in women means investing in business, and both can succeed when gender equity becomes rooted in corporate conduct.

# Notes

1 "Barbara Krumsiek to Step Down as President and CEO of Calvert Investments: Remains Chair of the Investment Firm," *Businesswire*, May 2014, http://www.businesswire.com/news/home/20140530005341/en/Barbara-Krumsiek -step-President-CEO-Calvert-Investments#.VfGaXfnBzGc.

2 Barbara Krumsiek, in discussion with Lisa Hetfield and Dana M. Britton, April 21, 2014.

3 Ibid.

4 "The Glass Ceiling," *Economist*, May 5, 2009, http://www.economist.com/node/13604240.

5 Barbara Krumsiek, in discussion with Lisa Hetfield and Dana M. Britton, April 21, 2014.

6 Calvert Investments, "Our Culture & People," n.d., http://www.calvert.com/choose-people.html (accessed September 12, 2014).

7 Calvert Investments, "Investing with Calvert Means Investing in Women," n.d., http://www.calvert.com/sri-women.html (accessed September 12, 2014).

8 Institute for Women's Policy Research, "Pay Equity & Discrimination," n.d., http://www.iwpr.org/initiatives/pay-equity-and-discrimination (accessed September 12, 2014).

9 American Association of University Women, "Graduating to a Pay Gap: The Earnings of Women and Men One Year after College Graduation," October 2012, http://www.aauw.org/files/2013/03/Graduating-to-a-Pay-Gap-The -Earnings-of-Women-and-Men-One-Year-after-College-Graduation-Executive -Summary-and-Recommendations.pdf.

10 Catalyst, "Women CEOs of the S&P 500," n.d., http://www.catalyst.org/knowledge/women-ceos-sp-500 (accessed September 12, 2014).

11 Nathaniel Flannery, "23 Global Companies with No Women on Their Boards," *Atlantic*, March 18, 2011.

12 Thomson Reuters, "Average Stock Price of Gender Diverse Corporate Boards Outperform Those with No Women," press release, July 10, 2013, http://thomsonreuters.com/press-releases/072013/Average-Stock-Price-of-Gender -Diverse-Corporate-Boards-Outperform-Those-with-No-Women.

13 Australian Government Workplace Gender Equality Agency, "The Business Case for Gender Equality," March 2013, https://www.wgea.gov.au/sites/default/files/business_case_web.pdf.

14 Calvert Investments, "The Calvert Women's Principles Initiative," 2014, http://www.calvert.com/NRC/Literature/Documents/sr_women_CWP_Initiative.pdf.

15 Davia Temin, "Making the Business Case for Gender Equality," *Forbes*, November 9, 2011, http://www.forbes.com/2010/11/09/gender-gap-business-case -diversity-forbes-woman-leadership-harvard-women-public-policy.html.

16 Catherine Rampell, "In Most Rich Countries, Women Work More than Men," *Economix* (blog), *New York Times*, December 19, 2012, http://economix.blogs .nytimes.com/2012/12/19/in-most-rich-countries-women-work-more-than -men/?_php=true&_type=blogs&_r=0.

17  Erin Kelly, Phyllis Moen, and Eric Tranby, "Changing Workplaces to Reduce
    Work-Family Conflict: Schedule Control in a White-Collar Organization,"
    *American Sociological Review* 76, no. 2 (2011): 265–290.
18  Calvert Investments, "The Calvert Women's Principles: A Global Code of Cor-
    porate Conduct to Empower, Advance and Invest in Women," n.d., http://www
    .calvert.com/NRC/literature/documents/4978.pdf (accessed September 12, 2014).

## Bibliography

American Association of University Women. "Graduating to a Pay Gap: The Earn-
    ings of Women and Men One Year after College Graduation." October 2012.
    http://www.aauw.org/files/2013/03/Graduating-to-a-Pay-Gap-The-Earnings
    -of-Women-and-Men-One-Year-after-College-Graduation-Executive-Summary
    -and-Recommendations.pdf.
Australian Government Workplace Gender Equality Agency. "The Business Case
    for Gender Equality." March 2013. https://www.wgea.gov.au/sites/default/files/
    business_case_web.pdf.
"Barbara Krumsiek to Step Down as President and CEO of Calvert Investments:
    Remains Chair of the Investment Firm." *Businesswire*, May 2014. http://www
    .businesswire.com/news/home/20140530005341/en/Barbara-Krumsiek-step
    -President-CEO-Calvert-Investments#.VfGaXfnBzGc.
Calvert Investments. "The Calvert Women's Principles: A Global Code of Corporate
    Conduct to Empower, Advance and Invest in Women." n.d. https://www.calvert
    .com/NRC/literature/documents/4978.pdf (accessed September 12, 2014).
———. "The Calvert Women's Principles Initiative." 2014. http://www.calvert.com/
    NRC/Literature/Documents/sr_women_CWP_Initiative.pdf.
———. "Investing with Calvert Means Investing in Women." n.d. http://www
    .calvert.com/sri-women.html (accessed September 12, 2014).
———. "Our Culture & People." n.d. http://www.calvert.com/choose-people.html
    (accessed September 12, 2014).
Catalyst. "Women CEOs of the S&P 500." n.d. http://www.catalyst.org/knowledge/
    women-ceos-sp-500 (accessed September 12, 2014).
Federal Glass Ceiling Commission. *Good for Business: Making Full Use of the Nation's
    Human Capital: The Environmental Scan: A Fact-Finding Report of the Federal Glass
    Ceiling Commission.* Washington, DC: U.S. Department of Labor, 1995.
Flannery, Nathaniel. "23 Global Companies with No Women on Their Boards."
    *Atlantic*, March 18, 2011. http://www.theatlantic.com/business/archive/2011/
    03/23-global-companies-with-no-women-on-their-boards/72664/.
"Glass Ceiling, The." *Economist*, May 5, 2009. http://www.economist.com/node/
    13604240.
Institute for Women's Policy Research. "Pay Equity & Discrimination." n.d. http://
    www.iwpr.org/initiatives/pay-equity-and-discrimination (accessed Septem-
    ber 12, 2014).
Kelly, Erin, Phyllis Moen, and Eric Tranby. "Changing Workplaces to Reduce Work-
    Family Conflict: Schedule Control in a White-Collar Organization." *American
    Sociological Review* 76, no. 2 (2011): 265–290.

Morrison, A. M., R. White, and E. Van Velsor. *Breaking the Glass Ceiling: Can Women Reach the Top of America's Largest Corporations?* New York: Perseus, 1987.

Rampell, Catherine. "In Most Rich Countries, Women Work More than Men." *Economix* (blog), *New York Times*, December 19, 2012. http://economix.blogs .nytimes.com/2012/12/19/in-most-rich-countries-women-work-more-than -men/?_php=true&_type=blogs&_r=0.

Temin, Davia. "Making the Business Case for Gender Equality." *Forbes*, November 9, 2011. http://www.forbes.com/2010/11/09/gender-gap-business-case-diversity -forbes-woman-leadership-harvard-women-public-policy.html.

Thomson Reuters. "Average Stock Price of Gender Diverse Corporate Boards Outperform Those with No Women." Press release, July 10, 2013. http:// thomsonreuters.com/press-releases/072013/Average-Stock-Price-of-Gender -Diverse-Corporate-Boards-Outperform-Those-with-No-Women.

# Roseline Marston

## Navigating Transition in an Employee-Owned Firm at A. D. Marble & Company

### Carolina Alonso Bejarano and Dana M. Britton

**Background**

After working as a marine biologist, Roseline Marston changed careers and made her way to the top at A. D. Marble & Company, a small environmental consulting and engineering firm. Marston took over as CEO of the company in 2005, and she successfully led A. D. Marble through a transition from a solely owned firm to an employee stock ownership plan (ESOP). As soon as she saw this process through, the market collapsed, and Marston watched other engineering companies file for bankruptcy one after the other. How did her leadership style facilitate the transition of her company from a conventional corporate structure into the more employee-centered model of an ESOP? As the CEO of an employee-owned company, how could Marston navigate A. D. Marble through one of the biggest financial crises in history?

### "I Wanted to Study Marine Biology"

The oldest of seven children, Roseline Marston became a leader early in life. She is the daughter of a successful Puerto Rican doctor, who spent long hours at the hospital while she was growing up. She spent much of her childhood and teenage years in San Juan helping her stay-at-home mother raise her six brothers and sisters. This is where she began to learn to lead:

I helped raise my brothers and sisters from day one. And if you look at my upbringing, in terms of where the leadership part came up, I can honestly tell you that I don't know if it was something I was born with or if it was the situation that I was put into that made me develop an "I will never follow" attitude. During the time that my mom was either always pregnant and having a kid or taking care of a baby, I helped with [all my brothers and sisters]. I was about eleven years old when my little brother was born, the seventh, and I came up with this system where the three oldest will take care of the three youngest, so my mom will have time to take care of the baby. So it was sort of a system that I designed to help my mom and to help things run smoother in the house.[1]

This attitude—as well as her skills at designing and managing people and meeting goals—served her well in her later career.

Marston learned from her father the importance of having a career and of having passion for what you do. Her mother had been a secretary when she met Roseline's father and started having children right away. When Roseline was about seven, she recalls that her mother "wanted to do something more" and so went back to school. This was not easy given her growing family:

My mom sometimes had problems getting the babysitter to come and take care of us, so we would actually go to classes with her and sit in the back with coloring books. My mom would try to hide us all, and we would sit quietly because we couldn't speak while the professor was speaking. I remember that I started listening to what the teacher was saying, so I learned about physics and chemistry very early on. I was mesmerized about how these numbers appeared on the board, and I loved writing on the blackboard anyway. It was the old blackboard with the chalk and eraser, and for me that was pretty exciting.

Marston's mother ultimately got a master's degree in clinical psychology, but she was never allowed to work outside the home and never had her own practice. The message her mother sent her was one of determination but also one of living a different life; she told her daughter to earn her own money and never depend on anyone for anything. These were lessons Marston took very much to heart.

Apart from the young Marston's family role and her parents' unconditional support, sports also gave her the strength and motivation to always seek to excel. Because she lived on an island, her parents encouraged her to swim from the age of three. She loved swimming but quickly found that she was not fast enough to do it at a competitive level. Seeing her determination, her mother and her coach encouraged her to take up synchronized swimming. She joined the local team at nine, made the national team at thirteen, and kept competing for the Puerto Rican national team through her sophomore year at Cornell University in 1989.

Marston followed her dream to become a marine biologist and pursued a degree in biology. She remembers this experience as being very formative, and not only in an academic sense. A young woman in a new country, Marston soon realized that language and cultural differences were going to be major difficulties that she would have to overcome. She remembers,

> My first lecture was a biology lecture. First of all, I wasn't expecting three hundred students to be sitting there. I went to Catholic school. Classes were no more than twenty kids, if that. I brought my book, thinking, "I'm going be able to follow with the book." And the professor just started talking, and I went into shock for forty-five minutes. Next thing I know, I called my parents and said, "This was a huge mistake. I can't do this. I did not understand a word he was saying. How am I going do this?" And my mom said, "You can do this," and she encouraged me to keep going. I kept calling and telling her I couldn't and couldn't, and then at one point, she said, "Okay, Roseline, you know what? I'll send you a ticket. You can come back here, and you can go to the University of Puerto Rico." And that was a little bit of a wake-up call. I said to myself, "Wait a minute. I really don't want to do that. I really, really need to do this."

During her first semester, her grades were so poor that she was placed on academic probation. Marston had two choices: "I could either just give up and go to University of Puerto Rico, or I could raise my GPA. I don't even remember how low it was, but it was incredibly low, and I had to bring it up to a 3.2."

Not only did she have to learn English—and do it fast—but she also had to find the nerve to speak English despite the racist comments of her colleagues, who mocked her for being an immigrant ("Did you come in on a boat?") and made fun of her for mixing up words. She describes one incident in detail:

> I remember one time I was sitting at the common study room at Cornell. It was very quiet, and I was doing my calculus homework with my pencil and my eraser. Now, in Spanish, "eraser" is *goma*, but it's the same translation as "rubber." So you can call it "rubber" or "eraser." For us, it's the same thing. When I was doing my homework, I happened to lose my eraser. I'm looking around, and I can't find it and just got the courage to ask, "Has anybody seen my rubber?" That was when I took a few steps back. Everybody was laughing so hard—I mean, there were people literally rolling on the floor. They thought it was hilarious.

Despite all of these challenges, Marston decided to stick it out. Marston stayed at Cornell and obtained her bachelor's degree in 1991. By her senior year, she was so comfortable with her English that she was asked to serve as a teaching assistant for a class on public speaking.

After Marston finished her bachelor's degree, she went to Nova Southeastern University in Florida and continued to pursue her dream of becoming a marine biologist. She graduated with a master's degree in oceanography and coastal zone management and then stayed in Florida working as a coastal biologist for five years. She loved the work of doing biological assessments, which meant she was "basically going into work in a wet suit and getting in a boat to go in the water."

## Straight to the Top

By 1997, Marston found herself living a life that was not cut out for her as a stay-at-home mom in the suburbs of Philadelphia. She and her then husband had left Florida so he could go to law school, and the initial plan was for her to stay at home to care for their young daughter, Stephanie, and their infant son, Andrew. Marston tried this arrangement for a year but soon realized, "I could not clean anymore! It was just driving me crazy." She needed to find a job, and she worried about her education becoming obsolete.

Because Marston thought the family would be moving back to Florida once her husband finished school, she did not spend much energy looking for a perfect job; after all, she was only going to work there for a couple of years. She found an opening at A. D. Marble & Company, an environmental consulting and engineering company that supports engineering projects to ensure that their needs are weighed appropriately against environmental constraints.[2] At the time, the firm had about fifteen employees. The job for which Marston applied was an entry-level environmental scientist position that did not pay much and for which she was overqualified:

> When they offered me the job at A. D. Marble, they said, "You know, this is an entry-level position. We can only pay $15.60 an hour, and we can't count your master's, and we can't count your years of experience because you're overqualified for the job." So I decided to take it anyway, because the headquarters were located in Rosemont, and my kids' day care was literally down the street. I didn't have any help. I had to figure everything out on my own. So I figured if I ever have to go pick up the kids [they're right down the street]. I had it all figured it out. So I accepted the job as an entry-level scientist, and after that, I started getting interested in how are things managed, as opposed to how are things done.

Marston moved up the ladder quickly at her new job and soon became a project manager, which allowed her to learn about work allocation and about the financials of the company. In 2002, after only four years of working with A. D. Marble, Marston became vice president, and in 2004, she became executive vice president.

As Marston moved up in the company, she worked more closely with its owner and founder, Anne Marble. Marble was a pioneer in her field. After working as a project manager in a company that did environmental work, she founded her own engineering company in 1985.[3] Very few women worked in the engineering world when Marble entered the scene. By the time Marston took over, things had changed somewhat, but she faced a boys' world nonetheless. Marble was (and remains) an important mentor for Marston, advising her that as a woman in a man's field, she had to "be 110 percent prepared, so they can see 80 percent. That's how it works."

Marble was also grooming Marston for leadership by moving her up in the company to progressively more responsible positions. During that time, Marston herself transitioned from being a manager to being a leader. She describes the difference:

> A manager is an outliner. A manager is someone who looks at things in black-and-white where something has to get done. You have to be organized, and you have to be structured. You have to follow your arrows and come up with your own outline to get there. A leader needs an empty piece of paper and needs to start dumping ideas in there. You need to have a lot of flexibility with yourself. You need to know that you are going to make mistakes, and you need to take risks. It's not as clear-cut as if you follow the management process. Leadership is not like that at all. To be a leader, you have to be smart and you have to be risky, but you have to have heart. There are certain decisions that you're going to make that are not going to be comfortable and you can't explain.

As a leader, Marston learned to trust her instincts and develop confidence in her own ability to make decisions. In only four years, these abilities brought her from entry-level scientist to executive vice president of the company.

In 2005, Anne Marble was ready to retire. She asked Marston to take over the leadership of A. D. Marble and become its president and CEO. Marble initially explored various options for selling the company:

> She looked into the possibility of selling the company to an engineering company that didn't have our services. We're strictly environmental, and the engineering work that we do is related to

the environmental work. We don't build bridges or highways. And it would've been a great deal—she would've gotten paid a lot of money for the expertise that we offered. But she realized that she was going to lose what she created. She also considered selling the company to a few employees. And the group started out being five of us, and it ended up being twelve—she kept inviting people to join. That wasn't going to work. So she eliminated that idea and shortly thereafter happened to go to a conference on employee ownership. All of a sudden, she got the answer. [She said], "I am going to sell it to the employees, but it's going to be through an ESOP."

Neither Marble nor Marston had any idea of how an ESOP should work, and they spent the next two years figuring out the transition of ownership and the concurrent transition of leadership. Ultimately they designed a three-year plan in which the business would transition from a woman-owned small business to a fully executed ESOP.

Employee stock ownership plans allow employees to participate in the ownership of companies by receiving shares of stock. Establishing an ESOP essentially gave Marble a way to sell the company to its employees. She established a trust, had an external evaluation done of the shares, and then had a market value placed on the company; and over time, Marble sold her shares to that trust. The company initially took out a loan to buy shares. In an ESOP, the company itself finances the shares, so individual workers do not have to put up any personal money or collateral. As the loan was repaid, the shares were distributed to all employees at the company on the basis of their relative compensation. ESOPs are treated by law as retirement plans, and workers receive the fair market value of their shares when they leave the company. ESOPs were rare in the United States until about 1974, but by 2014, seven thousand companies had ESOPs covering 13.5 million employees. ESOPs have certain tax benefits that make them a desirable way to transfer ownership of private companies, but they also have benefits for employees. Studies have shown that employees of ESOPs make higher wages, on average, and have more retirement income. ESOP companies are also, on average, more productive. But with diversified ownership of the company also comes accountability; ESOP participants (employees) are required by law to be allowed to vote their shares on major issues, such as closing or selling the company. And because the valuation of the company affects the value of their shares, the company must be much more transparent about its finances, and employees are more acutely aware of their company's financial situation than those in companies without employee ownership.[4] At A. D. Marble, both of these facts shaped the management environment for newly appointed CEO Roseline Marston.

## Leading an ESOP

Roseline Marston became president of A. D. Marble at the age of thirty-five. Apart from the difficulty of being a single mother with a full-time job (she divorced during the time she was taking over A. D. Marble) and a woman in a man's world, Marston, along with her executive team of two vice presidents and a chief financial officer, had the challenge of transitioning the company from a small, solely owned business to an ESOP that was 100 percent owned by the workers and managers. In the process, the firm would lose its status as a woman-owned, "disadvantaged" small business (which allowed it to compete more competitively for some government-funded contracts) to an employee-owned company without that status.[5] Marston had to accomplish all of this while also maintaining the culture of environmental and social responsibility that had always characterized A. D. Marble.

In addition to having shares in the company, employees at A. D. Marble also participate in a plan that awards bonuses based on company performance, and the company covers 100 percent of the health-insurance premiums for employees and their families. Within the constraints of this generous model, Marston had the challenge of remaining competitive against other businesses that did not have to pay for these benefits. To achieve this, she aimed to translate the intangible asset of employee ownership into tangible assets reflected in the company's bottom line:

We share our financials with our employees every month. [We show them] how much money we give the bank to show profit, how much we're going to put towards bonuses, how much we're going to save to invest, and how much we're going to put into our ESOP. Most importantly, we also let them know how they can change the numbers. The purpose of educating them on the financials is not so they can say, "Oh, I know our revenues"; it's so they can say, "I know how I can make that number better." That's what gets people motivated.

Communication at A. D. Marble goes beyond sharing financials. The company has offices in six cities, and Marston tours the offices on a regular basis and makes it a point to sit down to talk with the employees about the strategic plan, the budget, how the company is doing, and what kind of challenges they are facing. She also has people in every one of the offices to continue that communication and make sure things are running smoothly.[6]

As the ESOP model implies, employees at A. D. Marble are owners, and their opinions matter. Not only are they constantly informed about the firm's financial situation; they are also anonymously surveyed every year. Marston takes the results of the survey very seriously:

We look at those responses as part of the strategic planning meeting. What are we doing right? What are we not doing right? What kind of resources do we need that they don't have? Can we afford them? So we really dig into questions, and we look at what they say. I take the survey, and I write down everything that they write down. And if it repeats itself, I'll put a mark by it so I can see the ones to focus on. There's always something to improve. I used to take these surveys very personally because there is one question that says, "If you were president of A. D. Marble for one day, what would you do?" And some shots are taken. In the beginning, it wasn't an easy thing to hear, what some people had to say. But now, I admit that I do need to work more on certain things. So I work on improving myself too.

Beyond these individual surveys of employees, Marston is evaluated every two years in a process that involves her board, her core team, her direct reports, and randomly chosen employees from throughout the company.

Employees enjoy other benefits as well, including working in an environment in which work-life balance is a priority. Dealing with the challenges of being a single mother has made Marston especially sensitive to the importance of working in a flexible environment. But her understanding is broader than that:

> Yes, being a single mom makes me more sensitive to mothers, but I also have to take into account fathers and people who are taking care of their elderly parents or even people who have pets. So when you put these policies in place, you have to be very broad. We had five babies being born at the end of last year, so we had to set a room aside for lactating mothers so they could feel comfortable. But there were also fathers, and they needed to help out and they had to take time off; so we accommodate that, too.

Marston also understands that people are productive in different ways and at different times of the day, so as long as the employees are meeting their billable targets, the pipeline looks healthy, and the clients are happy, flexible schedules are the general rule at A. D. Marble:

> Our flexibility allows employees to do their work wherever they want, whenever they want. If you're more productive at ten o'clock at night after your kids go to bed, that only helps the company. So if you're not a morning person and you can't drive yourself into the office until ten, unless you have a meeting or somebody's waiting for you or you have to meet a client, our schedule is incredibly flexible. Our employees love it, and the only times we have had problems with people abusing it is when we also have problems with performance.

Generous benefits packages like these are not typical of small firms, though they are more common in ESOPs. But above and beyond the actual package of benefits, this normative emphasis on flexibility and trust in the employees is part of the culture at the company.

For the most part, Marston now leads the very employees she worked alongside before. This meant that Marston had to transition her own admittedly Type A leadership style into a mode that facilitated communication and flexibility. As the CEO of an ESOP, she has had the unique challenge of finding a balance between consensus and efficiency:

> It's not just that I can sit at my desk and say, "You're going to do what I say because I'm the boss." Yes, you can pull that card off once in a while when things get at a point where we need to make a decision, and we're going to move in this direction, but most of the time, those are not the type of decisions that you encounter. Most of the time what you encounter is how do you deal with consensus and how far to take consensus, because you can take it so far that you don't get to make a decision ever. If you don't take consensus, sometimes you can be looked as a "dictator," and [employees say], "Wait a minute, I own shares in this company, and she's making decisions without consulting." So you have the challenge of creating an environment that is really engaged and careful; but at the same time, you have to make money, so you can't just go into the office every day and be the cheerleader. It's almost like you have two choices; you have two models to follow, and you have to decide when you are going to pick the leadership model that says, "That's it, this is what we need to do," and when you are actually going to go out for consensus.

The constraints of the ESOP model have shaped Marston's leadership style in fundamental ways; by necessity, she adopted a style that is transparent, flexible, and collaborative.

From 2005 to 2008, Marston grew as a leader and completed a three-year plan to transition the company from a "small disadvantaged business" to an ESOP. Her plan was successful; the company was thriving and growing. Some of the clients who had gone elsewhere when the company lost its status as a woman-owned business were returning. The number of employees had more than doubled, to about eighty. By 2008, Marston felt satisfied and ready to throttle back. But September came, and the economy collapsed; businesses all around her were closing, and she found herself with the future of all of A. D. Marble's employee-owners in her hands. For Marston, the next six years were "definitely not boring." She faced the challenge of leading an employee-owned company while at the same time making decisions to downsize the company and reshape business strategies in a way that would allow it to survive the economic downturn.

## Resolution

In 2008, when the housing market took a dive and banks began to collapse, A. D. Marble & Company first felt the financial crisis on its private development side. The public sector, which was its biggest market, did not experience the downturn until later, so Roseline Marston had some time to maneuver before the wave hit her company. This, along with Marston's previous decision to serve on various boards (including the board of the American Council of Engineering Companies) was decisive for the future of the company: "We started anticipating what was going to happen and educating ourselves and being a part of it. I don't like being the person who gets told what is going to happen. I like being the person who gets involved in the decision making. I want to be one of the first people in the room to find out what's going on; so I sit on various boards that are part of our trade organizations, and that way, I have a say on behalf of the company." Knowing what was coming, Marston and her team revised the entire financial model of the company.

Marston and her team made several critical decisions. First, they drastically cut all of their budgets—except for marketing and business development. She describes her rationale: "The business-development budget, if anything, had to get bigger, because if we didn't market ourselves, then when things changed, we were not going to be in the forefront." Not everyone was convinced. She listened to critical advice, but in the end, she decided to trust her instincts. The fact of the matter was that the 2008 crisis was one like no other in recent history, and "unless you had a great adviser who lived through the Great Depression, you really were coming up with things on your own." Everybody had to reinvent themselves, and Marston soon realized that she was the one responsible for the company and that she had to start taking risks and making unpopular decisions. Especially as the leader of an ESOP, she was venturing into uncharted territory.

Marston knew she had to show profits every year in order to show the banks that A. D. Marble was financially solvent—crisis or no crisis. But that meant that she had to cut A. D. Marble's staff significantly: "We had to cut about 30 percent of our workforce because there was no work for them." At first, she saw this as an opportunity to clean house; but then the decisions got tougher and tougher, and it got to the point where they were picking among very talented staff. While she was making these decisions, Marston followed her motto of continuously communicating with the employees and with the management team: "It's about beginning to have those conversations at the Operations Team level early—not communicate that, 'By the way, guys, we have to cut down 30 percent by next month,' but really letting everybody know what is happening so there are no surprises. That's key."[7]

Marston was aware that by firing people, she was really shaking the foundation of trust that she and Anne Marble had built at A. D. Marble, and she did not want the general fear of being fired to drive the most talented people away: "I needed the buy-in of the people who stayed. I didn't want this fear of 'I'm going be next. I better find another job.'" Marston made use of the tradition of sharing the company's financials to maintain that trust:

> It's really giving the why and explaining to the employees that, "Look, in order to do what we need to do as a company, these are the things that need to happen. And these are the reasons why we made these decisions." So they can see every month what the numbers are like, and they all know what they mean, too, which is important so they understand what is going on.
>
> So it was a combination of that leadership where you say, "This is what we're going to do. I need you to trust me," and then there

was that other part that was showing how you can trust me and showing empathy. I cannot say that by any means it was easy. It must have been four years when I did not know on a Friday who was going to have to go, and I'll be honest with you, I was afraid for myself, too, because if my board of directors saw that I just kept cutting even though we were showing profits, and the banks were still supporting us, at what point do you say, "That's enough?"[8]

Marston's leadership style, her efforts, and her tough decisions paid off. In 2011, she asked the remaining employees to trust her and to wait for three years. And indeed in 2014 things started looking up again. Various projects started pouring in, and the company is now hiring. From a low of thirty employees, the company now employs fifty people in its six offices.

Marston successfully saw her company through the transition from a small business to an ESOP and through the economic downturn, and today she is looking at a bright future. On the other side of these crises and transitions, she has been more able to turn her attention back to the work the company does. The connection to her original love of marine biology is clear:

[Some of our work] can get monotonous if you're filling out forms [for environmental clearances] and doing the same thing over and over. Then all of a sudden something comes up, and we get to create a wetland. We get to create habitat for flora, fauna, and we also get to rehabilitate streams. I mean, there's nothing cooler than that. You have a stream that's eroding because of construction and development around the area; it's just deteriorating fast. So we come in, and we determine, Where was that stream? Where did it want to go? How is the hydrology working? What kind of habitats can we create in this stream for fish and for other animals? And then we go in and restore it. Five years later, we go and take an after picture, and it's really amazing.

Anne Marble's original vision has clearly endured under Marston's leadership, as the company continues to honor her core values. In fact, Marston recently turned down a project that, while it would have been lucrative, would have compromised the company's ethic of environmental stewardship.

Of what lies ahead for Marston, she says she is "ready for a celebration." In some ways, her experiences at A. D. Marble have brought her full circle:

> [The last few years of my life] have been about showing myself that no matter what my experiences were growing up or what happened in college, for me, it's about being real, it's about truth. It's about not just being, wandering around and letting things pass you by. It isn't always going to be success and great things. Sometimes you're going to stumble. But I have found that most of the obstacles that have been put in my way have been to get me to where I am. And I'm still going places.

## Notes

1  Roseline Marston, in conversation with Lisa Hetfield and Dana M. Britton, June 24, 2014. All quotations from Marston are from this interview unless otherwise noted. The authors thank Roseline Marston for her comments on an earlier draft of this case study.

2  A. D. Marble & Company, "Water Resources Engineering Services," n.d., http://admarble.com/services_water_resource_page.html (accessed August 15, 2014).

3  "Anne Marble Caramanico," LinkedIn, n.d., https://www.linkedin.com/pub/anne-marble-caramanico/27/7a8/603 (accessed August 10, 2014).

4  National Center for Employee Ownership, "How an Employee Stock Ownership Plan (ESOP) Works," n.d., http://www.nceo.org/articles/esop-employee-stock-ownership-plan (accessed August 15, 2014).

5  The Small Business Administration designates firms as "small disadvantaged businesses" if they are 51 percent or more owned by one or more disadvantaged persons and if they are "small" according to standards concerning employees and receipts. Disadvantaged small businesses enjoy certain advantages in bidding for government-funded contracts. For the purposes of this designation, A. D. Marble had qualified as a disadvantaged small business because it was owned by a woman and had fewer than the maximum employees and revenues for its sector. When the company became an ESOP, it lost this designation.

6  Julie Cressman, "Executive Insights Interview with Roseline Marston—Part 2," YouTube, March 9, 2012, http://youtu.be/xUl-vtFxa6A, video.

7  Julie Cressman, "Executive Insights Interview with Roseline Marston—Part 3," YouTube, March 9, 2012, http://youtu.be/8hoxPiKBS-Q, video.

8  Ibid.

## Bibliography

A. D. Marble & Company. "Water Resources Engineering Services." n.d. http://
admarble.com/services_water_resource_page.html (accessed August 15, 2014).

"Anne Marble Caramanico." LinkedIn, n.d. https://www.linkedin.com/pub/anne
-marble-caramanico/27/7a8/603 (accessed August 10, 2014).

Cressman, Julie. "Executive Insights Interview with Roseline Marston–Part 2." You-
Tube, March 9, 2012. http://youtu.be/xUl-vtFxa6A. Video.

———. "Executive Insights Interview with Roseline Marston—Part 3." YouTube
Video, March 9, 2012. http://youtu.be/8hoxPiKBS-Q. Video.

National Center for Employee Ownership. "How an Employee Stock Ownership
Plan (ESOP) Works." n.d. http://www.nceo.org/articles/esop-employee-stock
-ownership-plan (accessed August 15, 2014).

# Subha Barry

## Changing the Cultural DNA at Merrill Lynch

### Grace Howard and Dana M. Britton

### Background

Merrill Lynch, the wealth-management division of the Bank of America Group, is the largest brokerage in the world, employing more than fifteen thousand financial advisers, with around $2.2 trillion in assets.[1] Founded in 1914 by Charles Merrill, who was joined by his friend Edmund Lynch the following year,[2] the company was once best known for its part in bringing Wall Street to Main Street and for helping to finance and grow the grocery chain Safeway.[3] Over the years, the company shifted from being a US-based retail securities broker to a diversified global financial services company. Merrill Lynch quickly became one of the largest investment firms in the country and expanded worldwide. In 2008, at the height of the financial crisis, it was acquired by Bank of America, which has retained the Merrill Lynch name for its wealth-management group.

Subha Barry joined Merrill Lynch in 1989. Beginning as one of the few women (and the only woman of color) in her branch office, she built a successful career as a broker and began to rise through the ranks. Making the risky choice to abandon that success, she conceived and founded the Multicultural and Diversified Business Development Group at Merrill Lynch and later became the company's global head of diversity. How did her efforts help to transform Merrill Lynch from a company that marketed exclusively to, as she put it, "the country-club set" into one that recognized diversity as a viable business strategy? How did her own background as an immigrant inform her approach to reaching communities that had traditionally been ignored by mainstream banks and brokerages? And how did she aim to translate this emphasis on the importance of diversity into the culture of Merrill Lynch itself?

## Barry's Early Life and Career

Subha Barry grew up in India. She recalls that her father, a corporate executive, had hoped that his first child would be a boy. When he had a daughter instead, he still raised her, in many ways, as though she were a boy. Because of this, Barry was able to learn and grow skills that boys learned as a matter of course. She says, "Growing up in India as a woman conditions you to appreciate gender in a very unique way. In the community I grew up in, in the family I grew up in, girls were raised to be wives and mothers."[4] Barry was not docile, submissive, or quiet—she had many opinions and felt comfortable articulating them. She says, "The good thing about that was my father, . . . neither of my parents, but especially my father, never put me down, never ever said, 'You're a girl. Keep quiet.' That was never said and done." However, once she entered puberty, she felt family and social expectations shift; suddenly she was expected to behave like a docile and submissive woman. Luckily, she believes her early childhood experiences and education had instilled the "bad habits" that helped her to become a successful professional woman.

Barry received a bachelor's degree in accounting from Bombay University in India, then came to the United States and earned a master's degree in accounting and a master's in business and public management from Rice University.[5] She describes herself during this period as having grand aspirations. Before leaving India to come to the United States, she would often tell her friends and family that she would become the chief executive officer of a company one day.

Barry married at a young age and, after she completed her education, began working as a commodities trader at a small firm. She was one of a very small number of women working for the company. The firm lacked a maternity-leave policy, and so when Barry gave birth to her first child, she was forced to go on sick leave. She recalls,

I took sick leave to have a baby, and I went back to work in less than two weeks. My husband took paternity leave, my mother was there, we had a nanny, and I went back to work. And so I knew that there was a whole bunch of betting going on about whether I would be back and how many weeks it would take for me to get back. And what they didn't realize was that through my assistant, I had actually bet against them. I raked in the dough. I always remember saying, "You guys, you don't even know what the heck you're doing. I've taken the other side of your bet [laughing], and I'm making the money, because I know what I'm going to do!"

Barry responded to her coworkers' assumptions with humor, while at the same time taking less than two weeks of leave. She ultimately decided she wanted to make a change, however. Commodities trading came with too many high and lows, and the roller-coaster lifestyle was not amenable to raising a family. Though she had no prior experience in the field, Barry thought working in private wealth management would be the right career move. So she set out to find another job.

## Getting the Job at Merrill Lynch

Barry and her husband moved to Pennington, New Jersey, and then to Princeton after she started working for Merrill Lynch, because they thought it would be a great place to raise children. In 1989, Barry interviewed with several companies and was offered two positions. Her first choice, Merrill Lynch, was hesitant to extend an offer, however. She says,

I went back for interview after interview after interview, and I remember the manager saying to me, "Well, you know, we're just not completely comfortable." I know what they were thinking: "Here's this Indian girl. A: she's young, B: she doesn't have any natural networks in this country, and C: she's got an accent, she kind of looks different. Not really a lot of . . . data points here that would point to success in this field," based on their prior experience. But remember, their lens had been a typical white male lens. And that's who the majority of my colleagues were.

Despite the grueling interview process and the company's hesitancy, Barry wanted to work for Merrill Lynch. She believed its training program surpassed those at other companies, a fact that would give her a tremendous leg up in her career. After many interviews, Barry used her two other job offers as leverage, boldly telling the hiring manager, "Well, I've got offers from two of your competitors, and I'm going to take one of those offers. And I will make it my life's mission to take every good account away from your office." Her gutsy threat was effective. Merrill Lynch hired her as a financial adviser.

## Working at Merrill Lynch

As a woman of color, Barry was a rarity at Merrill Lynch, whose workforce was overwhelmingly white and male. Like a number of Wall Street firms, Merrill Lynch faced charges of discrimination during the 1980s and 1990s. In 1998, the company paid $600,000 to settle claims by eight women brokers that they were systematically discriminated against in account assignments, promotion, and pay. As a result of the terms of the settlement of this case, *Cremin v. Merrill Lynch, Pierce, Fenner & Smith* (957 F.Supp. 1460 [N.D. Ill. 1997]), ultimately 904 women, or about 31 percent of the 2,900 women employed in the company's domestic brokerage business from 1994 to 1998, filed gender-discrimination claims against the company. The claims were settled in arbitration.[6]

This was the context into which Barry was hired when she became the first person of color in Merrill Lynch's Princeton office—which had more than one hundred financial advisers at the time. There were only five or six other women working there, all of whom were white. Between 1989 and 1995, Barry built her "book of business" (the set of client accounts she managed). She was eventually very successful, but she faced some unique challenges. She did not have a preexisting network of contacts from which to draw—the country-club crowd or even undergraduate classmates, for example, that her white male colleagues had. As such, her book of business was different from many of her colleagues'. Barry managed accounts for corporate executives, Indian physicians and technology entrepreneurs, and lots of women. Her book contained many more professionals than was typical of her coworkers, which Barry suggests is because she had grown up with a corporate executive for a father—it fell within her comfort zone to work with professionals. Though she did not join Merrill Lynch with a "natural" network, Barry cobbled together a remarkably successful book of business.

Barry gave birth to her second child, a son, in 1995. In that same year, she was offered the position of managing the flagship office in the Merrill Lynch headquarters in Princeton, a position that required that she run the office while at the same time continuing to work with her own clients. She took the promotion, though in essence this meant she was working two full-time jobs in addition to raising her two children.

Two years after Barry was promoted, she was diagnosed with cancer—Stage IIIB Hodgkin's lymphoma, a cancer of the lymphatic system that affects the immune system. She calls this as a "defining moment." Barry's diagnosis forced her to reflect on her life. She realized that with two young children at home, two full-time jobs, and a husband with a thriving career, she had not been taking care of herself—as she put it, "I put everything else ahead of me. And—and my body essentially said, 'I can't keep up anymore.'" Though she had the support of her family and was able to afford a nanny, Barry was still left with a long to-do list—she was a self-described "workaholic." Though she had been successfully maintaining a very demanding work schedule for years, walking on the work-life balance tightrope, the cancer diagnosis tripped her up. She needed to make some changes.

After Barry was diagnosed with cancer, she immediately offered to step down as the office manager. She felt she could not do justice to both jobs in addition to undergoing medical treatment, which included chemotherapy and surgery. Barry remembers that her manager, who had been so reluctant to hire her in the first place, said, "I don't want you to make that decision right now. . . . I will take over for you in your office. I will come to your office when you're not there. I will handle all of the routine, operational things that you have to do as a manager on a day-to-day basis. You go get your treatments. You get better." She continues, "He actually forced me not to make that decision under—in a stressful time.

Completely took that off my plate, supported me through it for the six months."

Even so, Barry continued working throughout her treatment. She scheduled her chemotherapy for Thursday evenings, would recover over the weekend, and would return to work on Monday. When she was too sick to operate a car, she had her mother or husband drive her to work and pick her up. After six months, her boss asked her if she would like to continue on as manager, and she accepted. Finally over the hurdle of this health crisis, Barry felt as though she could return full-time to the job, although this time with some small adjustments made so that she would have more support performing two full-time jobs.

In 2000, Barry's cancer returned, however. This was a pivotal moment. She recounts, "When [the cancer] recurred, I began to really look at my life and put it in perspective. I looked at what I had accomplished: I was very successful, I was one of the top hundred producers in the company, I had a great book of business, my office was thriving and doing very well, and my children were well. [But still] I felt like I . . . was not going to be leaving enough of a legacy if I were to die." The next stage of her career was to be about establishing that legacy and, in the process, taking her company in an entirely new direction.

## Finding Her Legacy

Barry had already been able to accomplish so much in her career. As an immigrant, an Indian woman, her successes in business had defied all expectations. Yet even after eleven years at the company, her office, and her industry more generally, remained almost entirely white and male dominated. When she asked her manager why, considering her immense success for the company, they had not hired other women like her, he replied, "I got lucky once. I'm not pushing my luck again." Her great successes had not caused an institutional cultural shift at Merrill Lynch. She was still seen as an exception, an anomaly. The company continued to hire as it always had and market to the same narrow group of customers. This is where Barry found her passion.

Barry knew that her own success in building a different, and more diverse, set of client accounts had not been a fluke. Always a believer in the value of data, Barry saw trends in the shifting demographics of the United States. She noted,

> The 2000 Census data was starting to really show the emergence of this population change in this country—and yet our office stayed predominantly white and predominantly male. I thought to myself, there's a huge opportunity; there are wealthy Indian doctors and Indian technology entrepreneurs. Same in the Chinese community. Hispanics are a huge part of the population. If you look at business owners, across the board, all these communities have large numbers of business owners. Women are emerging as a huge market opportunity. And yet we continued to focus on the country-club crowd.

Barry not only wanted to take advantage of this business opportunity—this emerging untapped market—but also hoped that by doing so, she would be able to change the culture of financial advising at Merrill Lynch. If advisers' "natural networks" meant that they found it difficult to imagine clients outside the country-club pool, maybe Barry could help the company engage with more diverse communities. Barry also hoped she could lay the groundwork for other "nontraditional" financial advisers to engage with their own networks, which had been generally excluded from engaging in the kind of wealth management that Merrill Lynch had to offer.

In 2002, Barry approached her then CEO, Stan O'Neal, to propose a plan for a multicultural marketing division at Merrill Lynch. She envisioned a group of advisers who would reach out to diverse communities and market the company's services. The CEO said, "If you believe in this so much, give up your book of business and go build it." Barry was pleased with her CEO's support, knowing that for the first three or four years of the project, she would need senior-level support in order to drive the project and help it to be as successful as she knew it could be. Even so, this was a tremendously risky decision. Barry had spent years cultivating her remarkably successful set of accounts. She had about two hundred clients, worth approximately $2.5 billion. Leaving her current job to pursue the new project would also mean that she would have to take a 40 percent cut in pay—though she negotiated for one and half times that amount if her idea succeeded and made money for the company. She was taking a chance, one that many of her colleagues warned her against. But Barry was confident. In her own words, "At that moment in time, I was convinced that there was a bigger calling for me. And so I gave up my book, and I began to build this business ground up."

## Creating the Multicultural and Diversified Business Development Group

Barry believed that the strategy she was building would give Merrill Lynch an edge over other companies—granting it first access to ever-growing immigrant communities that had until that point been largely neglected by the wealth-management industry. She explains,

> There's a certain mentality that goes hand in hand with being an immigrant. There is this drive to succeed and accumulate wealth and create success—for yourself and your next generation and the one before you. And so from that perspective, the company that readies itself to be the provider of choice for those communities will win big. So if Hispanics are going to be the minority majority in this country, the reality is the proportion of Hispanics who build great wealth is going to increase dramatically. And who's going to do business with them?

She began with the South Asian community—the immigrant community that she already knew best. Barry went to the largest Merrill Lynch offices in the states where 70 percent of South Asians live in the United States: New Jersey, New York, California, Illinois, and Texas. She made presentations to the financial advisers at these strategically chosen offices to spread the word about her new initiative and to recruit financial advisers to join in the effort.

Barry's strategy involved three elements. The first was recruiting and training advisers. The first people to step up to join her efforts were the advisers from diverse communities who had been hired, the newcomers at the company, who used the project to help develop networks. Her core team was relatively small, ten people at most. From her own experience, Barry knew that marketing to immigrant communities required different skill sets than those the advisers used with their typical clients. This meant that she and her team had to develop a training program, one that focused on cultural competency and identifying the needs of the client population. The training included information on demographics, cultural nuances, and the general wealth priorities of these communities. For example, Barry explains, "education is a huge driver [in the South Asian community]. So saving for children's education was a key way in which to approach this marketplace. [Unlike the company's traditional base, for South Asians], it may be less about retirement, more about the immediacy of being able to send their kids to the very best schools, whether or not the scholarships were available."

Once community wealth priorities had been identified, the next step was examining existing Merrill Lynch products and services and formulating new ways to package them so that they made sense and would be attractive to these potential clients. For example, Barry knew that a large a number of South Asian immigrants owned hotels and motels. Rather than financing their businesses with loans from banks, however (which would have been unlikely to give them credit, at least initially), these entrepreneurs often drew on pools of capital generated in their families and their communities. As such, they lacked the credit history of the typical small business owner with whom Merrill Lynch worked. This made it difficult for them to engage with more formal financial services institutions. Barry set about filling this need: "We didn't create a new mortgage product. We just took the existing one and repackaged it in a way that allowed for us to draw on additional things that they could pledge as collateral. Because it was quite easy for them to say, 'Well, you know, my brother has this motel on which he doesn't have any lien, and he'll be willing to pledge it against this loan.' So while they may not have had the credit history, we had other things that we could draw on." Barry understood that success for the company with these populations meant understanding the structure of new sources of wealth and the priorities of these growing populations. She and her team (re)designed products in ways that would make them attractive in these specific contexts.

Once Barry's group's business in the South Asian communities began to grow, she and her team reached out to Hispanic communities, African American communities, women, gays and lesbians, and people with disabilities. They learned more about these populations to better understand their unique financial needs, just as they had done with the South Asian community. For example, they saw that one of the biggest challenges faced by the gay and lesbian community in the area of wealth management was estate planning. Lacking the legal ability to manage assets as married couples (and the tax benefits that come with that ability), for example, gay and lesbian couples faced challenges in titling assets so that transfers to partners could occur without facing tax penalties. Barry and her team developed a guidebook with tips to help guide gays and lesbians through this process. This allowed Merrill Lynch to engage with and educate the community as a client pool that other companies had neglected. According to Barry, "The fact that we got the business was a by-product of helping them with something else that was a problem." Under her leadership, Merrill Lynch became the first major financial services company to recognize that these diverse communities had wealth and that their wealth was worthy of attention and management.

Beyond training advisers and developing products, Barry understood that Merrill Lynch needed to establish partnerships with organizations in these communities. For example, Merrill Lynch partnered with the Indus Entrepreneurs, an organization of South Asian technology entrepreneurs, and with the Hotel/Motel Owners Association, the Indian Physicians' Association, and the Association of Indian Technologists. In the Hispanic community, it partnered with community organizations and Catholic churches. In the African American community, it partnered with historically black colleges and universities and Alpha Kappa Alpha, a sorority. The company also created and participated in community events. For example, in Miami, Merrill Lynch sponsored an art fair called Arte Américas Miami, featuring art by Latin American artists. This partnership strategy paid tremendous dividends. Barry says, "By allowing our clients and their communities to see a reflection of themselves within Merrill Lynch, we created a comfort zone for them that [made] us their financial services partner of choice."[7]

Just as Barry had predicted, her Multicultural and Diversified Business Development Group was a great success. By engaging with these untapped markets, in a span of only three years, Barry and her team brought in $8 billion in assets and $45 million in revenues. She was very careful to document their success: "Everything was measured down to the last dollar. . . . It couldn't just be, 'Oh, it's doing really well. Oh, this is a story somebody told.' It had to be documented very cleanly. Because otherwise you—you lack credibility." Her efforts paid off for her personally as well; as she had negotiated, the 40 percent cut in pay she had taken as a condition of starting the project had indeed been replaced plus 50 percent.

After the initial proof of Barry's success, her team continued to work to disseminate the strategy across the company, and ultimately their efforts informed Merrill's Lynch's efforts to pursue global markets. She explains, "[The lessons you learn] working with a Chinese market or the South Asian market in this country [apply] globally. You could do the same thing in London, Hong Kong, and Singapore, where there's a preponderance of these populations. The lessons learned here were translated immediately to other communities and other Merrill Lynch facilities around the world."

### Barry's Next Career: The Challenge of Institutionalizing Diversity at Merrill Lynch

Barry's cancer recurred in 2002 and again in 2004, yet she continued to work steadily, taking time out for a stem-cell transplant in 2002 and experimental gene therapy in 2004 and 2006. Once the success of her project was clear, she began to feel some push-back. Now that the opportunities to make money and generate clients were clear, it seemed that everybody wanted to get involved. Managers and advisers who had initially been reluctant, who were quite comfortable catering to the country-club crowd, began to see what they had missed. Some thought that they could implement these changes and pursue the project's goals without Barry and her team and so went after the business on their own. She recalls,

> I remember the manager in the Miami office, at one point in time, actually believing that they could have done this whole thing without us. There were two very specific forums where the manager said, "I think I want to handle this on my own. I don't think I need you and your team." And [when they tried], they made the simplest of mistakes. That would not have happened had they had somebody from my team coaching them. So the reality is, will there come a tipping point at which they no longer need us? Absolutely. But it takes [training and experience] first.

Though her efforts had built success for the company, she felt that the broader understanding of diversity that had informed her work was not yet a part of the culture.

Barry also saw the paradox of her own success within the context of a company that was still, in terms of the composition of its workforce, much like the one she had joined in 1989. She says, "We liked the money that was coming in from these diverse communities, but we weren't really doing our fair share of creating enough diversity in the midst of our employees." Merrill Lynch's workforce was still disproportionately white and male. Though she had found success in this work environment, she knew that she had been an exception. She recalls, "While I had the sheer gumption to essentially ramrod through brick walls to get where I wanted to be, it was really unfair to expect everybody to have that. I looked around me and realized that while I was successful, there were still very few models like me. There were some new, more diverse advisers, but the problem was that they were not succeeding. Without networks, they were dying on the vine. Expecting them to have to walk through brick walls the way I did was not fair." The same initial unease that management had expressed about Barry continued to exclude other immigrants, women, and people of color from employment with the company. Those few who were employed came to work in a culture still dominated by white men.

Barry felt that other people should not have to "get lucky" to succeed professionally, and she saw that it was bad for business. She says, "To me diversity and inclusion means being able to attract and retain the best talent with no holds barred! Doing that will ensure that we remain innovative, competitive and successful creators of value in perpetuity."[8] In 2005, she was asked to take over as global head of diversity, in her own words, "to look at how we could drive a better culture within the company." She accepted the challenge of applying the lessons of her enormously successful efforts to create a more diverse client base to the project of creating a more diverse culture within Merrill Lynch itself.

## Resolution

Not only had Barry learned a great deal about diversity problems in the financial services sector over the course of implementing the Multicultural and Diversified Business Development Group; she had seen with her own eyes the barriers that prevented Merrill Lynch from becoming a truly diverse company. Early in her career, she recalls speaking with a very wealthy couple on the phone who wanted to come meet her to do business:

> They came in and—remember, my last name is Barry. They are shocked that I'm an Indian woman. I thought we had a great meeting, but at the end, they wanted to meet my manager and get a few minutes alone with him. And essentially they said, "We're really not comfortable working with an Indian woman. We would prefer somebody white." That hurt. My manager found somebody else for them, and I remember saying to him, "How could you do that? How could you not say to them, 'We really don't do business with people like you in this office?'" And he said to me, "I'm sorry. Business is business. Can't turn it away." I had a sense of, this is morally wrong. Somebody has to be the first one to say, "I'm not going to listen to that. I don't think that's right. Let's not do it."

Drawing on her personal experiences the skills and expertise that she had learned from organizing the Multicultural and Diversified Business Development Group and her own research, Barry went to work to improve diversity at Merrill Lynch.

Barry's strategy involved several key elements. First, she and her team began by attempting to change the company's climate for women and people of color. They started by transforming the adviser subgroups from the Multicultural and Diversified Business Development Group into a number of "professional networks" within the company. Over time, these came to include the Women's Professional Network, the Black Professional Network, the Hispanic Professional Network, the Parents' and Carers' Professional Network, the South Asian Professional Network, the East Asian Professional Network, and the Asian, Middle Eastern, and North African Professional Network. These groups not only continued the work of expanding and diversifying Merrill Lynch's client base but were also intended to help employees in the minority in the company to develop their own business networks and provided opportunities for support, training, mentorship, and fostering cultural awareness and appreciation at work. Barry and her team also developed numerous initiatives to help address work-life balance issues that disproportionately burdened women in the company. For example, during her tenure as global head of diversity, she developed on-site child care, child- and elder-care support, and in-home and facility-based backup care for employees. She also introduced a program to help new parents transition back to work and on-location health and wellness programs. Merrill Lynch began to offer paid maternity and paternity leave.[9]

Barry understood, however, that truly changing the culture at Merrill Lynch would require altering the ideas and practices of the predominantly white and male advisers and managers who had always formed the bulk of the company's workforce. So the second part of her strategy focused on initiatives that would help build understanding of difference and the value of diversity. For example, as part of a training program about physical disabilities, the company's senior executives were invited to a lunch. When they arrived, they found themselves in a dark room with no windows. The lights were not on, and the tables were not set with chairs:

> So we're all sort of standing around looking at each other, and then in come two people in wheelchairs, one of whom is clearly sight impaired also. They wheel themselves right up to the table, and they look at us and they say, "Please have a seat." We're looking around, going, "There's no chairs here. Can we get some chairs?" They said, "You mean you don't bring your own chairs?" The lights weren't on, and we said, "Could you turn the lights on?" And the woman in the wheelchair said, "I really don't need the light. Do you need a light?" It was an awkward feeling. And then she said, "Every day, because you live in a world that is customized to you, you never question the cost of accommodating everything you need. The chair, the light . . . You never stop to think. And yet when it comes to me, you're thinking about accommodation?" It was a very eye-opening experience. So one of the things we tried to do was we tried to build in lots and lots of . . . training modalities that allowed people to experience what difference felt like.

The third aspect of Barry's strategy focused on further diversifying the company. Under her leadership, Merrill Lynch intentionally reached out to more diverse pools of potential employees. It held job fairs for ex-military personnel; sent Merrill Lynch bankers to visit schools, give talks, and meet with students; and delivered educational sessions at college campuses. It also partnered with campus organizations. For example, Barry believes that Merrill Lynch's partnership with Howard University made it the "employer of choice for Howard students seeking careers in financial services."[10] Merrill Lynch offered merit-based awards—scholarships and fellowships— for students, including fellowships for racial minorities interested in financial services.

Of the initiatives that Barry worked on during her tenure as head of diversity at Merrill Lynch (and later at the Federal Home Loan Mortgage Corporation), she is particularly proud of the creation of an internship program for people with cognitive and physical disabilities. In one case, she educated herself about autism and looked at the jobs in her company at which people on the autism spectrum would be particularly skilled:

> Mortgage data testing is very repetitive work, looking for patterns, and people on the spectrum are really good at it. The challenge is that they are sometimes quirky and not always socially adept. But we spent our training dollars not on trying to train the people on the spectrum but rather on training the teams that received them. And one of the results that really was astonishing was the employee satisfaction of those teams, without exception, far exceeded the broader population. By putting somebody with this kind of disability in their midst, you created a greater sense of team. They felt better about themselves, about their teams, and about the company than they did before this person was put in there.

By 2008, programs like these that were focused on transforming the culture of Merrill Lynch had borne some fruit. The Leadership in Diversity & Inclusion awards program, which Barry initiated at the company in 2006, solicits nominations from Merrill Lynch employees to recognize those who have improved diversity and inclusion at the company. In the first year of the award, there were over 170 submissions from offices around the globe. Two years later, there were over 700.[11]

However, though the company is more diverse than when Barry began her career in 1989, the process of culture change within it has been slow. Its workforce (and that of firms in the finance sector generally) remains overwhelmingly white and male. In 2013, Merrill Lynch paid $160 million, the largest ever award in a racial discrimination case, to settle a class-action lawsuit filed by African American employees and another $39 million to settle a similar case brought by women at both Bank of America and Merrill Lynch.[12] Certainly the company is not alone in facing charges that its culture is exclusionary and that discrimination is a persistent problem, as recent high-profile lawsuits by women in finance suggest.[13] The fact that Barry was able to blast through "brick walls" did not in itself mean that those walls, built over the course of Merrill Lynch's more than one-hundred-year history, had ceased to exist. Indeed, Barry herself acknowledges that she faced less resistance in founding the Multicultural and Diversified Business Development Group than in her work with diversity inside Merrill Lynch. One of the key lessons of her story is perhaps that companies are far more willing to embrace diversity as a market opportunity than to address the exclusions at the heart of their own cultures.

When Bank of America acquired Merrill Lynch in 2008, it offered Barry a position. She decided it was time for a change, however. She took a job as senior vice president and chief diversity officer at the Federal Home Loan Mortgage Corporation (more commonly known as Freddie Mac), which was in turmoil after the financial crisis. Barry stayed there for a year, applying many of the same strategies she had learned at Merrill Lynch to improve diversity. Ultimately, however, she found the move from a private company to a public one restrictive and the commute too demanding while also raising a high-school-aged son. Barry decided to retire. She has since taught at Columbia University's School of International and Public Affairs, serves on a number of corporate and community boards, and continues to be a powerful advocate for diversity and a mentor to others.

Barry's work at Merrill Lynch left an enduring legacy. Part of the secret of her success, she believes, is her collaborative style of leadership, which is also infused with a respect for the value of diversity:

> It's really about building the right team. I focused a lot on how you bring people together. I found that usually it meant there were people with strengths that stood out, but they also had weaknesses. The weaknesses forced them to lean on others, and the strengths gave them the courage to lead with that strength. My job as the leader of the team was to find people with complementary strengths and weaknesses, so they would weave together, like two hands coming together. And as a leader, it becomes really important, learning to give credit away [to the team]. The generosity of heart and spirit is so important. And believe me, there's enough to go around. Hoarding it for yourself does nothing.

Barry's leadership with Merrill Lynch in the Multicultural and Diversified Business Development Group convincingly demonstrated that investment in diversity is good for business. Her work as global head of diversity helped to advance the conversation about diversity within the company and at the same time open the door for others like her. Though the process of change is not complete, Barry's efforts to change attitudes and reshape culture have helped, as she hoped, "to integrate diversity into the 'cultural DNA' at Merrill Lynch."[14]

## Notes

1 Merrill Lynch, "About Us," n.d., http://www.ml.com/index.asp?id=7695_8134 (accessed December 1, 2103).

2 Reuters, "Timeline: History of Merrill Lynch," September 15, 2008, http://www.reuters.com/article/2008/09/15/us-merrill-idUSN1546989520080915.

3 "When Finance Was for the 99%," *Economist*, January 4, 2014, http://www.economist.com/news/books-and-arts/21592594-how-charismatic-visionary-persuaded-nation-wall-street-was-force-good-when.

4 Subha Barry, in conversation with Lisa Hetfield and Dana M. Britton, October 30, 2013. All direct quotes from Barry are taken from this interview unless otherwise noted.

5 "Executive Profile: Subha V. Barry," *Bloomberg Businessweek*, n.d., http://investing.businessweek.com/research/stocks/people/person.asp?personId=23836548&ticker=FMCC (accessed December 1, 2013).

6 Ameet Sachdev, "Panel Finds Sex Bias at Merrill Lynch," *Chicago Tribune*, April 21, 2004, http://articles.chicagotribune.com/2004-04-21/business/0404210258_1_discrimination-merrill-lynch-wages-and-promotions; Ann Wozencraft, "Bias at the Bull: Merrill Lynch's Class-Action Settlement Draws a Crowd," *New York Times*, February 27, 1999, http://www.nytimes.com/1999/02/27/business/bias-at-the-bull-merrill-lynch-s-class-action-settlement-draws-a-crowd.html.

7 Merrill Lynch, "Transcending Boundaries in 2008: Diversity & Inclusion at Merrill Lynch," 2008, http://web.archive.org/web/20100215001121/http://www.ml.com/media/77086.pdf, 16.

8 Ibid., 6.

9 Ibid., 14.

10 Ibid., 12.

11 Ibid., 6.

12 Patrick McGeehan, "Merrill Lynch in Big Payout for Bias Case," *DealBook* (blog), *New York Times*, August 27, 2013, http://dealbook.nytimes.com/2013/08/27/merrill-lynch-in-big-payout-for-bias-case/; Patrick McGeehan, "Bank of America to Pay $39 Million in Gender Bias Case," *DealBook* (blog), *New York*

*Times*, September 6, 2013, http://dealbook.nytimes.com/2013/09/06/bank-of
-america-to-pay-39-million-in-gender-bias-case/.

13  See, for example, Sheelah Kolhatkar, "A Lawsuit Peeks inside the Goldman
Sachs 'Boys' Club,'" *Bloomberg Business*, July 2, 2014, http://www.bloomberg
.com/bw/articles/2014-07-02/a-lawsuit-peeks-inside-the-goldman-sachs-boys
-club; and David Streitfeld, "Ellen Pao Suit against Kleiner Perkins Heads to
Trial, with Big Potential Implications," *New York Times*, February 23, 2015,
http://www.nytimes.com/2015/02/23/technology/ellen-pao-suit-against
-kleiner-perkins-heads-to-trial-with-big-potential-implications.html.

14  Merrill Lynch, "Transcending Boundaries in 2008," 6.

## Bibliography

"Executive Profile: Subha V. Barry." *Bloomberg Businessweek*, n.d. http://investing
.businessweek.com/research/stocks/people/person.asp?personId=23836548&
ticker=FMCC (accessed December 1, 2013).

Kolhatkar, Sheelah. "A Lawsuit Peeks inside the Goldman Sachs 'Boys' Club.'"
*Bloomberg Business*, July 2, 2014. http://www.bloomberg.com/bw/articles/
2014-07-02/a-lawsuit-peeks-inside-the-goldman-sachs-boys-club.

McGeehan, Patrick. "Bank of America to Pay $39 Million in Gender Bias Case." *Deal-
Book* (blog), *New York Times*, September 6, 2013. http://dealbook.nytimes.com/
2013/09/06/bank-of-america-to-pay-39-million-in-gender-bias-case/.

———. "Merrill Lynch in Big Payout for Bias Case." *DealBook* (blog), *New York
Times*, August 27, 2013. http://dealbook.nytimes.com/2013/08/27/merrill-lynch
-in-big-payout-for-bias-case/.

Merrill Lynch. "About Us." n.d. http://www.ml.com/index.asp?id=7695_8134
(accessed December 1, 2103).

———. "Transcending Boundaries in 2008: Diversity & Inclusion at Merrill Lynch."
2008. http://web.archive.org/web/20100215001121/http://www.ml.com/media/
77086.pdf.

Reuters. "Timeline: History of Merrill Lynch." September 15, 2008, http://www
.reuters.com/article/2008/09/15/us-merrill-idUSN1546989520080915.

Sachdev, Ameet. "Panel Finds Sex Bias at Merrill Lynch." *Chicago Tribune*, April 21,
2004. http://articles.chicagotribune.com/2004-04-21/business/0404210258_1
_discrimination-merrill-lynch-wages-and-promotions.

Streitfeld, David. "Ellen Pao Suit against Kleiner Perkins Heads to Trial, with Big
Potential Implications." *New York Times*, February 23, 2015. http://www.nytimes
.com/2015/02/23/technology/ellen-pao-suit-against-kleiner-perkins-heads-to
-trial-with-big-potential-implications.html.

"When Finance Was for the 99%." *Economist*, January 4, 2014. http://www
.economist.com/news/books-and-arts/21592594-how-charismatic-visionary
-persuaded-nation-wall-street-was-force-good-when.

Wozencraft, Ann. "Bias at the Bull: Merrill Lynch's Class-Action Settlement Draws
a Crowd." *New York Times*, February 27, 1999. http://www.nytimes.com/1999/
02/27/business/bias-at-the-bull-merrill-lynch-s-class-action-settlement-draws
-a-crowd.html.

# Contributors

**CRYSTAL BEDLEY** holds an MA in sociology and is currently a doctoral student in sociology at Rutgers University. She received a BS degree in journalism, specializing in news editing, from the University of Colorado–Boulder. Her research interests include the negotiation and maintenance of multiracial identities, racial attitudes toward inequality, and gender/racial equity in higher education. In her dissertation, "The Ethnically Ambiguous Generation," she is investigating processes of racialized meaning construction in advertising by studying how multiracial persons are conceived by advertisers, how racial/ethnic diversity/ambiguity are incorporated into TV commercials and online images/video, and how these racial messages are interpreted by consumers. As a graduate assistant at Rutgers University, she engaged in evaluation research to understand the experiences of women-of-color faculty and programmatic effectiveness. As an academic adviser for the Ronald E. McNair Post-Baccalaureate Program, Bedley has developed and taught interdisciplinary courses on the topics of the research process, methodology, and graduate education preparation.

**CAROLINA ALONSO BEJARANO** holds a law degree from Los Andes University in Bogota and a master's in gender and social politics from the London School of Economics and Political Science. She is a collective owner, editor, and translator of Sangria Legibilities, a bilingual publishing house based in New York City and Santiago de Chile. She is currently pursuing her PhD in women's and gender studies at Rutgers, where she explores the intersection of decolonial theory and migration studies, specifically as it relates to the production of immigrant illegality in the United States. In her doctoral work, she examines how the colonial history of New Jersey influences current anti-immigration legislation in the state, while conducting ethnographic and organizing work with the undocumented Latin American community in Freehold, New Jersey.

**DANA M. BRITTON** is the director of the Center for Women and Work and a professor of labor studies and employment relations at Rutgers University. She received her PhD in sociology from the University of Texas at Austin. She is interested in the ways organizations, both historically and presently, structure and reproduce gender inequalities at work across the multiple dimensions of gender, race, class, and sexuality. One of her current projects, funded by a National Science Foundation grant, focuses on gender and the transition between associate and full professor, particularly for university faculty in the science, technology, engineering, and math disciplines. She is the author of *At Work in the Iron Cage: The Prison as Gendered Organization* and *The Gender of Crime*, as well as many articles on gender and work. She is editor emerita of the journal *Gender & Society* (2006–2011). As director of the Center for Women and Work, she is involved in research and programs that promote economic and social equity for women workers, their families, and their communities.

**LISA HETFIELD** is the associate director and director of development for the Institute for Women's Leadership (IWL) at Rutgers University. The institute is a consortium of nine members focused on advancing women's leadership and examining ways to educate leaders to pursue equity and social justice. Hetfield has worked at Rutgers since 1990, when she joined the university as the director of development for Douglass, the college for women at Rutgers. In that role, she worked to raise over $11 million for the 75th Anniversary Campaign for Douglass. She began her work with the Institute in 1995 and since that time has directed fund-development activities, raising over $6 million for leadership programs, research, and endowment. She is a cofounder of several leadership programs at IWL, including the Rutgers Executive Leadership Program for Professional Women. Hetfield holds an MA in women's and gender studies from Rutgers University and a BA in English from Carnegie-Mellon University.

**GRACE HOWARD** is a PhD candidate and Excellence Fellow in the Department of Political Science at Rutgers University, with specializations in women and politics, public law, and political theory. After graduating with a BA in political science from Virginia Commonwealth University, Howard worked in the field of women's health, which led to her interest in the politics of reproduction. Her research interests include reproductive law, criminology, criminal justice, critical race theory, law and society, constitutional law, feminist theory, and drug policy. She is a Graduate Fellow with the Rutgers Center for Race and Ethnicity and is the author of the forthcoming article "The Limits of Pure White: Raced Reproduction in the Methamphetamine Crisis." Her current work examines pregnancy-specific crime in the United States and state-mandated informed consent.

**LAURA LOVIN** is a researcher at the Weeks Centre for Social and Policy Research–London South Bank University, where she studies the transnational journeys, the quests for employment, and the trials of resettlement of immigrant workers from Romania in two major sites of global capitalism, the cities of London and New York. Her project was awarded the 2015 Marie Skłodowska-Curie Fellowship by the European Commission. She received her PhD in women's and gender studies from Rutgers University. Her areas of specialization include contemporary feminist theories, transnational mobilities, cultural politics and policy, and eastern European feminisms. Lovin's articles and reviews have appeared in anthologies and journals published in the United States and Europe. She taught women's and gender studies courses at Rutgers–New Brunswick and Rutgers–Newark.

**KATHLEEN E. McCOLLOUGH** is a PhD candidate in media studies at Rutgers University. She works at the Institute for Women's Leadership at Rutgers on its Women, Media, & Technology initiative and is a seminar fellow at the Institute for Research on Women at Rutgers for 2014–2015. McCollough also worked as a graduate assistant for the News Measures Research Project, where her team developed assessment tools for local journalism, and as a Tow-Knight research fellow, where she coauthored a research report on the current system for local and state-level news in New Jersey. Her dissertation studies feminine labor and intimacy within a participatory culture through an ethnographic study of the US scrapbook industry.

**ROSEMARY NDUBUIZU** is a fifth-year PhD candidate in Rutgers University's Women and Gender Studies program. Her dissertation explores how black female domestic space is a privileged site for creative destruction. She argues that America's recent public and subsidized multifamily housing reforms cloak creative destruction within presumably neutral discourses such as the language of concentrated poverty, the culture of poverty, and undeserving poor. Ultimately this language constructs black female domestic space as an incubator of deviance and social waste. She ethnographically explores this phenomenon by analyzing how Washington, DC's housing advocates respond to creative destruction's three interventionist arguments. Committed to community-engaged scholarship, Ndubuizu remains connected to community organizing through her active involvement with Organizing Neighborhood Equity (ONE DC).

**AMANDA ROBERTI** is a PhD candidate in the Political Science Department at Rutgers University–New Brunswick. She studies women and politics, and public policy. Her research analyzes issue framing of abortion regulations in US state legislatures, specifically focusing on woman-centered frames. Roberti has instructed a variety of courses in her relevant subfields, including Gender, Law & Public Policy; American Government; Leadership & Global Citizenship; and Introduction to Women's Studies. She is also the coordinator of the Douglass Residential College Public Leadership Education Network (PLEN), which is a program that promotes young women's leadership in public policy. Before attending Rutgers–New Brunswick for her PhD program, she earned a master of arts in political science, with a concentration in women's and gender studies, from Rutgers University–Newark. Though she was born and raised in New Jersey, Roberti also lived and worked as a paralegal in Philadelphia for six years, before entering into her master's program, earning a paralegal certification from Peirce College. She earned her BA from Kutztown University in Pennsylvania, majoring in political science and philosophy.

**STINA SODERLING** is a doctoral candidate in women's and gender studies at Rutgers University. She has a bachelor's degree from Smith College in women's studies and international relations. Her research and teaching interests include queer theory, environmental justice and ecofeminism, and feminist perspectives on the prison system. Her dissertation, "In the Crevices of Global Capitalism: Rural Queer Community Formation," is an interdisciplinary study of the phenomenon of rural intentional queer communities in North America, focusing on questions of access to land. The project is based on ethnographic fieldwork in rural Tennessee, as well as archival research and oral histories. It draws on queer theory, feminist environmental studies, new materialism, and settler-colonial studies. Teaching is a central component of Soderling's work as a scholar, and she has taught both introductory and upper-level undergraduate courses at Rutgers University and Mount Holyoke College on topics including queer studies, environmental justice, and feminist food politics. She has also been the coordinator for the prison-to-college efforts of the Progressive Education Initiative, a volunteer-run organization providing education to incarcerated women.

# Index

CPSIA information can be obtained at www.ICGtesting.com
Printed in the USA
BVOW06*2241120416

444011BV00001B/2/P